D0984639

LAW AND PUBLIC CHOICE

LAW AND PUBLIC CHOICE

A Critical Introduction

Daniel A. Farber and
Philip P. Frickey

The University of Chicago Press / Chicago and London

Daniel A. Farber and Philip P. Frickey are professors of law at the University of Minnesota.

The University of Chicago Press, Chicago 60637
The University of Chicago Press, Ltd., London
© 1991 by The University of Chicago
All rights reserved. Published 1991
Printed in the United States of America

00 99 98 97 96 95 94 93 92 91   5 4 3 2 1

Library of Congress Cataloging-in-Publication Data

Farber, Daniel A., 1950–
    Law and public choice : a critical introduction / Daniel A. Farber
and Philip P. Frickey.
        p.   cm.
    Includes bibliographical references and index.
    ISBN 0-226-23802 (cloth). — ISBN 0-226-23803-2 (pbk.)
    1. Law—Economic aspects.   2. Law—United States—Economic
aspects.   3. Social choice.   I. Frickey, Philip P., 1953–
II. Title.
    K487.E3F37   1991
    338.4′734—dc20   90-44285
                                                                                 CIP

∞ The paper used in this publication meets the minimum requirements of the American National Standard for Information Sciences—Permanence of Paper for Printed Library Materials, ANSI Z39.48-1984.

This book is printed on acid-free paper.

To my parents

———

To my father
and the memory of my mother

DAF

PPF

CONTENTS

ACKNOWLEDGMENTS   ix
INTRODUCTION   1

1   INTEREST GROUPS AND THE POLITICAL PROCESS   12
     I.   The Impact of Interest Group Theory   13
     II.   Interest Groups and Political Science   17
     III.   The Economic Theory of Legislation   21
     IV.   Normative Implications   33

2   ARROW'S THEOREM AND THE
     DEMOCRATIC PROCESS   38
     I.   Arrow's Theorem and Its Implications   38
     II.   Republicanism   42
     III.   Chaos and Coherence in Legislatures   47
     IV.   Public Choice and Legislative Deliberation   55

3   ECONOMIC REGULATION AND THE CONSTITUTION   63
     I.   Economic Rights and the Constitution   64
     II.   Federalism   73
     III.   The Delegation Doctrine   78

4   STATUTORY INTERPRETATION   88
     I.   Legislative Intent   89
     II.   Legislative History   95
     III.   Ambiguous Language and Rational Choice   102
     IV.   Statutory Evolution   106

5   INTEGRATING PUBLIC CHOICE AND PUBLIC LAW   116
     I.   Existing Strands of "Due Process
         of Lawmaking"   118
     II.   Expanding the Influence of Public Choice
         in Public Law   132

EPILOGUE: BEYOND THE ECONOMIC SPHERE   145
INDEX   155

ACKNOWLEDGMENTS

Of the many persons who provided us with support in this project, a few deserve special mention. William Eskridge, Richard Posner, and Suzanna Sherry read large portions of the manuscript in one form or another, and provided many helpful suggestions. Robert Stein, as our dean, provided special support, both financial and otherwise, to our endeavors. Our spouses were understanding when our attempt to write about self-interested politics became self-absorbing.

Some portions of this book appeared in different form in three articles of ours: *The Jurisprudence of Public Choice*, 65 Tex. L. Rev. 874 (1987); *Integrating Public Choice and Public Law: A Reply to DeBow and Lee*, 66 Tex. L. Rev. 993 (1988); and *Legislative Intent and Public Choice*, 74 Va. L. Rev. 423 (1988). Much smaller fragments of the book have appeared in different form as parts of three articles by Daniel Farber: *Democracy and Disgust: A Comment on Public Choice*, 65 Chi.-Kent L. Rev. 161 (1989); *Statutory Interpretation and Legislative Supremacy*, 78 Geo. L.J. 281 (1989); and *Review Essay: Environmentalism, Economics and the Public Interest*, 41 Stan. L. Rev. 1021 (1989).

INTRODUCTION

*T*raditionally, law has been divided into two subfields: private law, which involves private transactions such as contracts, wills, and deeds; and public law, which involves broad issues of public policy. This dichotomy needs to be taken with a grain of salt because the two categories are hardly airtight: contract law, for example, involves public policy issues relating to consumer protection. Still, even today, there is a noticeable difference between the law of wills, which is mostly concerned with helping individuals plan their estates, and discrimination law, which is intended to change rather than facilitate private conduct.

The focus of public law is legislation. Constitutional law studies the limits on legislative power; administrative law studies how statutes are implemented by agencies; fields like discrimination law and environmental law focus on how to apply particular federal statutes. Yet, even though legislation is central to public law, legal scholars have only recently begun to devote serious attention to the legislative process. This book is intended to help fill that gap, by considering how some of the "new learning" from the social sciences can illuminate issues of public law.

If we are to understand how legislation is involved in making public policy, we cannot simply take for granted that the legislature represents the public interest. Realistically, we must also consider the possibility that a statute represents private rather than public interests, because of the undue influence of special interest groups. Alternatively, a statute may fail to represent any identifiable "public" interest because the public itself is too fragmented to generate any coherent public policy. These questions have been the focus of a body of work by economists and political scientists often labeled as public choice.

Public choice theory is a hybrid: the application of the economist's methods to the political scientist's subject. For many people, it was a relatively obscure field until 1986, when James Buchanan was awarded the Nobel prize in economics for his work on public choice. Most people—including many legal scholars—had never heard of public choice before the Buchanan prize. Most of what they then heard seemed dismaying: a cynical portrayal of politics of the kind one would expect from practitioners of the "dismal science" of economics.

Cynicism about politics is not new in American life. It was many years ago that Mark Twain referred to members of Congress as the only truly native class of American criminals. But Twain did not buttress his remarks with masses of equations, nor did James Buchanan seem to have a Twainian twinkle in his eye. Unlike Twain's, the observations of the public choice theorists seemed deadly serious. Of course, many public choice scholars rightly contend that their purpose, far from being cynical, is merely to describe dispassionately the operation of the political process. Normative judgments are for others.[1] Yet, if their descriptions of politics are correct, certain normative conclusions seem inevitable, and those conclusions are generally not happy ones.

The initial response to public choice by even the intellectually sophisticated was typified by Abner Mikva, one of the nation's leading federal appeals judges. Judge Mikva said he "found it hard to read or profit from the 'public choice' literature." Perhaps, he said, he was "still one of those naive citizens who believe that politics is on the square, that majorities in effect make policy in this country, and that out of the clash of partisan debate and frequent elections 'good' public policy decisions emerge." He added that not even five terms in that notorious den of inequity, the Illinois state legislature, had prepared him for the political villainy depicted in the public choice literature.[2]

Judge Mikva is not alone in finding the public choice literature unpalatable. At least on initial acquaintance with the public choice literature, the reader is likely to come away with a feeling of despair about the political process. Sometimes the legislature is portrayed as the playground of special interests, sometimes as a passive mirror of self-interested voters, sometimes as a slot machine whose outcomes are entirely unpredictable. These images are hardly calculated to evoke respect for democracy.[3]

1. Although this dichotomy between normative and "positive" theory is conventional among social scientists, it is not universal. Buchanan, for example, views the two as closely connected. *See* Buchanan, *Richard Musgrave, Public Finance, and Public Choice*, 61 PUB. CHOICE 289, 290 (1989).

2. Mikva, *Foreword to Symposium on The Theory of Public Choice*, 74 VA. L. REV. 167, 167 (1988).

3. When we say that this image is conveyed by some of the public choice literature, we do not mean that any one writer explicitly endorses all aspects of this view of politics. Any given public choice theorist would undoubtedly introduce qualifications and exceptions to this description of politics. Rather, this view is the common core of much of the writing on public choice as it existed, say, about ten years ago.

The legal scholar who comes closest to adopting this view outright is Judge Frank Easterbrook. He has argued, for example, that because it relies on majority voting, the Supreme Court's opinions will necessarily be incoherent, Easterbrook, *Ways of Criticizing the Court*, 95 HARV. L. REV. 802, 811–32 (1982); that legislative outcomes are likely to be either incoherent or the result of arbitrary agendas, Easterbrook, *Statutes' Domains*, 50 U. CHI. L. REV. 533, 547–48 (1983); and that much legislation purporting to reflect the public interest is in fact the product of special interest groups, Easterbrook, *Foreword: The Court and the Economic System*, 98 HARV. L. REV. 4, 15–18 (1984).

Judge Mikva's ire was aroused not only by the content of public choice theory but also by its mathematical style. Mathematics, he said, "has always held a strong allure for many social scientists," but "[d]espite its seductiveness . . . the postulates of mathematics usually provide only fools' gold for human problems."[4] In short, he concluded, public choice might aptly describe the behavior of computers but not of the flesh-and-blood politicians who make our laws.[5]

Mikva's irritation is all the more impressive because of its context. He was writing the introduction to a symposium on law and public choice, yet his message seemed to be that the symposium was a waste of paper because its subject matter was intellectually (if not morally) bankrupt.

As the very existence of this book makes clear, we disagree with Judge Mikva's preemptory dismissal of public choice. But his assessment of public choice, while hostile, is not without basis. As he says, much of public choice theory is forbiddingly abstract and mathematical, seemingly far removed from the emotions, ideologies, and personalities that dominate the political news. There is also a basis for Mikva's charge of cynicism: public choice theorists often *have* taken a rather jaundiced view of democracy. In one of the contributions to the same symposium, William Riker (a political scientist) and Barry Weingast (an economist) made several observations about democratic politics. The legislator, they said, is "a placeholder opportunistically building up an ad hoc majority for the next election."[6] Moreover, there is a "fundamental inescapable arbitrariness to majority rule."[7] The decisions of legislatures are "determined mainly by the *agenda,* and related institutions, by which legislative leaders determine the order in which the alternatives arise for a vote."[8] In short, they say, "the notion of a 'will of the people' has no meaning."[9]

Most of our readers probably do not regard this as an accurate portrayal of American government. Why, then, is public choice worth serious attention? There are at least five reasons.

First, the questions raised by public choice are critically important. If Riker and Weingast are accurate in their portrayal of democracy, then the rest of us have been far too sanguine in our attitude toward the political process. If majority rule is a sham behind which self-seeking agenda setters dictate the content of legislation, then we must question whether democracy itself has any inherent worth. It is tempting simply to brush these questions aside,

---

4. Mikva, *supra* note 2, at 176.

5. *Id.* at 177.

6. Riker & Weingast, *Constitutional Regulation of Legislative Choice: The Political Consequences of Judicial Deference to Legislators,* 74 VA. L. REV. 373, 396 (1988).

7. *Id.* at 374.

8. *Id.* at 385 (emphasis in original).

9. *Id.* at 395.

as Judge Mikva does. But public choice scholars can claim support in a mass of empirical studies, as well as in sophisticated mathematical models. Given the seriousness of the issues at stake and the substantial support mustered by public choice scholars, their views of government deserve careful consideration.

Second, even if views like those of Riker and Weingast do not fully capture the realities of government, they may still represent some important tendencies. All legislators may not be self-seeking, all legislative decisions may not be arbitrary—but in designing governmental institutions, we need to take these possibilities into account. Perhaps we can design legal doctrines that will encourage legislators to rise above special interests or rules that can make legislative outcomes more principled. So, for example, public choice may be relevant to current disputes about election financing or to judicial rulings about legislative procedures.

Third, public choice deserves attention because it has already begun to have an important influence on the law. Several influential judges—most notably Justice Scalia on the Supreme Court and Judge Frank Easterbrook on the U.S. Court of Appeals for the Seventh Circuit—have drawn on public choice insights in their own writings. Both judges have strongly criticized current methods of interpreting key federal statutes. They argue that judges should cease looking for the "legislative intent" behind a statute, either because legislation is mindless or because legislative records are deliberately distorted. Under the influence of public choice, other important legal scholars have called for radical changes in constitutional doctrine in order to limit economic regulation. Some of these scholars have sought to undo the New Deal and make deregulation a matter of constitutional law. To ignore public choice is to leave the intellectual battleground in possession of these scholars.

Even if highly pessimistic assumptions about the political process do not lead directly to new legal doctrines, accepting these premises could not help but affect the judicial function. Knowing that legislative actions are generally either self-serving or random might not convey a new intellectual direction to public law, but this knowledge would be bound to have a dispiriting effect. How can a judge take seriously the job of interpreting legislation while believing that the legislature is morally bankrupt? How willingly would judges leave policy decisions to a Congress they believed to be mindless or indifferent to the public interest? If we come to accept this nihilistic vision of politics, judges might still go through the motions of deference to legislatures, but they will surely find it hard to muster much enthusiasm for the task.

Fourth, in accusing public choice of caricaturing politics, Mikva himself presents a caricature of public choice. Mikva's charges against public choice do have a grain of truth, but he ignores may nuances. Like Riker and

Weingast, many public choice scholars do portray legislation as arbitrary and legislators as self-seeking. But this is only one segment of public choice scholarship. Other scholars have given more complex and balanced portraits of the political process. The most dramatic, stark versions of public choice have received the most publicity, but they are not necessarily the most useful or even the most representative of current work in the field.

Finally, even one-sided and simplistic theories have their uses. No theory can capture the richness and diversity of political institutions, but without a theory, we may be overwhelmed by fascinating facts and unable to orient ourselves. Just as even a crude, inaccurate map can provide a general orientation, even a badly flawed theory can provide some badly needed coherence. Public choice can at least provide us with some overall concept of the dynamics of democratic government. So long as we remember that the theory is incomplete, it can provide a useful framework for analysis. The danger lies only in confusing the map with the territory.

For all these reasons, public choice deserves to be taken seriously. In this book, we have attempted to offer a balanced appraisal of public choice and some of its implications for the American legal system. Although we are sharply critical of some portions of the public choice literature, the book is not intended as an exercise in debunking. Rather, we have attempted to assemble the most accurate possible picture of the dynamics of government decisionmaking. Only by getting a clear picture of how government works can we begin to think sensibly about how it should work.

We will begin in chapters 1 and 2 by surveying some of the findings of public choice theory. Chapter 1 deals with the role of interest groups, while chapter 2 covers more abstract studies of decisionmaking procedures. As legal scholars, we are most interested in, and therefore give the most attention to, those aspects of public choice theory with possible application to legal issues. The remainder of the book explores some of these applications. In chapter 3, we consider proposals that constitutional law be radically modified in light of public choice theory. Chapter 4 discusses the possible applications of public choice to problems of statutory interpretation. Chapter 5 then discusses other useful contributions of public choice to public law. Finally, in the Epilogue, we move away from the specific findings and premises of public choice to consider how some of its general implications might help judges in deciding difficult cases. At this point, we will no longer be dealing with a true "application" of public choice. Instead, we will use public choice, with its emphasis on the importance of institutional structures, as a source of inspiration for resolving some hard cases.

Our approach to public choice reflects our general views about the role of theory in law. For the past decade, legal scholarship has been dominated by the search for grand theory. In their search for the magic key that will unlock all the secrets of the legal system, scholars have turned to sources like public choice theory, French literary theory, feminism, and microeconomics. This quest for abstract theory has taken many scholars increasingly far from the careful attention to particular cases which used to be the hallmark of legal scholarship. In our view, the pendulum has now gone too far toward abstract theory.

This book itself is proof that we take theory seriously and view it as important to law. But we also value the traditional attachment of legal scholars to "the particular." We have tried to balance our investigation of political theory with a pragmatic assessment of the implications of theory for particular cases. As pragmatists, we find theory usually helpful and sometimes enormously illuminating, but the limits of theory and the demands of the empirical must always be kept in mind. Jurisprudentially, then, we align ourselves with those who believe in "practical reason" or "legal pragmatism" as opposed to grand theory.

Even apart from our jurisprudential reservations, we believe that caution is required in applying public choice to actual legal problems. Public choice theory is far from mature. The application of economic methods to political questions already has proved fruitful, and we can expect further insights from this approach, but current formulations of public choice are still far from definitive. It is premature to draw firm conclusions about how public law should respond to public choice theory. But it is not too early, in our view, to begin the task of integrating public choice and public law.

One of the difficulties in seeking to link public law and public choice is that both are really labels for complex entities with rather unclear boundaries. Public law clearly encompasses constitutional law and general theories of statutory interpretation, but lawyers might disagree about whether income tax or antitrust law should be considered part of "public" law. Similarly, the term "public choice" may also suggest a greater degree of unity than actually exists. Under the rubric of public choice we will be discussing a variety of different approaches such as heuristic theories of legislative behavior, mathematical models of collective decision processes, and empirical studies of roll call votes, with little concern about defining the exact line between public choice and allied fields of economics and political science. Some of what we will have to say about public choice may apply more to the "Rochester School" than to the "Virginia School," or vice versa. Because this book is aimed at the general reader, we will not make fine distinctions between these various schools of thought.

Because public choice is a new field—and also because it straddles several disciplines—the definition of the field itself is hotly disputed. Some political scientists are understandably uncomfortable with a definition of public choice in terms of economic methodology. They might prefer to define it as the study of how governments supply "public goods" such as national defense or environmental protection. Consequently, they may also be inclined to distinguish *public* choice form theories of *social* choice (the study of collective decisionmaking processes) and theories of *rational* choice (any analysis postulating that individuals act rationally to maximize their preferences). For other purposes, these are important distinctions. For purposes of this book, however, we have not found such line-drawing useful. We rely upon Dennis Mueller's definition of public choice "as the economic study of nonmarket decision making, or simply the application of economics to political science,"[10] a definition widely accepted in the legal literature.[11]

When we speak of the relationship between public law and public choice, then, we are really talking about several fields of law in which the role of legislatures is crucial, on the one hand, and several fields of scholarship that make use of economic methodology, on the other. At this relatively early stage of the interaction between public choice and public law, making these terms more precise would complicate the discussion to very little purpose. Our goal is not a detailed topographical map, but simply a guide—designed with the agenda of public law in mind—to some newly discovered, and as yet poorly explored, intellectual territory.

We will begin our examination of public choice by investigating the role of self-interest in politics. Some public choice models portray the political process as an arena of pure greed, in which self-interested voters, avaricious politicians, and self-seeking interest groups meet to do business. Much of the early public choice literature embraced this viewpoint. As we will see in chapter 1, however, recent scholarship gives us good grounds for rejecting this model of politics as informing the content of public law. To view politics as wholly deliberative would be quixotic, but there is (perhaps surprisingly) solid evidence that voters and politicians are actually motivated in part by factors other than greed. Careful statistical studies have shown that ideology—beliefs about the public interest—does indeed influence congressional votes.

If interest group theory suggests the possibility that legislation is likely to be malign, another branch of public choice theory suggests the equally unpleasant possibility that legislation is random and arbitrary. Building on Kenneth Arrow's pioneering work, theorists have shown that under plausible circumstances a majority can be led to adopt absolutely any possible decision. (Notably, these results do not depend on whether legislators are self-interested or motivated by ideology.) It was this body of work that Riker and Weingast relied on when they decried the arbitrariness of majority rule.

In chapter 2, however, we offer another perspective on this body of liter-

---

10. D. MUELLER, PUBLIC CHOICE II 1 (1989).

11. *See, e.g.*, Mashaw, *The Economics of Politics and the Understanding of Public Law,* 65 CHI.-KENT L. REV. 123, 124 (1989); Miller, *Public Choice at the Dawn of the Special Interest State: The Story of Butter and Margarine,* 77 CALIF. L. REV. 83, 85 n.4 (1989).

ature. It is true that majority rule, in and of itself, is not a sufficient basis for coherent decisionmaking. In our view, however, this finding does not debunk democracy, but instead shows that democracy rests on a much richer institutional basis than pure majoritarianism. Democracy simply cannot be reduced to the precept that whatever is preferred by "50 percent plus one" should be the law. No actual democracy works on this basis. All democracies use complex institutions such as political parties, committees, and procedural rules in order to implement some variety of majority rule. The real lesson of public choice theory is that these are not just accidental features of democratic government, but instead are basic to the whole enterprise. Our normative vision of democracy must reflect these institutional realities if our aspirations are to be anything more than quixotic fantasies.

At about the same time that public choice emerged as a major influence on legal theory, another political theory known as republicanism also became influential. Summarizing republicanism is no easy task, though we attempt a brief description in chapter 2. Superficially, the portrayal of government by republicanism is the antithesis of public choice. Republicanism praises legislatures as forums for public deliberation and civic virtue. [12] Public choice theory can be read to suggest that republicanism is false as a portrayal of the actual legislative process, and that as a normative vision it demands more of legislatures than they can possibly be expected to attain. Despite the apparent conflict between these two forms of political theory, we believe that there is a deeper connection between them. Properly understood, public choice theory can support the republican vision of deliberative democracy.

While chapters 1 and 2 reject the deep pessimism of some portions of the public choice literature, that literature does dramatically portray problems which are all too prevalent. The institutions necessary for legislative deliberation can easily break down, and special interest groups are eager to exploit their weaknesses. In the remainder of the book, we explore possible ways in which the legal system can combat the pathologies of the democratic process.

Some legal scholars have interpreted the implications of public choice as a basis for renewed judicial activism. If legislatures are at best erratic and at worst corrupt, let the judges make public policy. This has been the argument for resurrecting the judicial doctrines of the pre–New Deal Supreme Court, when the Court sought to protect property rights from government regulation. We are skeptical of this invitation to conservative activism. In chapter 3, we critique the arguments for reviving pre–New Deal judicial doctrines.

---

12. For a brief introduction to republicanism, see Michelman, *Law's Republic*, 97 YALE L.J. 1493 (1989).

Our key criticism is that the difference between "bad" special interest legislation and "good" public interest laws is too subjective and political to form a sound basis for constitutional doctrine. Although these scholars are right to be concerned about special interest legislation, dramatically revamping constitutional law is not the answer.

We are also skeptical of proposals for a radical revision of methods of statutory interpretation. Justice Scalia and others have argued that courts should not concern themselves with legislative intent, in part because of public choice theory. We argue in chapter 4 that the idea of legislative intent remains tenable despite public choice theory, and that Scalia is too cynical in his views about the legislative process. In a constructive vein, we suggest a model of statutory interpretation which combines legal pragmatism with public choice methodology.

Legal pragmatism is also the key to the final chapter, in which we offer some new suggestions for modifying American public law in light of public choice and its allied disciplines. We do not advocate sweeping changes in public law. Rather, we think public choice will be most useful as a basis for incremental adjustments in the legal system. One area for reform is campaign finance, which we consider briefly. We also illustrate at some length how judges might use the insights of public choice in deciding specific cases.

In particular, we think courts need to be more sensitive to considerations of legislative structure and process. On the whole, courts generally have tended to consider the constitutionality of laws with little regard to when they were passed, by whom, or how. If there is one clear practical lesson from public choice, it is the importance of structure and process. Yet courts often ignore the setting of legislation. The same constitutional tests are applied to decrepit city ordinances as to modern congressional statutes. Using the Court's controversial sexual privacy decisions as an example, in an epilogue we show that greater sensitivity to structure and process could have led the Court to a much more satisfactory resolution of the cases, furthering democratic deliberation without imposing a judicial value judgment on the public. We certainly don't argue that public choice and its allied disciplines can "solve" the issues of abortion or gay rights. What the social sciences may be able to do, however, is to show courts how they can help the public come to grips with the issues better.

This book offers a guided tour of many aspects of public choice and some of their possible applications. It does not purport to give a grand theory, and such a theory would be inconsistent with our general philosophical views. On the other hand, there is a unifying perspective. For lack of a better description, we would like to call it a neo-Madisonian view of the political system.

Some aspects of Madison's thought closely tracked modern public choice theory.[13] Where modern theorists speak of interest groups, Madison spoke of factions. He was keenly aware of the threat that factions can pose in a democracy. In *The Federalist No. 10,* he said that the "latent causes of faction are thus sown in the nature of man," but "the most common and durable source of factions has been the various and unequal distribution of property." Like today's public choice theorists, Madison was also skeptical in *The Federalist No. 10* that the virtue of politicians would be a sufficient cure: "It is in vain to say that enlightened statement will be able to adjust these clashing interests, and render them all subservient to the public good." Instead, Madison sought institutional methods of controlling the influence of factions. As he explained in *The Federalist No. 51,* the system of checks and balances is intended to provide the institutional protections against factions and compensate for the possible inadequacies of civic virtue. "Ambition must be made to counteract ambition. The interest of the man must be connected with the constitutional rights of the place." It is necessary, therefore, to "divide and arrange the several offices in such a manner as that each may be a check on the other—that the private interest of every individual may be a sentinel over the public rights."

Although he obviously had never heard of Arrow's Theorem, Madison anticipated the other major branch of public choice theory in his thoughts about legislative instability.[14] In *The Federalist No. 62,* he spoke of the "propensity of all single and numerous assemblies to yield to the impulse of sudden and violent passions" and the consequent need to control the "mutability in the public councils." Again, he sought a solution to instability through institutional arrangements, thereby anticipating the work of recent public choice theorists.

These elements of Madison's thought are echoed in modern public choice theory. But there is also a strongly republican tinge to his thought. Cass Sunstein has written at length about the role of legislative deliberation in Madison's political theory.[15] Madison's skepticism about human virtue is familiar fare. One of his best known statements (found in *The Federalist No. 51*) is that "[i]f men were angels, no government would be necessary. If angels were to govern men, neither external nor internal controls on government would be necessary." But he did not rely wholly on institutional protections. Unlike many of today's public choice theorists, he also understood the importance of civic virtue. As he said in *The Federalist No. 55:*

> As there is a degree of depravity in mankind which requires a certain degree of circumstances and distrust, so there are other

13. Some of the parallelisms between Madison and public choice theory are explored in THE FEDERALIST PAPERS AND THE NEW INSTITUTIONALISM (B. Grofman & D. Wittman eds. 1989).

14. *See* Mayton, *The Possibilities of Collective Choice,* 1986 DUKE L.J. 948, 953–54.

15. *See* Sunstein, *Interest Groups in American Public Law,* 38 STAN. L. REV. 29 (1985).

qualities in human nature which justify a certain portion of esteem and confidence. Republican government presupposed the existence of these qualities in a higher degree than any other form. Were the pictures which have been drawn by the political jealousy of some among us faithful likenesses of the human character, the inference would be, that there is not sufficient virtue among men for self-government; and that nothing less than the chains of despotism can restrain them from destroying and devouring one another.

Like Madison, we believe that no theory of government can ignore the powerful forces of individual self-interest and the critical role of institutional design. It is equally one-sided, however, to lose sight of the role of civic virtue. As Judge Mikva admitted, "Certainly, crooks have held public office." But the "biggest crook" Mikva had known in public life had a passion for protecting the interests of the elderly, though he had nothing to gain by doing so.[16]

In this book, we try to steer a middle course between cynicism and romanticism. Public choice theory can help us understand the all-too-real pathologies of government, and it is well to consider how best to avoid them. Just as in medicine, however, the most effective ways to treat the disease may rely on the patient's own strengths. Indeed, some important parts of our government structure can best be understood as part of the political "immune system," designed specifically to combat problems such as special interest influence and legislative incoherence. One of the most pressing problems now facing our legal system is how to strengthen this immune system, so that democratic government can realize its potentials rather than succumb to its pathologies.

16. Mikva, *supra* note 2, at 169.

O N E

Interest Groups and the Political Process

"*W*ould you say the government is pretty much run by a few big interests looking out for themselves or that it is run for the benefit of all the people?" A University of Michigan research institute has been asking Americans that question for over two decades. In 1964, less than a third adopted the "interest group" theory of politics. By 1982, over sixty percent did.[1]

Not surprisingly, some legal scholars have also begun to adopt an increasingly negative view of the government.[2] These scholars have been influenced not only by the public mood, but also by social science research. The literature on interest groups is indeed rich and suggestive, but a simplistic reading of that literature threatens to distort public law.

We will begin this chapter by showing how this literature is already affecting public law. Then we will turn to a detailed survey of the literature itself, to see what it really shows about the influence of interest groups in American government. Finally, we will ask whether interest group politics is inevitably harmful to society.

As we noted in the Introduction, how to define "public choice" is itself sharply disputed. Under our definition, interest group theory is part of public choice because it involves the use of economic premises and methodology to

1. *See* Sorauf, *Caught in a Political Thicket: The Supreme Court and Campaign Finance,* 3 CONST. COMM. 97, 114 (1986).

2. For analyses largely reflecting the view of interest group dominance, see Easterbrook, *Foreword: The Court and the Economic System,* 98 HARV. L. REV. 4, 15–18, 51 (1984) ("[o]ne of the implications of modern economic thought is that many laws are designed to serve private rather than public interests"); Epstein, *Toward a Revitalization of the Contract Clause,* 51 U. CHI. L. REV. 703, 713–15 (1984) ("interest-group theory of legislation provides powerful evidence of the persistence and extent of legislative abuse"); Macey, *Promoting Public-Regarding Legislation Through Statutory Interpretation: An Interest Group Model,* 86 COLUM. L. REV. 223, 224, 229–36, 245 (1986) ("special interest groups tend to dominate"); Wiley, *A Capture Theory of Antitrust Federalism,* 99 HARV. L. REV. 713, 723–26, 769–73 (1986). Miller, *Public Choice at the Dawn of the Special Interest State: The Story of Butter and Margarine,* 77 CALIF. L. REV. 83 (1989), is an excellent case study of rent-seeking legislation using a public choice perspective. Roin, *United They Stand, Divided They Fall: Public Choice Theory and the Tax Code,* 74 CORNELL L. REV. 62 (1988), applies public choice theory in the context of tax legislation. For more general discussions of public choice and public law, see Hirshman, *Postmodern Jurisprudence and the Problem of Administrative Discretion,* 82 NW. U.L. REV. 646 (1988); Rose-Ackerman, *Progressive Law and Economics—and the New Administrative Law,* 98 YALE L.J. 341 (1988).

study political institutions. Under some other definitions, however, the subject of interest groups is not part of public choice, nor are studies about how economic interests affect legislative or popular voting. We do not think much turns on whether a subject is labeled as "public choice" or as something else. Determining the effect of interest groups in American government is crucial. Deciding whether to label the inquiry as part of public choice may be important to some social science scholars in defining their particular disciplines, but for our purposes is only a matter of semantics.

I. The Impact of Interest Group Theory

Some readers may wonder why the social science literature about interest groups is relevant to law. If you think of judges as simply applying existing legal rules, the judges' political worldview doesn't seem very relevant. But legal rules are often unclear and conflicting, thus requiring judges to take a more creative role. A basic issue in "hard cases" is how much judges should defer to other branches of government rather than trying to solve problems themselves. Their willingness to defer to the legislature or the executive may depend on how they perceive those branches.

Public law is currently premised on the assumption that legislators are competent to make public policy. For example, in the constitutional law, deference to the legislature has been the norm, unless some specific constitutional right is threatened. Courts do not second-guess legislatures on issues like tax policy, welfare reform, or safety regulation. But what if the tax code is just designed to enrich particular industries, welfare reform to enrich social workers, and safety regulations to benefit unions? Why *shouldn't* courts decide for themselves whether these statutes make sense?[3]

Our very constitutional structure can be traced to a Madisonian concern about the influence of interest groups in the political process.[4] In the modern world, as well, contrasting visions of the representative process animate quite different versions of public law.[5]

One view of the political process is often called "pluralism." According to pluralists, legislative outcomes simply reflect private political power. Although it may be mechanical and rather disheartening, it is no new view that "[t]he balance of . . . group pressure *is* the existing state of society."[6] Public law theorists who accept the empirical accuracy of this conception have two options. They may celebrate pluralism. Or, if they find pluralism em-

---

3. *See, e.g.,* B. Siegan, Economic Liberties and the Constitution (1980); Epstein, *supra* note 2.

4. *See* Sunstein, *Interest Groups in American Public Law,* 38 Stan. L. Rev. 29 (1985).

5. *See, e.g.,* Sullivan, *Unconstitutional Conditions,* 102 Harv. L. Rev. 1413, 1468–76 (1989).

6. A. Bentley, The Process of Government 258–59 (1908).

pirically accurate but morally repulsive, they may favor judicial activism to protect those who lose in the political power struggle. Either way, trying to promote legislative deliberation is useless, since the mechanistic process of legislation leaves no room for a thoughtful legislative response.

Those who believe that legislators have some autonomy face a different menu of theoretical possibilities. Some may find the idea of the "public interest" itself either incoherent or a tyrannical imposition upon dissenters. They may want judges to promote pluralism by undercutting legislator independence. Believers in "republicanism" may embrace the public interest as a goal. They might want judges to rewrite election laws to insulate legislators from powerful private interests. To republicans, legislative deliberation may properly result in the rejection or reformation of "bad" private preferences.

So far, the Supreme Court has not fully embraced either pluralism or republicanism. Its various constitutional strategies—sometimes creating rights immune from legislative interference, at other times protecting politically powerless minorities from disadvantageous statutes, occasionally attempting to promote more careful deliberation about public policy, and frequently deferring to the legislature's judgment—reflect some appreciation of the richness and complexity of public policy formation.[7] The Court's decisions reflect a respectful yet practical understanding of the legislative process— for example, that a representative cannot be expected to understand every bill voted upon, that the remarks of a sponsor are often useful in construing the legislation despite the sponsor's obvious lack of objectivity, and that legislation is often the product of compromise. But there are also decisions invalidating statutes because of demonstrable legislative irrationality or prejudice, as well as decisions refusing to adhere to a legislator's interpretation that deviates substantially from the statutory language.[8] The Supreme Court's mediating path between the drastic alternatives of rigid pluralism and legislative independence indicates at least some appreciation for the problem of faction, while maintaining a degree of respect toward Congress and the state legislatures.

Some work on public choice, however, suggests that the Court might have done better to have adopted a rigid pluralism. Public choice models often treat the legislative process as a microeconomic system in which "actual political choices are determined by the efforts of individuals and groups to

7. For some illustrative cases, see Hawaii Hous. Auth. v. Midkiff, 467 U.S. 229, 241–42 (1984); Rogers v. Lodge, 458 U.S. 613, 627 (1982); Hampton v. Mow Sun Wong, 426 U.S. 88, 116 (1976); Lyng v. International Union, 485 U.S. 360, 370–74 (1988).

8. The Court's understanding of the legislative process is illustrated by Board of Governors v. Dimension Fin. Corp., 474 U.S. 361, 373–74 (1986); City of Cleburne v. Cleburne Living Center, 473 U.S. 432, 450 (1985); Regan v. Wald, 468 U.S. 222, 236–37 (1984).

further their own interests,"[9] efforts that have been labeled "rent-seeking."[10] Thus, "[t]he basic assumption is that taxes, subsidies, regulations, and other political instruments are used to raise the welfare of more influential pressure groups."[11] Although this assumption is obviously simplistic, its very simplicity creates the possibility of constructing powerful formal models. The similarity between pluralism and these economic models is obvious.

Several leading legal scholars have been influenced by this vision of the role of special interests. The economic theory of legislation recounted by William Landes and Richard Posner is firmly grounded in that tradition:

> In the economists' version of the interest-group theory of government, legislation is supplied to groups or coalitions that outbid rival seekers of favorable legislation. The price that the winning group bids is determined both by the value of legislative protection to the group's members and the group's ability to overcome the free-rider problems that plague coalitions. Payments take the form of campaign contributions, votes, implicit promises of future favors, and sometimes outright bribes. In short, legislation is "sold" by the legislature and "bought" by the beneficiaries of the legislation.[12]

Judge Posner himself has shown considerable restraint in his attitude toward public choice theory.[13] But other scholars have enthusiastically argued for changes in public law in light of the public choice literature.[14]

9. Becker, *A Theory of Competition Among Pressure Groups for Political Influence*, 98 Q.J. ECON. 371, 371 (1983). *See generally* Macey, *The Theory of the Firm and the Theory of Market Exchange*, 74 CORNELL L. REV. 43 (1988).

10. "Rent-seeking refers to the attempt to obtain economic rents (i.e., payments for the use of an economic asset in excess of the market price) through government intervention in the market." Macey, *supra* note 2, at 224 n.6.

11. Becker, *supra* note 9, at 373–74.

12. Landes & Posner, *The Independent Judiciary in an Interest-Group Perspective,* 18 J.L. & ECON. 875, 877 (1975). In describing this article, an economist has commented: "In this setting, an independent judiciary can increase the value of the legislation sold today by making it somewhat immune from short-run political pressures that might try to thwart or overturn the intent of the legislation in the future. And this is apparently what the founding fathers had in mind when they established an independent judiciary in the Constitution. In the Landes-Posner theory the First Amendment emerges 'as a form of protective legislation extracted by an interest group consisting of publishers, journalists, pamphleteers, and others who derive pecuniary and non-pecuniary income from publication and advocacy of various sorts' [citation omitted]. By such fruit has the dismal science earned its reputation." D. MUELLER, PUBLIC CHOICE II 244 (1989).

13. *See* Posner, *Theories of Economic Regulation,* 5 BELL J. ECON. & MGMT. SCI. 335 (1974), which evaluated the relative merits of "the traditional public interest theory of regulation and the newer economic theory" and concluded that not only had neither approach any demonstrated empirical support, neither had "been refined to the point where it can generate hypotheses sufficiently precise to be verified empirically." *Id.* at 357. *See also* R. POSNER, THE FEDERAL COURTS 262–67, 271, 286–93 (1985).

14. *See* Aranson, Gellhorn, & Robinson, *A Theory of Legislative Delegation,* 68 CORNELL

Although public choice has not yet radically altered contemporary public law, we are hardly ready to dismiss that possibility. One obvious analogue would be Chicago School economics. Two decades ago, the Chicago School would not have seemed likely to change antitrust law profoundly. Today, antitrust law hews closely to the Chicago "party line." The same could happen with public choice.

Even legal scholars who do not embrace the "new pluralism" may fall under its sway. For example, Cass Sunstein, a leading "republican" scholar, proposed an enhanced judicial role in promoting legislative deliberation insulated from powerful factions. One obvious question, as Sunstein recognized, is whether such legislative deliberation is even possible. He correctly noted that "[t]he state of political and economic theory on [legislative behavior] remains surprisingly crude." Yet, he said, "[f]ew would contend that nationally selected representatives have been able to exercise the [deliberative] role." Instead, there is "mounting evidence that the pluralist understanding captures a significant component of the legislative process and that, at the descriptive level, it is far superior to its competitors."[15]

What is the "mounting evidence" that led to Sunstein's pessimism about the feasibility of legislative deliberation about the public interest? He cited some political science studies of legislative motivations and alluded to "the economic literature" attempting "to explain legislative behavior solely by reference to constituent pressures."[16] That literature has pessimistic implications not only regarding the deliberative qualities of legislatures, but also regarding the likelihood that voters will be influenced by anything but raw self-interest. As we will see, Sunstein's forebodings are consistent with some of the best-known work in each area. We believe, however, that the

---

L. REV. 1, 21–67 (1982); Bruff, *Legislative Formality, Administrative Rationality,* 63 TEXAS L. REV. 207, 214–18 (1984); Elliott, *Constitutional Conventions and the Deficit,* 1985 DUKE L.J. 1077, 1086–95; Krier & Gillette, *The Un-Easy Case for Technological Optimism,* 84 MICH. L. REV. 405, 421–23 (1985); Rapaczynski, *From Sovereignty to Process: The Jurisprudence of Federalism After Garcia,* 1985 SUP. CT. REV. 341, 374–80, 392, 396–405; Spitzer, *Multicriteria Choice Processes: An Application of Public Choice Theory to Bakke, the F.C.C. and the Courts,* 88 YALE L.J. 717 (1979); Wiley, *supra* note 2. *See also* Ackerman, *Beyond Carolene Products,* 98 HARV. L. REV. 713, 728 (1985) (majorities "pay the bill for tariffs, agricultural subsidies and the like," while congressmen "deliver the goods to their well-organized local constituents"); Cass, *The Meaning of Liberty: Notes on Problems Within the Fraternity,* 1 NOTRE DAME J.L. ETHICS & PUB. POL'Y 777, 790 (1985).

15. Sunstein, *supra* note 4, at 48.

16. *Id.* at 48 nn.78–80. Sunstein remarked that "[s]uch interpretations have been attacked as too reductionist," Sunstein, *id.,* at 48, thus anticipating some of what follows in this chapter. *See also* Kelman, *On Democracy-Bashing: A Skeptical Look at the Theoretical and "Empirical" Practice of the Public Choice Movement,* 74 VA. L. REV. 199 (1988); Stewart, *Regulation in a Liberal State: The Role of Non-Commodity Values,* 92 YALE L.J. 1537, 1548–49 (1983).

prospects for democracy are not so dim as some theorists would have us believe. Legislators are indeed influenced by special interests, but they need not be mere pawns.

II. Interest Groups and Political Science

Interest groups are obviously important in the political process, so one would expect to find sustained study of their influence by political scientists. In fact, however, attention to special interests has fluctuated rather dramatically in the political science literature.

In 1935 a classic case study of E. E. Schattschneider concluded that special interest groups profoundly shaped the Smoot-Hawley Tariff of 1930.[17] By the early 1950s,[18] a pluralistic interpretation of politics had emerged, in which legislative outcomes were said simply to mirror the equilibrium of competing group pressures:

> [t]he legislature referees the group struggle, ratifies the victories of the successful coalitions, and records the terms of the surrenders, compromises, and conquests in the form of statutes. Every statute tends to represent compromise because the process of accommodating conflicts of group interest is one of deliberation and consent. The legislative vote on any issue tends to represent the composition of strength, i.e., the balance of power, among contending groups at the time of voting. What may be called public policy is the equilibrium reached in this struggle at any given moment, and it represents a balance which the contending factions of groups constantly strive to weight in their favor.[19]

This model received important support from Robert Dahl's famous study of New Haven politics in which he found a pluralistic dispersion of power among groups, which promoted stability and orderly change in response to the political preferences of the community.[20]

Other writers soon challenged the pluralist notion of the political centrality of interest groups. A survey of Washington lobbyists carried out in the late 1950s concluded that interest groups did not dominate the federal political process.[21] Bauer, Pool, and Dexter's detailed examination of tariff

---

17. E. SCHATTSCHNEIDER, POLITICS, PRESSURES AND THE TARIFF (1935).

18. *See* D. TRUMAN, THE GOVERNMENTAL PROCESS (1951); E. LATHAM, THE GROUP BASIS OF POLITICS (1952).

19. E. LATHAM, *supra*, at 35. Schattschneider, whose Smoot-Hawley Tariff study reached pluralist conclusions, stopped far short of this mechanical conception of politics. "It is hard to imagine a more effective way of saying that Congress had no mind or force of its own or that Congress is unable to invoke new forces that might alter the equation." E. SCHATTSCHNEIDER, THE SEMISOVEREIGN PEOPLE 37 (1960).

20. R. DAHL, WHO GOVERNS? (1961).

21. L. MILBRATH, THE WASHINGTON LOBBYISTS (1963).

legislation between 1953 and 1962 echoed this finding. They described lobbying groups as usually underfinanced, poorly organized, overworked, and often cancelling each other out.[22] Indeed, they concluded that lobbyists were more like "service bureaus" for legislators than "agents of direct persuasion."[23]

These conclusions about the relative unimportance of interest groups became "something approaching a new conventional wisdom" in political science.[24] With few exceptions, political scientists then paid little attention to interest groups until recently. Some theoretical advances were made by Theodore Lowi, James Q. Wilson, and Michael Hayes, suggesting that interest group activity should differ depending upon the distribution of the costs and benefits of proposed legislation.[25] This work was grounded in the "[c]ommon sense [notion] that groups might well be pivotal to certain kinds of issues and largely peripheral to others."[26] Notwithstanding these insights, one scholar complained in 1983 that interest group studies were "badly in need of empirical research and conceptual development."[27]

The rather discouragingly weak political science literature received a major boost in 1986, when Kay Lehman Schlozman and John T. Tierney published the first systematic study of interest group politics in twenty years.[28] A short summary cannot do justice to the rich information and anal-

22. R. BAUER, I. POOL, & L. DEXTER, AMERICAN BUSINESS AND PUBLIC POLICY (1963).

23. *Id.* at 350–53. In short order, Theodore Lowi explained that these conclusions about the impotence of interest groups in influencing 1950s tariff legislation could not fairly be compared to Schattschneider's finding that groups dominated the passage of the 1930 tariff (see *supra* note 17), because both studies were time-bound and of modest value for developing generalized group theory. Lowi, *American Business, Public Policy, Case-Studies, and Political Theory,* 16 W. POL. 677 (1964). For a brief overview, see M. HAYES, LOBBYISTS & LEGISLATORS: A THEORY OF POLITICAL MARKETS 8–10 (1981).

24. M. HAYES, *supra* note 23, at 2. *See id.* at 10–17.

25. *See* Lowi, *supra* note 23; J. WILSON, POLITICAL ORGANIZATIONS (1973); M. HAYES, *supra* note 23.

26. M. HAYES, *supra* note 23, at 3. Although Hayes's constructs are sophisticated and insightful, he recognized that they "cannot do justice to the full complexity of the legislative process," *id.* at 159, and are potentially impossible to test empirically. *Id.* at 161.

27. Sinclair, *Purposive Behavior in the U.S. Congress: A Review Essay,* 8 LEGIS. STUD. Q. 117, 126 (1983). The publication of Sinclair's complaint coincided with the appearance of two important books on interest groups. *See* INTEREST GROUP POLITICS (A. CIGLER & B. LOOMIS eds. 1983); A. MCFARLAND, COMMON CAUSE: LOBBYING IN THE PUBLIC INTEREST (1984).

28. K. SCHLOZMAN & J. TIERNEY, ORGANIZED INTERESTS AND AMERICAN DEMOCRACY (1986). In addition to examining information collected by others, Schlozman and Tierney interviewed 175 Washington representatives of interest groups and categorized about 7,000 organizations apparently involved in politics and the nearly 3,000 political action committees registered with the Federal Elections Commission. *Id.* at xii–xiii. Public law theorists tempted to accept simple generalizations about interest group politics should consider closely why Schlozman and Tierney attempted such a broad-gauged study: "By undertaking a systematic inquiry across the entire pressure scene we are able to pose questions that would be, quite sim-

ysis they provide. We will only note those principal findings most pertinent to public law theory.

Schlozman and Tierney concluded that, despite the recent growth in broad-based groups such as Common Cause, interest group politics is skewed dramatically toward narrow economic interests. There are few lobbyists for consumers but many for producers. Moreover, Schlozman and Tierney found little support for the "conventional wisdom" of scholars like Bauer, Pool, and Dexter about the supposed organizational and political weaknesses of interest groups. Today, many groups have substantial resources and engage in sophisticated political strategies, including active involvement in electoral politics. Contrary to another finding of Bauer, Pool, and Dexter, groups are not always active on both sides of an issue. Earlier studies focused too much on whether groups were able to kill legislation or push bills through Congress, ignoring whether the group was able to influence the details of legislation—for example, to soften a disfavored bill.

Nevertheless, Schlozman and Tierney reject the simple-minded view that groups control Congress. Group influence is likely to be strongest when the group is attempting to block rather than obtain legislation; when the group's goals are narrow and have low visibility; when the group has substantial support from other groups and public officials (who are themselves important figures and not merely referees of the group struggle); and when the group is able to move the issue to a favorable forum such as a sympathetic congressional committee. "Depending on the configuration of a large number of factors—among them the nature of the issue, the nature of the demand, the structure of political competition, and the distribution of resources—the effect of organized pressure on Congress can range from insignificant to determinative."[29]

Schlozman and Tierney confirm the frequently central role of interest groups. But their work also demonstrates that this process is too complex for simple predictive modeling. To be sure, "[t]he activities of organized interests build into the American political system a minoritarian counterweight to some of its more majoritarian tendencies," and "the minorities thus benefited—while not unanimous in their interests—are disproportion-

---

ply, impossible to answer were we to concentrate on a smaller portion of the whole. The realm of organized interest politics is so vast—encompassing so many different kinds of organizations and so many different avenues of influence—that it is possible to locate an example to illustrate virtually any reasonable generalization one might put forward. Only by taking a more global view can we get a sense of the relative frequencies within this world of astonishing political diversity." *Id.* at xiii.

29. *Id.* at 317. In addition to demonstrating the empirical invalidity of any reductionist theory of interest group influence in Congress, Schlozman and Tierney debunked any generalized theory that administrative agencies are inevitably captured by the interests they regulate. *See id.* at 276–78, 339–46.

ally but not uniformly affluent ones."[30] Yet the less advantaged, Schloz-man and Tierney concluded, "are nonetheless heeded in the making of policy" because they are somewhat active in group politics, because they sometimes benefit from the activities of narrower groups, "electoral and social movements are more hospitable to their interests," and because "those in government sometimes take up the cudgel on their behalf."[31] This last point is worth considering at greater length:

> The orthodox group theorists erred in ignoring the independent leadership and influence exercised by public officials. Contrary to what the group theorists would have us believe, the government is not some kind of anemometer measuring the force of the prevailing organized interest breezes. At various times and under various cir-cumstances, various governmental institutions and actors have adopted the causes of the less advantaged and broad publics.[32]

Why do public officials sometimes oppose powerful groups? Another body of literature has contemplated legislative behavior. In "one of the most influential essays in recent years,"[33] David Mayhew assumed that federal representatives "are interested in getting reelected—indeed, in their role here as abstractions, interested in nothing else."[34] Mayhew acknowledged that "[a]ny such assumption necessarily does violence to the facts,"[35] and that "a complete explanation (if one were possible) of a [representative's] or any one else's behavior would require attention to more than just one goal."[36] Yet Mayhew forcefully argued that the actions of federal legislators could profitably be understood by use of the "simple abstract assumption" that representatives are "single-minded seekers of reelection."[37]

As Mayhew noted, this assumption about legislators' motives is not nec-essarily inconsistent with democratic norms. Responsiveness to broad constituencies is not only an important aspect of representation, it also helps ameliorate the influence of special interests, as Schlozman and Tierney indi-cated. Yet fixation on reelection has its drawbacks. It may lead legislators to spend their time on pork barrel legislation for their districts and on personal contact with voters and casework for constituents, rather than on addressing hard policy issues.[38]

---

30. *Id.* at 403.

31. *Id.*

32. *Id.* at 402.

33. Matthews, *Legislative Recruitment and Legislative Careers,* in HANDBOOK OF LEGISLA-TIVE RESEARCH 17, 32 (1985).

34. D. MAYHEW, CONGRESS: THE ELECTORAL CONNECTION 13 (1974).

35. *Id.*

36. *Id.* at 15.

37. *Id.* at 5.

38. *See id.* at 49–61, 81–158; M. FIORINA, CONGRESS: KEYSTONE OF THE WASHINGTON ESTABLISHMENT (2d ed. 1989).

Because Mayhew's model is based on economic methodology, much of the discussion in the next section is applicable to his study. In particular, the demonstrated importance of legislators' ideology cuts against Mayhew's model. Moreover, empirical studies suggest, not surprisingly, that Mayhew's behavioral assumption is too simplistic.[39]

Surely closer to reality—although not as intellectually elegant—is Richard Fenno's suggestion that the behavior of members of Congress is dictated by three basic goals: achieving reelection, gaining influence within the House, and making good public policy. In Fenno's view, "[a]ll congressmen probably hold all three goals," but each representative has "his own mix of priorities and intensities—a mix which may, of course, change over time."[40] These goals are interconnected: a legislator's primary goal may be obtaining policy-making influence, not reelection for its own sake—but of course the former requires the latter.[41] This analysis fits well one federal representative's comment, in response to Fenno's remark that "[s]ometimes it must be hard to connect what you do here [in your district] with what you do in Washington." The reply was: "I do what I do here so I can do what I want to do there."[42] Sorting out these conflicting motives may be difficult because many actions serve both interests at once.

In the final analysis, contemporary political science research concerning interest groups and legislator behavior suggests a complex political world ill-fitting any simple formula. To be sure, the national political process appears vulnerable on a variety of fronts, including domination largely by narrow economic interests and reelection posturing by representatives. These concerns are reinforced by another body of research about interest groups conducted largely by economists.

III. The Economic Theory of Legislation

Economists, like political scientists, have held varying views of the political process. Until about twenty years ago, economists somewhat naively as-

39. *See* Kozak, *Decision-Making on Roll Call Votes in the House of Representatives*, 9 CONGRESS & THE PRESIDENCY 51 (1982) (voting is not a function of a single determinant); Smith & Deering, *Changing Motives for Committee Preferences of New Members of the U.S. House*, 8 LEGIS. STUD. Q. 271 (1983) (new members of 97th Congress reported preferences for committee assignments that represented mixed goals of reelection, policy impact, and prestige); Thomas, *Electoral Proximity and Senatorial Role Call Voting*, 29 AM. J. POL. SCI. 96 (1985) (as election approaches, federal senators seeking reelection tend to change voting patterns in direction of views of probable opponents, but even those senators attempt simultaneously to satisfy goals of reelection and of achieving preferred policy outcomes).

40. R. FENNO, CONGRESSMEN IN COMMITTEES 1 (1973). Fenno focused on members of the House of Representatives. He also acknowledged a fourth goal, setting up a career beyond the House, and a potential fifth, aggrandizing personal gain.

41. *See* Dodd, *Congress and the Quest for Power*, in CONGRESS RECONSIDERED (L. Dodd & B. Oppenheimer 1st ed. 1977). *See also* A. MAASS, CONGRESS AND THE COMMON GOOD 70–71 (1983) (reelection seen as a constraint to achievement of other goals).

42. R. FENNO, HOME STYLE: HOUSE MEMBERS IN THEIR DISTRICTS 199 (1978).

sumed that politicians were solely interested in furthering the public interest. Like some "pluralist" political scientists, economists then embraced the belief that legislation is generally a product of special interest groups.[43] This economic theory, which is most closely associated with George Stigler[44] and other members of the Chicago School, has increasingly influenced legal scholars. In this section, we will sketch the major arguments underlying the economic approach to legislation, consider the plausibility of the assumptions made by economists, and review the extensive empirical tests of the theory.

The core of the economic models is a jaundiced view of legislative motivation. In place of their prior assumption that legislators voted to promote their view of the public interest, economists now postulate that legislators are motivated solely by self-interest.[45] In particular, legislators must maximize their likelihood of reelection.[46] A legislator who is not reelected loses all the other possible benefits flowing from office.

The question, then, is what do legislators have to do to get reelected? In other words, what determines the outcomes of elections? Economic models can be classified into two groups, depending on how they answer this question.

Models in the first group assume that legislators attempt to maximize their appeal to their constituents. These constituents, in turn, vote according to their own economic self-interest.[47] Thus, those models suggest that legisla-

---

43. For excellent, balanced reviews of the literature, see Mashaw, *The Economics of Politics and the Understanding of Public Law*, 65 CHI.-KENT L. REV. 123, 141–50 (1989); Posner, *supra* note 13. Michael Hayes states: "For all their promise, these theories ultimately represent a reversion to the naive pressure model so effectively refuted by Bauer, Pool, and Dexter. Ironically these economists, not having read [Bauer, Pool, and Dexter], never fell prey to the new conventional wisdom it helped to create; unfortunately they also failed to benefit from its insights." M. HAYES, *supra* note 23, at 18.

44. *See* G. STIGLER, THE CITIZEN AND THE STATE: ESSAYS ON REGULATION (1975); Stigler, *The Theory of Economic Regulation*, 2 BELL J. ECON. & MGMT. SCI. 3 (1971).

45. *See* Shepsle, *Prospects for Formal Models of Legislatures*, 10 LEGIS. STUD. Q. 5, 12–13 (1985). As Landes and Posner state, *supra* note 12, at 877: "In the economists' version of the interest-group theory of government, legislation is supplied to groups or coalitions that outbid rival seekers of favorable legislation. . . . Payment takes the form of campaign contributions, votes, implicit promises of future favors, and sometimes outright bribes." Thus, as they note later, when interpreting statutes, "The courts do not enforce the moral law or ideals of neutrality, justice, or fairness; they enforce the 'deals' made by effective interest groups with earlier legislatures." *Id.* at 894.

46. *See, e.g.,* Sinclair, *supra* note 27. Stigler suggests that legislators would vote according to the public interest if they could, but that the need to be reelected makes this impossible. Stigler, *supra* note 44, at 11.

47. Some empirical evidence suggests that legislators are also influenced by the ideology of their constituents. *See* Kau, Kennan, & Rubin, *A General Equilibrium Model of Congressional Voting*, 97 Q.J. ECON. 271 (1982).

tive votes can be easily predicted from the economic interests of constituents.[48]

Models in the second group give a greater role to special interest groups. Because voters don't know much about a legislator's conduct, elections may turn on financial backing, publicity, and endorsements. These forms of support, as well as other possible benefits including outright bribes, are likely to be provided by organized interest groups, which thereby acquire the ability to affect legislative action.

The economic theory of interest groups can be traced to Mancur Olson's theory of collection action.[49] Olson pointed out that political action generally benefits large groups. For example, everyone presumably benefits from improved national security. But any single person's efforts to protect national security normally can have only an infinitesimal effect. Hence, a rational person will try to "free ride" on the efforts of others, contributing nothing to the national defense while benefiting from other people's actions.

This "free rider" problem suggests that it should be nearly impossible to organize large groups of individuals to seek broadly dispersed public goods. Instead, political activity should be dominated by small groups of individuals seeking to benefit themselves, usually at the public expense.[50] The easiest groups to organize would presumably consist of a few individuals or firms seeking government benefits for themselves, which will be financed by the general public. Thus, if Olson is correct, politics should be dominated by "rent-seeking" special interest groups.

The various economic theories of legislation have in common their rejection of ideology as a significant factor in the political process.[51] They assume that ideology, defined simply as individual beliefs about the public interest, influences neither voters nor legislators. The heart of the economic

---

48. *See* Weingast, Shepsle, & Johnsen, *The Political Economy of Benefits and Costs: A Neoclassical Approach to Distributive Politics,* 89 J. POL. ECON. 642 (1981) (explanation of pork barrel politics based on constituent interest); Peltzman, *Constituent Interest and Congressional Voting,* 27 J.L. & ECON. 181 (1984).

49. *See* M. OLSON, THE LOGIC OF COLLECTIVE ACTION: PUBLIC GOODS AND THE THEORY OF GROUPS (1965). Olson attempts to explain the ability of groups to overcome free riding on the basis of their ability to provide direct, nonpolitical services to members. *See id.* at 132–34. Other possible explanations are discussed in Finkel, Muller, & Opp, *Personal Influence, Collective Rationality, and Mass Political Action,* 83 AM. POL. SCI. REV. 885 (1989).

50. *See, e.g.,* Macey, *supra* note 2, at 231–32. As Becker points out, most groups involved in politics may suffer from free rider problems. What is important is the relative rather than absolute degree of free riding, since this determines the relative power of the group. *See* Becker, *supra* note 9, at 380.

51. Olson conceded that "[t]here is to be sure always *some* ideologically oriented behavior in any society, and even among the most stable and well-adjusted groups." M. OLSON, *supra* note 49, at 162. He went on to suggest, however, that in the United States this behavior is relatively minor. *Id.*

approach is the assumption that self-interest is the exclusive causal agent in politics. (This may seem a cynical perspective, but in some ways it may actually be unduly optimistic, because it ignores the dark side of ideology as exemplified by the Nazis and other hate groups. There are worse forces in the human psyche than greed.)

Clearly, these economists have identified some important political realities. Legislators with more affluent constituencies often vote differently from those with blue collar or unemployed constituents. Those from agricultural districts often have different views from those from manufacturing centers. This is consistent with the assumption that legislators represent their constituents' economic interests. Moreover, as the political science literature indicates, special interest groups do appear to play a major role in the legislative process.[52] Thus, the economic model appears to have a certain amount of explanatory power—which is not surprising, because it parallels some common sense observations about politics.

On the other hand, public choice ignores some other common sense observations about politics. Some crucial features of the political world do not fit the economic model. It does not account for ideological politicians like Reagan and Thatcher. Most notably, it does not account for popular voting. Elections provide a classic example of the incentives to free ride. Given the number of voters, the chance that an individual vote will change the outcome is virtually nil.[53] Since voting is costly in terms of time and inconvenience, no economically rational person would vote. Indeed, the likelihood of casting a decisive vote is about the same as that of being run over by a car in the process of going to or from the polls.[54] Yet, millions of people do in fact

---

52. As Olson would predict, these groups generally represent relatively concentrated economic interests. In contrast, consumers—the most widely dispersed economic interest—remain unrepresented. *See* K. SCHLOZMAN & J. TIERNEY, *supra* note 28, at 74–87, 111, 128, 387–89. On the other hand, even if members of large diffused groups are individually less likely to attend to, and base their votes on, recent legislation, the greater size of the group is a countervailing factor. *See* Wittman, *Why Democracies Produce Efficient Results,* 97 J. POL. ECON. 1395, 1407–8 (1989). *See also* Blais, Couiseneau, & McRoberts, *The Determinants of Minimum Wage Rates,* 62 PUB. CHOICE 15, 19 (1989) (finding that diffuse groups have more influence than labor unions).

53. The chance that a single vote will decide an election goes down rapidly with the number of voters. The exact formula depends on the particular statistical assumptions. Roughly speaking, if a district contains 500,000 voters, the likelihood of such a close election is somewhere between 1 in 700 and 1 in 500,000. *See* Foster, *The Performance of Rational Voter Models in Recent Presidential Elections,* 78 AM. POL. SCI. REV. 678 (1984). Using the larger probability, we would expect in any given district to have one such House election every 1,400 years (once every million years if we use the other figure). And even then, only the identity of one House member has been changed, which can be expected to have only a tenuous impact on public policy.

54. D. MUELLER, *supra* note 12, at 350.

vote.[55] A theory that cannot even account for people going to the polls,[56] let alone explain how they vote once they get there,[57] can hardly claim to provide a complete theory of politics.

Public choice's inability to account for voting is important for two reasons. First, if public choice cannot explain such a fundamental aspect of political behavior as voting, can we trust its explanations of other political behavior? Second, because much of what politicians do is either constrained or motivated by electoral results, a theory that cannot explain the behavior of voters may also be unilluminating when it comes to some aspects of politicians' behavior. Successful politicians must have their own models about how voters behave, and these models cannot be based on public choice. So even a model of legislators' behavior must incorporate a non–public choice model of voting in order to predict legislative events.

In a recent article, Professors DeBow and Lee have tried to plug this hole in public choice theory.[58] They admit that ideology and self-interest are not coterminous, and that people are not single-minded seekers of either. But they suggest that popular voting behavior is nonetheless largely compatible with public choice. As we understand their argument, voting provides the pleasure of expressing an opinion on a matter of public importance at a relatively low cost. The very impotence of the vote allows people to express their ideological viewpoints at minimal personal sacrifice. For example, someone who thinks that taxes should be raised can express that view by voting for a candidate who advocates a tax increase. This vote is "cheap"

---

55. As Margolis points out, not only do most people vote, but "generally the propensity to vote increases with education." Thus, "the voters more likely to be aware of the argument that voting is not rational are in fact particularly likely to vote." H. MARGOLIS, SELFISHNESS, ALTRUISM, AND RATIONALITY: A THEORY OF SOCIAL CHOICE 17 (1982).

56. Apart from the common sense objections to the "rational voter" model, more rigorous empirical studies fail to support it. For example, the model predicts that voter turnout should be strongly related to the closeness of the election, since in close elections the voter's "taste" for voting is reinforced by the increased likelihood of affecting the result. The data reveal only a rather weak relationship between turnout and closeness. Furthermore, the electoral margin starts to affect turnout when elections are not terribly close and the chance of an individual voter affecting the result is still almost zero. *See* Foster, *supra* note 53, at 688. For a recent survey of the literature, see D. MUELLER, *supra* note 12, at 348–69.

57. No reason exists to believe that the economically irrational forces that propel people to the voting booth cease to operate once they are inside. *See* Kalt & Zupan, *Capture and Ideology in the Economic Theory of Politics*, 74 AM. ECON. REV. 279, 282 (1984). The empirical evidence suggests that voters are influenced by both their own economic interest and their view of the national economy, but that the latter has more effect on election results. *See* Markus, *The Impact of Personal and National Economic Conditions on the Presidential Vote: A Pooled Cross-Sectional Analysis*, 32 AM. J. POL. SCI. 137 (1988). There is some evidence that ideological voting is on the increase. *See* M. FIORINA, *supra* note 38, at 90.

58. DeBow & Lee, *Understanding (and Misunderstanding) Public Choice: A Response to Farber and Frickey*, 66 TEX. L. REV. 993 (1988).

since the voter can rest free of any concern that her vote might actually make a difference and result in the candidate's election, which might ultimately result in a tax increase costly to the voter. The same vote would become more costly (and hence less likely) in a very close election where a single vote might make a difference to the outcome.

This seems a bit farfetched. Voting is time-consuming and bothersome; an individual could find many more efficient ways to express her ideology at less overall expense, such as scribbling a postcard and mailing it to a legislator, or shouting out the window. Moreover, if DeBow and Lee are correct, it should not matter whether the total votes cast determine who holds public office. People should be just as happy to vote so long as the votes are tallied and reported in the newspaper—indeed, they should be happier, because then votes inconsistent with their economic self-interest would be even less likely to cost them anything![59]

Why is it so difficult to admit that people vote out of political commitment, not personal satisfaction? Popular voting is rational largely in a Kantian, not an economic sense.[60] DeBow and Lee do readily acknowledge the "Virginia School criticism of the claim that voters vote their economic self-interest, *narrowly defined*," citing an article by Brennan and Buchanan.[61] DeBow and Lee continue to argue, however, that a public choice theorist would expect "the average person to pursue objectives in his political behavior that are different from those pursued in his market behavior *simply* because the costs of such pursuits differ between the political process and the market process."[62] They have seemingly missed the thrust of Brennan and Buchanan's remarks: "Public choice theory, in simply assuming that voters behave rationally and in a manner analogous to that in which market agents can be presumed to operate, is . . . at risk entirely on logical grounds."[63]

---

59. Actually, the ideal method of expression would be to lock yourself in a room, make sure that no one else was in the house, and then shout your political views at the empty house, free from any concern that anyone might hear and implement your views. This would insure that your self-expression could not possibly result in the implementation of any of the potentially costly policies that you might favor.

60. That is, voting is rational because society is better off if everyone does it, even if no one individual's decision to vote has any impact. Thus, people would agree to the recognition of a moral duty to vote when determining social rules behind the Rawlsian "veil of ignorance." *See generally* J. RAWLS, A THEORY OF JUSTICE 333–42 (1971) (arguing in favor of some similar "natural duties"). Such conduct is socially rational but not rational in the sense economists use the term, since any given individual could increase his welfare by allowing others to incur the costs of political participation.

61. *See* DeBow & Lee, *supra* note 58, at 998 n.23 (citing Brennan & Buchanan, *Voter Choice*, 28 AM. BEHAV. SCIENTIST 185 (1984) (emphasis added)).

62. DeBow & Lee, *supra* note 58, at 997 (emphasis added).

63. Brennan & Buchanan, *supra* note 61, at 200.

We doubt that DeBow and Lee have made the case for the premise that voting is economically rational because it is impotent. We also doubt that this premise rescues the public choice theory of voting from tautology, in the sense that you can explain anything if you postulate a "taste" for that behavior. DeBow and Lee seek to avoid the tautology by postulating a single taste which can then be gratified with methods of varying cost. Nevertheless, their account cannot be empirically falsified and hence must be considered tautological. Suppose, for example, that in some population a more costly method of political activity (carefully monitoring legislators or organizing political action groups) was actually preferred to voting. This would disprove the DeBow-Lee hypothesis only if we knew that these individuals valued the self-expression involved in voting and the other activities equally. But we have no independent measure of the amount of "self-expression" purchased through these activities. So, if individuals choose a course of conduct despite a higher price, we can infer that not only do they have a "taste" for political self-expression, but they put a higher value on that "flavor" of self-expression than on the self-expression involved in voting. Without some independent measure, not only of the cost of each activity, but of its "self-expression value," we can account for *any* pattern of activities within the public choice framework.

In short, we agree with another theorist that "[i]deology plays a role in political choice that has no real parallel in ordinary private choice on how to spend on consumer goods."[64] Besides failing to explain the behavior of voters, the economic model also fails to explain how voters and interest groups control legislators. In the model, voters and interest groups seek to use legislators as their agents, while legislators (like all economic actors) seek to further their own goals. Economists have a well-developed theory of agency. This theory suggests strongly that the behavior of agents is unlikely to correspond perfectly with the preferences of their principals.[65] On the basis of general economic theory, then, it seems likely that legislators will sometimes "shirk," acting in accord with their own preferences, rather than those of voters or interest groups.

The economic model clearly overlooks important aspects of the political process. Nevertheless, a theory may make unrealistic assumptions but prove highly useful in making predictions. Even a physicist, when seeking to describe a complex physical system, will often make simplifying assumptions that are known to be at best approximations. The basic assumptions of microeconomic theory are notoriously unrealistic, but most economists feel that the predictions are sufficiently accurate to justify the continued use of

---

64. H. MARGOLIS, *supra* note 55, at 95.

65. For details concerning this argument and citations to the economics literature on agency, *see* Kalt & Zupan, *supra* note 57, at 282–84.

the assumptions. The ultimate test of an economic model is its predictive ability. How well does the economic theory of legislation perform empirically? Despite the common assumption to the contrary in the legal literature,[66] the supporting evidence is quite thin.[67]

Two types of evidence are commonly cited in support of the theory. The first consists of studies showing that some particular law in fact benefits a discrete economic group.[68] For example, environmental regulation may favor firms owning large plants over those owning small plants;[69] this finding has been cited as showing that even legislation apparently in the public interest is really the product of special interests. Such evidence is not entitled to much weight. To begin with, the finding of differential impact is often dubious.[70] Economists disagree, for example, over whether federal trucking regulation benefited the owners, the drivers, or both.[71] If economists cannot always determine the economic impact of legislation after the fact, interest groups must also sometimes find it difficult to determine whether to support proposed legislation.[72] Moreover, showing that a law benefits a certain group hardly establishes that this support caused the passage of the law. Differential economic impact only suggests that the passage of a law *could* possibly have an economic explanation. But ideological forces may be an alternative explanation.

The other type of empirical study attempts to meet this criticism by using

66. *See* Easterbrook, *supra* note 2, at 16 n.16, 45 n.101; Macey, *supra* note 2, at 224 n.224.

67. Our conclusion in this regard is in agreement with Judge Posner's earlier survey of the literature. *See* Posner, *supra* note 13, at 352–55.

68. *See* Macey, *supra* note 2, at 232 n.46; Easterbrook, *supra* note 2, at 45 n.101.

69. *See* Pashigan, *The Effect of Environmental Regulation on Optimal Plant Size and Factor Shares*, 27 J.L. & ECON. 1 (1984). (For a debate on the validity of Pashingan's methodology, *see* Evans, *The Differential Effect of Regulation Across Plant Size: Comment on Pashigan,* 29 J.L. & ECON. 187 (1986), and Pashigan, *Reply to Evans, id.* at 201.) A similar study of OSHA can be found in Bartel & Thomas, *Direct and Indirect Effects of Regulation: A New Look at OSHA's Impact,* 28 J.L. & ECON. 1 (1985). *But see* Kelman, *supra* note 16, at 251–63 (critiquing Bartel & Thomas); Leone & Jackson, *The Political Economy of Federal Regulatory Activity: The Case of Water Pollution Controls,* in STUDIES IN PUBLIC REGULATION 248 (G. Fromm ed. 1981) (finding no relationship between legislators' votes and compliance costs for local industry). Note that if a law would help one group of firms at the expense of a second group, either the passage or defeat of the law can be cited as proof of the economic theory, because the researcher can always attribute the outcome to the influence of one of the contesting groups.

70. Posner points out the difficulty of tracing the economic effects of regulation. *See* Posner, *supra* note 13, at 355.

71. *See* Rose, *The Incidence of Regulatory Rents in the Motor Carrier Industry,* 16 RAND J. ECON. 299, 300–303 (1985); Kim, *The Beneficiaries of Trucking Regulation, Revisited,* 27 J.L. & ECON. 227 (1984).

72. For example, physicians, who lobbied hard against Medicare legislation, received an unanticipated financial windfall from its passage. *See* K. SCHLOZMAN & J. TIERNEY, *supra* note 28, at 18.

the economic model to predict the votes of individual legislators. Typically, the researcher finds several rough measures of a law's economic effects on constituents or campaign contributors. The researcher then studies whether the votes of individual legislators are statistically related to these economic impacts. In general, as predicted by the model, these studies do find positive relationships between legislative behavior and economic variables.[73] They fail to show, however, that noneconomic factors are not even more important.[74]

Other studies have focused on noneconomic factors. They also find positive relationships. In fact, ideology (usually measured by the annual ratings given by the Americans for Democratic Action) seems to be an even better predictor than economics. Even on purely economic matters, ideology is a strong predictor of legislators' votes.[75] For example, in consider-

73. *See* Netter, *An Empirical Investigation of the Determinants of Congressional Voting on Federal Financing of Abortions and the ERA*, 14 J. LEGAL STUD. 245 (1985); Primeaux, Filer, Herren, & Hollas, *Determinants of Regulatory Policies Toward Competition in the Electric Utility Industry*, 43 PUB. CHOICE 173 (1984); Frendreis & Waterman, *PAC Contributions and Legislative Behavior: Senate Voting on Trucking Deregulation*, 66 SOCIAL SCIENCE Q. 401 (1985); Kau & Rubin, *Voting on Minimum Wages: A Time-Series Analysis*, 86 J. POL. ECON. 337 (1978); Danielsen & Rubin, *An Empirical Investigation of Voting on Energy Issues*, 31 PUB. CHOICE 121 (1977); Silberman & Durden, *Determining Legislative Preferences on the Minimum Wage: An Economic Approach*, 84 J. POL. ECON. 317 (1976). Other studies are discussed in M. HAYES, *supra* note 23, at 44–46. In failing to detect any economic influence on passage of the Sherman Act, Stigler, *The Origin of the Sherman Act*, 14 J. LEG. STUD. 1 (1985), concluded that the reason must be that the Sherman Act was only a "moderate change" in public policy, *id.* at 7.

74. Many of the studies are done with statistical techniques (logit or probit analysis) that do not provide any convenient measure of how much of the variation in the dependent variable (here, legislative voting) is explained by the independent economic variables. (For an introduction to these variants of regression analysis, *see* R. PINDYCK & D. RUBINFELD, ECONOMETRIC MODELS AND ECONOMIC FORECASTS 273–318 (2d ed. 1981).) Other studies use traditional regression analysis for which R^2 provides a measure of how much legislative behavior is left statistically unexplained. (Regression analysis is explained in H. KELEJIAN & H. OATES, INTRODUCTION TO ECONOMETRICS 19–76 (2d ed. 1981).) These studies have come up with relatively low R^2s, indicating that either the data are poor or much of the legislative voting is left unexplained.

75. *See* Bernstein & Anthony, *The ABM Issue in the Senate, 1968–1970: The Importance of Ideology*, 68 AM. POL. SCI. REV. 1198 (1974) (ideology much more important factor than amount of defense spending in district generated by ABM); Bernstein & Horn, *Explaining House Voting on Energy Policy: Ideology and the Conditional Effects of Party and District Economic Interests*, 34 W. POL. Q. 235 (1981) (ideology much more important explanatory factor than constituent interest); Goldstein, *The Political Economy of Trade: Institutions of Protection*, 80 AM. POL. SCI. REV. 161, 173, 179–80 (1986) (free trade views more important in determining trade policy than interest groups); Kenski & Kenski, *Partisanship, Ideology, and Constituency Differences on Environmental Issues in the U.S. House of Representatives: 1973–1978*, 9 POL'Y STUD. J. 325 (1980) (similar finding with respect to environmental legislation); Mitchell, *The Basis of Congressional Energy Policy*, 57 TEX. L. REV. 591 (1979) (reporting

ing votes on natural gas deregulation, Professor Mitchell found that over ninety percent of the votes could be predicted simply by whether the congressman's ADA score was greater than forty-five percent. This simple rule predicted 361 out of 399 votes correctly.[76]

Given this evidence of the importance of noneconomic factors, validation of the purely economic model requires proof that it performs better than models that include noneconomic factors. The economic model has not done well in such tests. Studies that examine both economic and ideological influences generally conclude that ADA scores are substantial factors in predicting legislators' votes. Models that include both ideological and economic factors outperform purely economic models, even when legislation involves strictly economic issues.[77]

Some economists criticize these studies because ADA scores are themselves correlated with the legislators' constituencies. Hence, the ADA score may be indirectly measuring the makeup of a legislator's district rather than the legislator's own political views.[78] This is not an implausible criticism, but it appears to be ill-founded.[79] Several researchers have developed techniques of "cleansing" ADA scores of their association with constituent makeup.[80] (Essentially, the portion of the ADA score that can be correlated with constituent interests is eliminated, and the residue is treated as a measure of the legislator's ideology.) The cleansed scores were still found to be significantly related to legislative votes.[81]

---

that ideology is an *extremely* strong predictor of votes on energy legislation); Welch, *Campaign Contributions and Legislative Voting: Milk Money and Dairy Price Supports*, 35 W. POL. SCI. Q. 478 (1982) (ideology more important factor than campaign contributions). Another article suggests that political science case studies overestimate the influence of interest groups because such groups may influence decisions at one point in the legislative process which are cancelled out by later decisions. *See* Meier & Copeland, *Interest Groups and Public Policy*, 64 SOC. SCI. Q. 641 (1983).

76. Mitchell, *supra* note 75, at 598. *See also* Poole & Daniels, *Ideology, Party, and Voting in the U.S. Congress, 1959–1980*, 79 AM. POL. SCI. REV. 373 (1985) (liberal-conservative dimension used by interest groups to rate members of Congress is consistent with much roll call voting). For a related study, see Poole & Rosenthal, *A Spatial Model for Legislative Roll Call Analysis*, 29 AM. J. POL. SCI. 357 (1985). Their methodology is critiqued in Koford, *Dimensions in Congressional Voting*, 83 AM. POL. SCI. REV. 949 (1989).

77. Peltzman now concedes that inclusion of noneconomic factors increases a model's explanatory power. *See* Peltzman, *An Economic Interpretation of the History of Congressional Voting in the Twentieth Century*, 75 AM. ECON. REV. 656, 663, 666 (1985).

78. *See* Peltzman, *Constituent Interest and Congressional Voting*, *supra* note 48.

79. *See* Poole & Rosenthal, *The Political Economy of Roll-Call Voting in the "Multi-Party" Congress of the United States*, 1 EUR. J. POL. ECON. 45 (1985).

80. *See* Kalt & Zupan, *supra* note 57, at 288, 290–97. A somewhat more rigorous development can be found in Carson & Oppenheimer, *A Method of Estimating the Personal Ideology of Political Representatives*, 78 AM. POL. SCI. REV. 163 (1984); Poole & Rosenthal, *supra* note 79.

81. *See* Carson & Oppenheimer, *supra* note 80, at 173, 177; Kalt & Zupan, *supra* note 57, at

There are strong reasons to believe that the cleansed scores actually measure legislators' personal views on public policy, rather than indicating the influence of undetected economic factors. First, the cleansed scores correlate better with voting in off years than in election years. Politicians presumably feel freer to vote their own views when they aren't up for reelection. Second, any undetected economic factor would have to be entirely unrelated to the economic factors already taken into account.[82] (Illustratively, an undetected special interest group would have to be equally powerful in urban and rural districts, among union members and nonmembers, and among all income groups. Such an interest group is not easy to imagine.) Third, the cleansed scores correlate with a broad range of votes, including both economic and social issues. Again, it is hard to imagine economic groups with such diverse constellations of interests.[83] Thus, these results strongly suggest that one factor in determining how a legislator votes is simply that legislator's view of the public interest.[84]

Indeed, these results may underestimate the importance of ideology. Their statistical method essentially assumes that whenever a legislator's ide-

---

286–98; Kau & Rubin, *Self Interest, Ideology, and Logrolling in Congressional Voting*, 22 J.L. & Econ. 365, 379–81 (1979); Poole & Rosenthal, *supra* note 79. Another study found significant effects of constituent ideology after controlling for constituent economic traits. *See* Kau, Kennan, & Rubin, *supra* note 47, at 287. This and related work by Kau and Rubin are collected in J. Kau & P. Rubin, Congressmen, Constituents, and Contributors: Determinants of Roll Call Voting in the House of Representatives (1982). Another sophisticated technique, with similar results, was used in J. Kalt, The Economics and Politics of Oil Price Regulation: Federal Policy in the Post-Embargo Era 253–78 (1981) (using a technique that pools prior information and sample information). Another study, using a simultaneous equation model, found that much of the apparent effect of campaign contributions on legislative votes was actually due to the propensity of interest groups to contribute to legislators whose initial positions were sympathetic. *See* Chappell, *Campaign Contributions and Voting on the Cargo Preference Bill: A Comparison of Simultaneous Models*, 36 Pub. Choice 301 (1981).

82. For instance, Kau and Rubin took into account per capita income, unionization, racial composition, education, oil production, average age, defense spending, percentage of farmers, and welfare payments. Kau & Rubin, *supra* note 81, at 370. This is far from a complete list of major economic interests, but most other economic factors seem to have some correlation with at least one of these variables. For example, it is not easy to come up with economic interests that are equally powerful in rural and urban areas.

83. For example, Kalt and Zupan found that votes on legislation to control strip-mining are highly correlated with votes on issues such as the death penalty and sex education. *See* Kalt & Zupan, *supra* note 57, at 291. We are unable to imagine any group with an economic interest in all these issues.

84. A study of abortion and related social issues found only a modest correlation between legislators' votes and their constituents' preferences; on abortion, in particular, a representative's religion and race were powerful explanatory factors. *See* Page, Shapiro, Gronke, & Rosenthal, *Constituency, Party and Representation in Congress*, 48 Pub. Opinion Q. 741, 752 (1984).

ology correlates with the interests of his constituency, all of the causal power is to be attributed to constituency economic interest. A plausible argument can be made, however, that part of the effect of the economic makeup of the constituency is on constituency ideology, which in turn relates to the choice of legislator.[85] If so, constituency economic interest may have little direct effect on legislators' votes. If, as seems likely, the truth is somewhere in between the economic model and this ideological model, ideology may play a role of at least the same order of magnitude as economics in the political process.

The studies using "cleansed" ADA ratings are the best of the current crop of econometric tests of the economic model of legislation. That does not, of course, mean that they are foolproof. The results of these studies are reinforced, however, by two other important kinds of evidence. First, as we saw earlier, the political science literature on legislative behavior supports the conclusion that legislators are partly influenced by a desire to promote the public interest. While economists sometimes seem to trust only the results of econometric studies, we see no reason to be so parochial in our methodological assessments. Indeed, the fact that traditional political scientists have reached the same conclusions as the best econometric research is a particularly valuable confirmation precisely because the research methodologies are so different.

Second, detailed investigations of the adoption of particular statutes tend not to support explanations based solely on special interest influence. For example, it has been suggested that environmental statutes favor large firms over small ones.[86] In reality, the major influence on the legislation seems to have been a desire to appeal to environmentalist voters.[87] Similarly, the Glass-Steagall Act has been described by a prominent public choice analyst as the result of lobbying by New York investment bankers.[88] A recent study,

85. For empirical evidence on the significance of constituent ideology in explaining legislative votes, see Kau & Rubin, *Economic and Ideological Factors in Congressional Voting: The 1980 Election*, 44 PUB. CHOICE 385 (1984); Page, Shapiro, Gronke, & Rosenberg, *supra* note 84. *See also* Glazer & Robbins, *How Elections Matter: A Study of U.S. Senators*, 46 PUB. CHOICE 163 (1985) (senators change their positions to track the ideology of recently elected senators from their states). *See generally* Wattier, *Ideological Voting in 1980 Republican Primaries*, 45 J. POL. 1016 (1983) (ideology guides voters); sources cited in note 39 *supra*. A recent article suggests that it may be futile to attempt to separate a legislator's personal beliefs from those of the constituents, because an entrepreneurial politician can often find enough support groups in diverse districts to be elected when voter turnout is low. See Poole, *Recent Developments in Analytical Models of Voting in the U.S. Congress*, 13 LEGIS. STUD. Q. 117 (1988).

86. Easterbrook, *supra* note 2, at 16 n.16; Pashigan, *supra* note 69.

87. Elliott, Ackerman, & Millian, *Toward a Theory of Statutory Evolution: The Federalization of Environmental Law*, 1 J.L. ECON. & ORG. 313 (1985). Notably, the authors of this study concluded that these voters were not represented by organized interest groups at the time. *Id.* at 317.

88. Macey, *Special Interest Groups Legislation and the Judicial Function: The Dilemma of Glass-Steagall*, 33 EMORY L.J. 1, 20 (1984).

however, demonstrates that the statute is precisely what it appeared to be all along: the product of misguided populist impulses.[89]

Thus, we have three bodies of evidence that seem to point to the same conclusion: the most careful econometric work, the findings of traditional social scientists, and historical investigations of the public choice accounts of particular legislation. There is no such thing as conclusive evidence in the social sciences, but we can feel some degree of confidence in rejecting the economic model of legislation (at least, without significant modifications). No one would deny the importance of self-interest in the political process, but we can also be reasonably sure that self-interest is not the whole story.

A less grandiose version of the economic theory would simply postulate (1) that reelection is an important motive of legislators, (2) that constituent and contributor interests thereby influence legislators, and (3) that small, easily organized interest groups have an influence disproportionate to the size of their membership. In short, the model could be used to identify tendencies within the political system, rather than claiming to explain all of politics. Based on the empirical evidence, this less ambitious, weaker version of the theory seems far more supportable than the strong version.

Our best picture of the political process, then, is a mixed model in which constituent interest, special interest groups, and ideology all help determine legislative conduct.[90] Even in purely economic matters, ideology plays some role, while economics may have some impact even on social issues. It would be extremely useful to know more about the relative weights of these factors in various situations. Although a few writers have offered some suggestions about how the relative influence of interest groups may vary, the empirical evidence so far is spotty at best. The studies of tariff legislation discussed earlier in this chapter show that, even with a single type of legislation, the relative influence of special interest groups and ideology has varied over time. For now, the strongest (if somewhat vague) conclusion is simply that these relative weights seem somewhat correlated with the nature of the issue.

IV. Normative Implications

Much of the literature on interest groups conveys a strong flavor of disapproval. Suppose organized interest groups do have disproportionate political influence. What is so wrong with that?

89. Langevoort, *Statutory Obsolescence and the Judicial Process: The Revisionist Role of the Courts in Banking Regulation*, 85 MICH. L. REV. 672 (1987).

90. Undoubtedly many readers will find our conclusion unsurprising and wonder whether any scholar truly believes that economic factors overwhelm all others in the legislative process. Those who suspect us of creating a straw man out of the economic theory of legislation should see *A Bias Toward Bad Government?*, N.Y. Times, Jan. 19, 1986, § 3, p. 1, col. 2, at p. 27, attributing to Gordon Tullock, a leading public choice theorist, the view "that people act from

When economists describe special interest legislation as "rent-seeking," they mean that the legislation is not justified on a cost-benefit basis: it costs the public more than it benefits the special interest, so society as a whole is worse off.[91] We agree that, all other things being equal, this is undesirable. But all other things are not always equal. Some wealth transfers may be morally desirable, even though the process involves some inevitable degree of waste, if only the cost of printing the checks. (There is also a more subtle social cost, in that potential beneficiaries of such transfers will expend resources in lobbying for favorable legislation.) Only if we are willing to make cost-benefit analysis our sole norm can we categorically reject such wealth transfers.

Cost-benefit analysis cannot be the only standard for evaluating government decisions. For technical reasons, cost-benefit analysis—or more specifically, the underlying standard of economic efficiency—cannot be applied until a prior decision is made about how to distribute social entitlements. Without such a prior decision, the standard of economic efficiency can give inconsistent results.[92] It is also possible to have more than one economically efficient outcome, so that efficiency gives no basis for judging between them.

Some of the limits of the efficiency standard can be seen by considering a hypothetical world with only two individuals, Bush and Dukakis, neither of whom cares about the other. In state *A*, Bush holds all the wealth. In state *B*, Dukakis holds all the wealth. Both states are economically efficient: it is impossible to improve the welfare of either individual without harming the other at least as much. Since redistribution does not create new wealth, cost-benefit analysis cannot distinguish between these two states of the world. Hence, cost-benefit analysis cannot tell us whether state *A* or state *B* is more desirable.

The same kind of problem can also arise when intangible entitlements rather than ordinary "wealth" are at stake. Consider the decision to destroy a stand of redwoods. If lumber companies have the legal right to harvest the trees, environmentalists might not be willing (or able) to pay the companies

---

selfish motivations about 95 percent of the time. And they are no more high-minded as voters than as customers, selecting the candidate they think represents the best bargain for them just the way they select cars or detergent."

91. The standard underlying cost-benefit analysis is called Kaldor-Hicks efficiency.

92. This point is developed at greater length in Farber, *From Plastic Trees to Arrow's Theorem*, 1986 U. ILL. L.F. 337, 352–54. For a related argument against "wealth maximization" as a principle for social choice, see Keenan, *Value Maximization and Welfare Theory*, 10 J. LEG. STUD. 409 (1981). Note that these results do not contradict the Coase Theorem, which holds that in the absence of transaction costs, the parties will bargain to an efficient result. Given each initial allocation, the resulting bargain is efficient, but the two allocations produce *different* efficient bargains.

enough to get them to stop. A cost-benefit analyst would say that company profits were greater than the harm to the environmentalists, so logging would be economically efficient. Thus, the loggers can claim that their actions meet the "market" test of cost-benefit analysis: in a world of perfect markets, the logging would proceed because its benefits to them outweigh the costs to the environmentalists. Hence, the environmentalist attempt to ban the logging is rent-seeking.

The loggers' argument covertly assumes, however, that they have the right to control logging. If the environmentalists had the legal right to prevent logging, they might demand a much higher price to sell that right to the lumber companies. One reason for the disparity is that environmentalists are in a sense "wealthier" (they have a legal entitlement they didn't own before). Changes in wealth shift the demand curve. Now, the cost-benefit analysis may well show that logging is inefficient; the environmentalists wouldn't be willing to sell the logging rights at a price the firms would be willing to pay. If so, lobbying by the loggers would be rent-seeking. We can't decide whether the logging is economically efficient until we know who has the entitlement. Thus, cost-benefit analysis is indeterminate in this situation. We have to look elsewhere to decide whether we should allow the trees to be cut, or which side we want to accuse of being a rent-seeking special interest.

None of this is news to economists.[93] Even fervent believers in economic efficiency concede that "there is more to justice than economics."[94]

Because the efficiency standard is limited, rent-seeking can be justified when it advances other social values. From one perspective, legislation requiring handicapped access may be rent-seeking. It may well cost society more to give the access than the handicapped would be willing to pay to obtain it. (In fact, this is probably true; otherwise the market would already offer access to the handicapped.) But many people think that deeper issues of social justice are involved, and they are willing to sacrifice some of society's economic wealth to attain these goals. Calling a law "rent-seeking" means at most that it decreases society's total wealth, but this price may be worth paying.

Thus, the fact that interest groups obtain rent-seeking legislation does not *necessarily* mean that interest group politics is undesirable. Realistically, however, we must concede that at least some of the resulting legislation may be hard to justify based on *anybody's* view of social justice. As a society, we are made poorer by such legislation with no countervailing moral benefit.

The current federal budgetary woes suggest another reason to be con-

---

93. For example, the reversibility problem is discussed in Cooter, *Liberty, Efficiency, and Law*, 50 L. & CONTEMP. PROBS 141, 152–58 (1987).

94. R. POSNER, ECONOMIC ANALYSIS OF LAW 25–26 (3d ed. 1986).

cerned about interest group politics. We may be facing a version of the prisoners' dilemma game, in which choices that are individually rational become collectively disastrous.[95] (Prisoners' dilemma is a game theory situation in which two prisoners find it rational to "rat" on each other, though they would both be better off if they could trust each other to remain silent.) Suppose that the budgetary deficit will have serious economic consequences, and that everybody recognizes this fact. It is even possible that in the long run these economic consequences will outweigh whatever benefits interest groups now receive. Even if everyone knows this, however, it may be impossible to do anything about it. The struggle of the various interest groups in the end can make them all worse off.

For example, although farmers benefit from price supports, they might be willing to give up those supports if the budget could be balanced. The reason is that they are hurt even more by budget deficits, which unhinge exchange rates and destroy their foreign markets. If other interest groups were willing to agree to a cut in federal spending, the farmers would go along. But other groups haven't made such a commitment. If the farmers were to voluntarily give up price supports and other groups failed to go along, the farmers would then be faced with the worst of all worlds: no price supports and a budget deficit that is essentially unreduced. Thus, without a commitment from all the other interest groups, it would be crazy for the farmers to give up their price supports. The other interest groups all reason the same way, so no one is willing to give up their own "piece of the federal action." The result is that the deficit continues to mount, even though everyone agrees that serious action is called for.

Analytically, this problem is much like that of air pollution. Suppose catalytic converters cost $100, but that each catalytic converter would prevent $200 worth of air pollution damage. A law requiring converters is in everyone's interest. But without such a law, individuals may not find it in their rational self-interest to install converters. If any one person installs a converter, she has to pay the full cost of $100, but the $200 worth of cleaner air is enjoyed by everybody; the effect of one converter on her own air supply is negligible. If she does a personal cost-benefit analysis, she finds that she is paying $100 to obtain insignificant personal benefits. If she is economically rational—luckily, not everybody is—she won't install the converter, and, for the same reason, neither will everyone else. Special interest legislation, then, can be like air pollution: collectively irrational but individually rational.

Another concern about special interest legislation relates to equity. Not everyone is equally represented by organized interest groups. Indeed, all

95. Another explanation of the deficit may be that current generations are externalizing the costs onto their descendants.

other things being equal, one would expect that the wealthy would be willing to pay more for political influence, just as they are usually willing to pay more for other goods. Even apart from any connection with wealth as such, the process may exclude some politically disfavored groups, who are neither powerful enough to belong to the establishment, nor treated so badly that they are spurred to organize. Moreover, there is another form of inequity in that, because of the "free rider" problem, broadly diffused groups like consumers are likely to be underrepresented compared with producers.

The most fundamental concern about interest group politics, however, is that it corrodes the political system. As we saw earlier, for example, voting is not economically rational. People apparently vote because of some view of political obligation: it is part of their conception of themselves as citizens in a democracy. Interest group politics erodes such norms. If politics is just a fight for spoils, why bother to vote? And if politics is just a fight for spoils, why hold politicians to any higher standards than used car sellers? As we saw at the beginning of this chapter, this view of politics has become increasingly prevalent among the public. In the long run, it is not clear that a democratic society can function effectively once this perspective becomes thoroughly established.

Public choice theory can help us analyze the problem of interest group influence and seek ways to prevent excesses. It can also, unfortunately, contribute to the problem by reinforcing existing public cynicism about the political process.[96] In later chapters, we will return to the question of how public law should respond to the problem of special interests. First, however, we must consider another body of public choice theory that presents a serious challenge to conventional views of democracy.

96. *Compare* Kelman, *"Public Choice" and Public Spirit*, 87 PUB. INTEREST 80 (1987), *with* Brennan & Buchanan, *Is Public Choice Immoral? The case of the "Nobel" Lie*, 74 VA. L. REV. 179 (1988). For a more extended discussion by Kelman, see S. KELMAN, MAKING PUBLIC POLICY (1987).

T W O

Arrow's Theorem and the Democratic Process

As we've seen, public choice suggests that the political process may be corrupted by special interests. If this happens, political outcomes will represent only the self-interest of factions rather than the public interest. Another branch of public choice, growing out of the work of Kenneth Arrow, suggests an even more disturbing possibility: that political outcomes will be entirely incoherent and that the whole concept of the "public interest" is meaningless.

Arrow's Theorem and its various corollaries pose a dramatic threat to the legitimacy of political decisions. If we want the political process to reflect the combined preferences of voters, we seem to be doomed to disappointment. But if the process doesn't reflect the electorate's preferences, what claim does the outcome have to democratic legitimacy?

The first section of this chapter explores Arrow's Theorem and its implications. Next, we consider whether republicanism offers an escape from this prospect of legislative incoherence. We then review recent research on the incoherence issue. Finally, we suggest that these recent findings may open the door to a sort of synthesis of republicanism and public choice theory.

I. Arrow's Theorem and Its Implications

The incoherence issue stems from Arrow's Theorem. Arrow was interested in the problem of measuring social welfare. Given the varying preferences of individuals, when does a change make society as a whole better off? Rather than finding an answer to this question, he ultimately proved that no answer exists. More precisely, he showed that no method of combining individual preferences can satisfy basic requirements like the following:

> (a) *Minimum rationality.* If society prefers outcome A to outcome B and outcome B to outcome C, then society prefers A over C.
>
> (b) *The Pareto standard.* If one person prefers A over B and no one else cares, then society prefers A over B.
>
> (c) *Non-dictatorship.* Society's preferences aren't simply dictated by one person's desires.

(d) *Independence of Irrelevant Alternatives.* If *C* is not on the agenda, whether *A* is preferred to *B* should not depend on how either one compares with *C*.

(e) *Universal applicability.* The method has to work for any possible combination of individual preferences, not just a particular situations.[1]

These are seemingly modest aspirations. And yet, as Arrow showed, even these modest aspirations cannot be satisfied.

Arrow's proof is too complicated to go through here, but the heart of the difficulty can be seen from a simple example involving voting. Suppose that three legislators must vote on where to locate a new federal facility, and that their preferences are as follows:

Legislator 1 prefers Texas to Illinois, and Illinois to Florida.
Legislator 2 prefers Illinois to Florida, and Florida to Texas.
Legislator 3 prefers Florida to Texas, and Texas to Illinois.

Now, suppose they first decide between Texas and Illinois, with the winner to be paired against Florida. Legislators 1 and 3 prefer Texas, so it wins the first round. One the second round, legislators 2 and 3 combine to pick Florida over Texas, so the choice is Florida. Does the choice of Florida represent the "majority will"? No, because two of the three legislators actually prefer Illinois to Florida! In fact, unless procedural rules restrict how many motions can be made, the voting could continue forever. On a majority vote, Illinois loses to Texas, which then loses to Florida—but Florida loses to Illinois, so we're right back where we started! The legislators are trapped in a revolving door with no exit.

Arrow proved that the possibility of "cycling" can only be avoided at the expense of some equally undesirable flaw—for example, by making one legislator the dictator. If we are concerned about defining the "public interest," Arrow's Theorem presents a conceptual barrier to combining individual preferences into some overall measure of social welfare. If our concern instead is with voting methods, Arrow's Theorem shows that no method of voting is immune from breakdowns.

One might hope that, while cycling is a theoretical possibility, it would not occur very often. Later work, however, suggests that under plausible circumstances there will be a complete cycle in majority voting. Take any two outcomes *A* and *Z*, where a majority prefers *A* to *Z*. Although *A* would beat *Z* in a direct vote, a series of motions can always be made replacing *A* with other alternatives, which ultimately results in adoption of *Z*. A majority

---

1. For a summary of Arrow's work, see D. MUELLER, PUBLIC CHOICE II 384–99 (1989). If we could compare the intensity of preferences on some scale, then we could simply add up the individual scores to determine the social preference. Assumption (d) in the text indirectly precludes this.

would vote to drop *A* in favor of some other option, that option in favor of a third, and so forth, until finally *Z* is adopted. In other words, all of the alternatives cycle. This result is called the "chaos theorem."[2]

The chaos theorem gives enormous power to the agenda setter. The person in charge of the agenda can guarantee the adoption of *A* by pitting *A* and *Z* against each other in a direct vote. On the other hand, the agenda setter can obtain the passage of *Z* by scheduling a clever series of intermediate votes. What looks like majority rule is actually under the complete control of the person setting the agenda, who can exploit the possibility of a cycle to dictate the outcome.

Another problem with voting systems relates to strategic behavior. In our earlier hypothetical, legislator 1 essentially shoots herself in the foot by being too honest. By voting for Texas against Illinois in the first round, she makes a victory for Florida inevitable in the second round, although she would really prefer Illinois to Florida. But if she voted insincerely in the first round, picking Illinois over Texas even though her true preference is the opposite, she would ensure the victory of Illinois in the second round. Thus, by being a bit sneaky, she can obtain a final outcome more to her liking. This kind of strategic voting makes it even more difficult to interpret votes as reflecting majority sentiment in any straightforward way.

Concern about cycling and strategic behavior has made some social scientists skeptical about the meaningfulness of legislative choice. Perhaps the most notable example is Professor William Riker. Riker argues that voting is so susceptible to cycling and strategic behavior that outcomes cannot be understood as expressing the voters' values. Hence, "the meaning of social choices is quite obscure": they may reflect the voters' true values, successful strategic behavior, or the "accidental amalgam of what the manipulators (perhaps unintentionally) happened to produce."[3] Under the chaos theorem, he believes, any tiny change in the situation could lead to a wildly different outcome.[4]

If Riker is right, statutory interpretation becomes a rather desperate enterprise. Suppose a statute sets a deadline of January 1, and a court must decide whether Congress meant midnight of January 1 or the end of the day. If we say that Congress intended the midnight deadline, then presumably Congress would have agreed to a clarifying amendment ("on or before December 31"). Under Riker's view, if a Senator had proposed such an amendment, the result might well have been a July deadline instead, or perhaps an en-

---

2. *See* P. Ordeshook, Game Theory and Political Theory: An Introduction 71–82 (1986).

3. W. Riker, Liberalism Against Populism: A Confrontation Between the Theory of Democracy and the Theory of Social Choice 167 (1982).

4. *Id.* at 192.

tirely different bill! If so, it may be meaningless to say that Congress had *any* intention at all on the subject. Even if they did, we could never discover it, since in Riker's view the actual results tell us little or nothing about what the legislators wanted.[5] The whole idea that statutes have purposes or embody policies becomes quite problematic, since the content of the statute simply reflects the haphazard effect of strategic behavior and procedural rules.

Professor Riker's view of the meaningless of legislative outcomes has been echoed by Judge Frank Easterbrook:

> Because legislatures comprise many members, they do not have "intents" or "designs," hidden yet discoverable. Each member may or may not have a design. The body as a whole, however, has only outcomes. It is not only impossible to reason from one statute to another but also impossible to reason from one or more sections of a statute to a problem not resolved.
>
> This follows from the discoveries of public choice theory. Although legislators have individual lists of desires, priorities, and preferences, it turns out to be difficult, sometimes impossible, to aggregate these lists into a coherent collective choice. Every system of voting has flaws. The one used by legislatures is particularly dependent on the order in which decisions are made. . . . The existence of agenda control makes it impossible for a court—even one that knows each legislator's complete table of preferences—to say what the whole body would have done with a proposal it did not consider in fact.[6]

While "the order of decisions and logrolling are not total bars to judicial understanding," nevertheless "they are so integral to the legislative process that judicial predictions of how the legislature would have decided issues it did not in fact decide are bound to be little more than wild guesses."[7]

---

5. For a case study in which agenda control apparently did greatly influence a legislative outcome, see W. ESKRIDGE & P. FRICKEY, CASES AND MATERIALS ON LEGISLATION: STATUTES AND THE CREATION OF PUBLIC POLICY 369–77 (1988).

6. Easterbrook, *Statutes' Domains*, 50 U. CHI. L. REV. 533, 547–48 (1983).

7. *Id.* at 548. Judge Posner, though concerned about the implications of public choice theory, is less inclined than Easterbrook to take these implications to their logical extreme: "Public-choice theory makes the attribution of unified purpose to a collective body increasingly difficult to accept—though I think it is possible to overdo one's skepticism in this regard. Institutions act purposively, therefore they have purposes. A document can manifest a single purpose even though those who drafted and approved it had a variety of private motives and expectations." Posner, *Legal Formalism, Legal Realism, and the Interpretation of Statutes and the Constitution*, 37 CASE W. RES. L. REV. 179, 195–96 (1986–87).

Judge Easterbrook, too, has sometimes drawn back from the full implications of his position. *See* Easterbrook, *Ways of Criticizing the Court*, 95 HARV. L. REV. 802, 828 n.57 (1982) (although "the 'drafters,' as a group, may have no consistent intent," nevertheless the "written product may have a structure that governs questions of interpretation"). Note, however, that this more restrained statement predates the more full-blown skepticism of the *Statutes' Domains*

Professor Jerry Mashaw aptly summarizes the implications of this position as "indicating that collective action must be either objectionable or uninterpretable":

> A stable relationship between the preferences of individuals and the outcomes of collective choice processes can be obtained only by restrictions on decision processes that most people would find objectionable. At its most extreme, Arrovian public choice predicts that literally anything can happen when votes are taken. At its most cynical, it reveals that, through agenda manipulation and strategic voting, majoritarian processes can be transformed into the equivalent of dictatorship. In a more agnostic mode, it merely suggests that the outcomes of collective decisions are probably meaningless because it is impossible to be certain that they are not simply an artifact of the decision process that has been used.[8]

If legislative outcomes are unrelated to preferences, then the case for majority rule seems pretty shaky. At the more mundane level of legal practice, those who must interpret statutes are seemingly faced with an impossible task. Since statutes say nothing about the purposes of the legislators, it is hard to see how we can resolve ambiguities.

The recent public choice literature suggests that the picture is not quite this grim. Before turning to that literature, however, we need to consider whether we could escape the problem entirely by adopting a different philosophical perspective. Instead of looking for loopholes in Arrow's Theorem, perhaps we can sidestep the problem entirely by rejecting the concept of politics underlying the theorem. That is the prospect held forth by supporters of the political philosophy called republicanism.

II. Republicanism

"Republicanism," in the sense used here, is hardly a household word. It is also a somewhat unfortunate term, since the only meaning it suggests to the ordinary reader is misleading, inasmuch as the political philosophy called "republicanism" has no connection with the Republican party. The very obscurity of the term suggests just how much republicanism has been submerged in American political thought.[9]

---

article. On the bench, Judge Easterbrook has continued to find the concept of legislative intent problematic, but has seemed to acknowledge that courts may sometimes be able to find and implement something akin to such intent. *See In re* Sinclair, 870 F.2d 1341, 1342–45 (7th Cir. 1989); Premier Electrical Construction Co. v. National Electrical Contractors Ass'n, 814 F.2d 358, 364–65 (7th Cir. 1987).

8. Mashaw, *The Economics of Politics and the Understanding of Public Law*, 65 CHI.-KENT L. REV. 123, 126–27 (1989).

9. Readers who are not familiar with the republicanism literature would do well to start with

The dominant strand of American political philosophy has been liberalism—another misleading term, since philosophical liberalism is as much embraced by political conservatives as liberals. Because it embraces a broad range of political thought, liberalism is not easy to define. Its distinctive feature, however, is that it begins with the individual rather than the community. Liberals view individuals as having innate human rights regardless of any particular political system. Political conservatives may view these basic rights as involving property while political liberals may stress self-expression or equality. Both agree that these rights are constraints on government rather than creations of government. The familiar language of the Declaration of Independence embodies this view of rights: individuals are endowed by their creator—not by the law—with inalienable rights.

Liberalism also stresses "the pursuit of happiness." Individuals have interests that they seek to advance both in private life and in politics. Subject to its mandate to respect individual rights, government is designed to advance these interests. When individual interests clash, the political process should provide fair procedures for resolving disputes.

Philosophical liberalism is the dominant strain in current American thought, but it has not always enjoyed this status. In the eighteenth century, another political tradition was also highly influential. Historians disagree about the details, but the broad outlines of the story are clear.[10] During the era of the Revolutionary War, Americans were strongly drawn to the teachings of the seventeenth-century Opposition party in England. English thinkers such as James Harrington were appalled by the Crown's use of political patronage to expand executive power. Events that now appear to have been the origins of the modern party system at the time seemed to reflect only the decay of the existing constitutional scheme. The opposition thinkers decried the destruction of the old order, the rise of corruption, and the loss of civic virtue. Ultimately, the health of the republic rested on civic virtue—that is, on the willingness of individuals to sacrifice private interests to the common good. This school of thought, which sought to revive the classical virtues of the Roman republic, has become known as republicanism.

Before the Revolution, Americans were confident in the virtue of the people and satisfied that it provided a sufficient basis for democratic govern-

---

the symposium on the subject in the July 1988 issue of the *Yale Law Journal. See Symposium: The Republican Civic Tradition,* 97 YALE L.J. 1493 (1988). The articles by Michelman and Sunstein exemplify the efforts to modernize republicanism, while the commentators offer a number of probing challenges to that effort. Other good critiques of republicanism can be found in Fallon, *What Is Republicanism, and Is It Worth Reviving?,* 102 HARV. L. REV. 1695 (1989); Fitts, *The Vices of Virtue: A Political Party Perspective on Civic Virtue Reforms of the Legislative Process,* 136 U. PA. L. REV. 1567 (1988).

10. For a summary of the historical literature, see D. FARBER & S. SHERRY, A HISTORY OF THE AMERICAN CONSTITUTION ch. 1 (1990).

ment. Legislative abuses between 1776 and 1789 disillusioned many prominent Americans. Having lost faith in virtue as a sufficient basis for government, they turned to alternate theories of government. The republican influence remained, particularly among the anti-Federalists who opposed the new Constitution, but perhaps also among Federalists such as James Madison. One point of controversy is how much republicanism influenced the drafting and ratification of the Constitution.

The republican tradition contained disparate elements, including a belief in traditional social hierarchies and a militarist strand, as well as concerns about civic virtue and corruption. Modern political thinkers find some of these elements quite uncongenial, but have seized on others as a possible alternative to philosophical liberalism. In doing so, they have been primarily interested in creating an alternate normative scheme to liberalism, but they have also found elements of republicanism already in existence in contemporary political life.

Modern reconstructions of republicanism stress civic virtue. For modern republicans, political life is more than the use of government to further the ends of private life, as it is in liberalism. Rather, politics is a distinct and in some respects superior sphere. By participating in public life, citizens rise above their merely private concerns to join in a common enterprise. They put aside their own interests and enter a public-spirited dialogue about the common good. Once found, the public interest disciplines their private pursuits. Indeed, one of the most important tasks of government is to make the citizenry more virtuous by changing individual preferences.[11]

The republican vision of government is strikingly unlike that animating public choice. In public choice, government is merely a mechanism for combining private preferences into a social decision. The preferences themselves remain untouched. In republican thought, private preferences are secondary; they are if anything the products of government action rather than its inputs. As compared with public choice, republicanism views the role of government as far more creative. Rather than mechanically processing preferences, government involves an intellectual search for the morally correct answer. In a nutshell, as Frank Michelman has written:

> [M]ajoritarian politics cannot be only the individualistically self-serving activity "realistically" portrayed by economics-minded

11. In addition to the materials in the Yale symposium (see note 9, *supra*), good summaries of the modern republican position can be found in Sunstein, *Interest Groups in American Public Law,* 38 STAN. L. REV. 29 (1985); Michelman, *Foreword: Traces of Self-Government,* 100 HARV. L. REV. 4 (1986). For an argument for expanding participatory politics in place of liberal politics, see B. BARBER, STRONG DEMOCRACY (1984). On deliberation in Congress, see A. MAASS, CONGRESS AND THE COMMON GOOD (1983). Of course, civic virtue and dialogue are not necessarily linked: one could conceivably have either one without the other. It is easier, however, to have them together.

political scientists and theorists. Politics must also be a joint and mutual search for good or right answers to the question of directions for our evolving selves. In other words, . . . we must be able to imagine ourselves voting for the Endangered Species Act—that is, committing ourselves to the principle of sympathy, or solidarity, or immanence, or whatever principle we think is expressed by the Act—although we would not as individuals be willing (or bet that our constituents would be willing) to pay any measurable sums of money for the enactment of that principle; and although no one has offered us anything in exchange for our vote, explicitly or implicitly; and although we know well that we may someday find our own private projects inconvenienced or thwarted by the statute and the principle to which we are now committing ourselves.[12]

It would be hard to imagine a vision of politics much more distant from the rent-seeking models we discussed in the previous chapter, or from the chaos and cycling of Arrow's Theorem.

Much of republicanism's appeal lies in just this contrast with public choice. Where public choice theorists find voter turnout inexplicable, republicans find it a paradigm case of civic virtue. Where public choice theorists see self-interest behind every statute, republicans hope to find a quest for the public good. And where public choice theorists see haphazard cycling and strategic behavior, republicans discern the possibility of genuine political dialogue.

Republicans can escape from the dismal implications of Arrow's Theorem by rejecting the entire perspective on politics behind the theorem. Public choice sees politics as a machine, with preferences as the input and decisions as the output. For republicans, however, preferences are shaped by politics; dialogue and reason are the energizing forces behind political decisions. From a republican perspective, the only surprise about Arrow's Theorem is that Arrow could prove mathematically what republicans regard as an obvious truth: government cannot be regarded as simply the handmaiden of private preferences.

Some of the lessons of republicanism are attractive: that ideas as well as pocketbooks matter in politics, that civic-mindedness is more than a myth, and that government can be a moral teacher as well as a reflection of public opinion. While it is possible to overemphasize these elements of political life, it is equally wrong to dismiss them, as some public choice theorists have been prone to do. In short, republicanism can nicely complement public choice theory.

Nevertheless, where public choice theory risks cynicism, republicanism can verge dangerously on romanticism. Contemporary republicans admit

---

12. Michelman, *Politics and Values or What's Really Wrong With Rationality Review?*, 13 CREIGHTON L. REV. 487, 509 (1979).

that the political process is subject to rent-seeking and other flaws of the kind identified by public choice theory. They may overestimate, however, the extent to which the public deliberation can break the link between prior preferences and political outcomes. More generally, they overplay the contrast between political and personal life.

It is unrealistic to draw a sharp line between personal preferences and political values, placing the latter in a higher sphere.[13] Most people's personal preferences and political values are connected. Not all supporters of the Endangered Species Act are dedicated backpackers. But their appreciation of animals and plants is usually not limited to the voting booth, whether it takes the form of recreation in city parks, gardening, or watching National Geographic specials. It would be rather odd to meet an environmentalist crusader who had absolutely no personal interest in nature. Normally, we expect individuals' political values to have some relationship to their personal lives.

The very difference between a personal interest and a public value is often in the eye of the beholder. In seeking government price supports, is the owner of a Wisconsin dairy farm seeking a merely personal reward, or upholding the traditional values of the family farm? In supporting affirmative action, is a minority contractor seeking racial justice, or just a spot at the public trough? Where is the line between private preference and public value? These questions are far more difficult than republicans seem to assume.

It may also be a mistake to exalt the public sphere over the private. Republicans sometimes view the private sphere as limited to rather trivial consumption decisions (buying Nintendos, Walkmen, etc.). But private life contains a great deal more, much of it at least as worthy as political life: raising a family, viewing or creating art, healing the sick, or advancing human knowledge. It is not immediately obvious that attending political meetings is any more virtuous than these aspects of private life.

Besides undervaluing individual preferences, republicans may also overestimate the capacity of dialogue to transform those preferences. Where political positions are reinforced by self-interest, discussion rarely causes major changes. Regardless of argument, individuals are likely to cling to their own political views, not because those views are merely camouflage for self-interest, but because it is so tempting to embrace beliefs that are also in one's self-interest. In important political disputes, neither side is likely to have a knockdown argument. Often, the facts will be in dispute or clashing values will resist philosophical resolution. Thus, both sides will be able to maintain their prior positions in good faith. This is not to say that political

13. For an extended discussion of this issue, see Farber, *Environmentalism, Economics, and the Public Interest*, 41 STAN. L. REV. 1021 (1989).

debate is fruitless but only that it is no panacea. In modern societies, diversity of political preferences will be the rule rather than the exception.

Once the government has decided, the republican expectation is that individual preferences will fall into line.[14] While governments may sometimes give moral leadership, it is probably a mistake to overestimate the pliability of private preferences. Even totalitarian governments have great difficulties overcoming cultural patterns, as evidenced by Soviet failures to persuade farm workers of the glories of collective farming, not to mention the recent collapse of forty years of communist rule in Eastern Europe. Democratic governments are likely to be even less successful in remolding preferences; after all, the powers at their disposal are so much weaker. Public choice theory may err in seeing preferences as entirely exogenous, but it would also be a mistake to see them as subject to government control.

Because of its romanticism, uncritical acceptance of republicanism also carries risks. Being confident that the political process yields more valid results than private preferences, republicans may be overly inclined toward government intervention. From believing that pubic deliberation yields superior answers, it is only a small step to the desire to impose politically correct behavior on the ignorant populace. The dark side of republicanism is its potentially totalitarian tendency to subordinate individuals to the public good, as defined by governmental elites.

While republicanism can be a useful counterweight to public choice, it does not eliminate the Arrovian difficulty. So long as dialogue and public deliberation fall short of producing unanimity, the problem of producing a joint decision remains. The question, then, is whether this can be done without insuperable cycling and strategic behavior.

III.   Chaos and Coherence in Legislatures

Despite the hopes of republicans, fundamental differences in preferences will probably persist in the populace, and in the legislature itself, in spite of deliberation. Thus, we must take as given the existence of diverse preferences and then seek to determine the viability of democratic institutions.

As we saw at the beginning of the chapter, public choice theory has led some writers such as Judge Easterbrook and Professor Riker to conclude that legislative incoherence is inevitable given a diversity of preferences. The heart of the Easterbrook-Riker position in Arrow's Theorem, for it is cycling that most often creates the opportunities for strategic behavior and renders legislative outcomes suspect. Arrow's Theorem, despite its importance, may not have as much to say about legislative behavior as Easterbrook and

14. *See* Sunstein, *Legal Interference with Private Preferences,* 53 U. CHI. L. REV. 1148, 1154 (1986) ("the role of government is to shape preferences").

Riker seem to believe. As one scholar recently observed, "the theoretical results achieved by the formal analysis of legislative choice are markedly inconsistent with our empirical knowledge of legislatures such as the U.S. Congress."[15]

> Extant theory implies that stable outcomes typically do not exist, that the outcomes which do occur are inherently unpredictable, and that consistent policy choices by legislatures are not to be expected due to the prevalence of cyclical majorities. Schofield, for example, concludes from his survey of social choice theory that political processes are fundamentally chaotic and unpredictable, that almost anything can happen. But these theoretical expectations are clearly at odds with what we know empirically about most legislatures. Unless the observed stability of legislative processes is simply dismissed as illusory, this inconsistency between theory and observation poses awkward problems for formal theorists. How this inconsistency can be remedied is consequently a principal question on the research agenda now emerging in formal theory.[16]

The reasons for the gap between theory and reality are not entirely clear, but recent scholarship identifies the following major factors.

To begin with, Arrow's Theorem implies the existence of cycles only given certain conditions.[17] These conditions may not always apply. For example, cycling cannot occur if the members of the group have "unipeaked preferences." In a legislature, this can occur if legislators agree in advance on how to rank their choices on the same liberal-to-conservative scale. Each legislator's vote would be determined by how close a bill was to her own ideal location on the scale.[18] The likelihood of having sufficiently "well-behaved" preferences to avoid Arrow's theorem is presumably much greater in a small group like a legislative committee. Nevertheless, according to some recent work, the votes of members of the United States Congress are often determined by the legislator's position on a unidimensional, liberal-conservative spectrum.[19]

---

15. Panning, *Formal Models of Legislative Processes,* in HANDBOOK OF LEGISLATIVE RESEARCH 689 (1985).

16. *Id.* at 680–81. *See also* D. MUELLER, *supra* note 1, at 94 (outcomes more stable in practice than in theory); Shepsle, *Prospects for Formal Models of Legislatures,* 10 LEGIS. STUD. Q. 5, 10–11 (1985) ("neither interpretation" of the chaos theorem—that either there must be a dictatorial agenda setter or legislative outcomes must "wander anywhere"— "rings true in any real-world legislative context").

17. For recent summaries of the various methods of evading Arrow's result, see Farber, *From Plastic Trees to Arrow's Theorem,* 1986 U. ILL. L. REV. 337; Sen, *Social Choice and Justice: A Review Article,* 23 J. ECON. LITERATURE 1764, 1770–74 (1985).

18. *See* K. ARROW, COLLECTED PAPERS OF KENNETH J. ARROW: SOCIAL CHOICE AND JUSTICE 78–87 (1983); A. SEN, COLLECTIVE CHOICE AND SOCIAL WELFARE 166–72 (1970).

19. *See* K. Poole & H. Rosenthal, The Unidimensional Congress, 1919–1984 (1986) (un-

Unipeakedness avoids cycling by placing limitations on voter preferences. Cycling can also be eliminated by what may seem a rather brutal restriction of preferences: identical preferences for a majority of voters. In the abstract, this may seem an unlikely coincidence, but a strong two-party system effectively produces this result, since all members of the majority party normally vote together. A two-party system may also eliminate cycling at the electoral stage. Suppose that each party proposes a package of legislation as its platform. Voters are assumed to be more likely to vote for the package that is closer to their ideal. To maximize their chances of victory, both parties will propose the platform that maximizes voter welfare.[20] After the election, assuming that campaign promises are kept, the legislature enacts the program. Thus, the two-party system can help limit cycling by identifying a unique preferred result.

Cycling can also be prevented by voting procedures. One important focus of pubic choice concerns agenda setting, decisional structure, and arbitrary outcomes.[21] Legislatures apparently use a variety of structures, rules, and norms to ameliorate the problem of cycling majorities.[22] As a result, legisla-

---

published paper). Poole and Rosenthal suggest that this strong unidimensionality in roll call voting is attributable in part to earlier bargaining at the committee level and to optimizing behavior by political actions in models of incomplete information. "Unidimensionality 'solves' the following problems: (1) it allows horse-trading to occur among spatially adjacent actors in defining the midpoint on a given issue. Conditional on the midpoint, liberals and conservatives will look like they are voting in a consistent, nonstrategic fashion that maintains their voting histories . . . , thereby preserving their reputations . . . with their electorates; (2) from the viewpoint of voters and campaign contributors, a single index greatly simplifies decision problems in an information poor environment; similarly, the dimension greatly facilitates cue-taking by members of Congress, who, massive staffs notwithstanding, are clearly information overloaded when faced with hundreds of roll calls a year." *Id.* at 28. After criticizing their methodology, Kenneth Koford concludes that a unidimensional scheme explains 25–50% of votes, still a significant number. *See* Koford, *Dimensions in Congressional Voting,* 83 AM. POL. SCI. REV. 949, 954 (1989).

20. This model is discussed in D. MUELLER, *supra* note 1, at 196–216; Wittman, *Why Democracies Produce Efficient Results,* 97 J. POL. ECON. 1395, 1414–15 (1989).

21. For an overview of the literature, see Panning, *supra* note 15, at 676–78, 681–82. Legal readers may find the thoughtful discussion in Levmore, *Parliamentary Law, Majority Decisionmaking, and the Voting Paradox,* 75 VA. L. REV. 971 (1989), more useful. Agenda control and legislative decisional structure can also influence outcomes even when cycling majorities are not present, for example, by keeping popular alternatives entirely off the voting agenda. *See generally* Levine & Plott, *Agenda Influence and Its Implications,* 63 VA. L. REV. 561, 564 (1977) ("[A]genda or groupings in which alternatives are considered for adoption or elimination can be a major parameter in determining what a group will ultimately choose"). For some experimental confirmation of this hypothesis, see Wilson, *Forward and Backward Agenda Procedures: Committee Experiments on Structurally Induced Equilibrium,* 49 J. POL. 390 (1986).

22. These devices and norms have other consequences as well, such as their tendency to increase legislative bias in favor of the status quo. For a discussion of how the article I structure

tures possess "structure-induced equilibrium," to use the phrase coined by social scientists researching the impact of Arrow's Theorem in concrete legislative settings.[23] Although Judge Easterbrook acknowledges the importance of agendas in legislatures, he seems to view them as an additional source of arbitrariness and unpredictability.[24] The recent public choice literature suggests, however, that agenda rules make outcomes more predictable and therefore more understandable. Moreover, agenda rules increase the power of the legislative leadership, and having powerful leadership should increase the predictability and intelligibility of results.[25]

Thus, various institutional features of legislatures may promote stability and coherence. Even without these institutional features, instability in voting outcomes may not be as much of a problem in reality as it seems in theory. In carefully controlled voting experiments, political scientists have found that voting outcomes are fairly predictable and clustered even when the voters' preferences contain massive cycles. Theoretically, the results of voting should wander over all possible outcomes, but in reality voting has a strong tendency to favor compromise outcomes.[26]

These empirical results are paralleled by new, more sophisticated formal models.[27] In these new models, even when the preference scheme is saturated with cycles, voting outcomes remain stable and predictable.[28] These

---

of decisionmaking prevents cycling and favors the status quo, see Mayton, *The Possibilities of Collective Choice: Arrow's Theorem, Article I, and the Delegation of Legislative Power to Administrative Agencies,* 1986 DUKE L.J. 948, 954–58.

23. *See* Shepsle & Weingast, *Structure-Induced Equilibrium and Legislative Choice,* 37 PUB. CHOICE 503–19 (1981); *see also* Shepsle & Weingast, *Uncovered Sets and Sophisticated Voting Outcomes with Implications for Agenda Institutions,* 28 AM. J. POL. SCI. 49, 69 (1984) (concluding that "only in the simplest of institutions . . . does the cyclicity of the majority-rule preference relation directly characterize outcomes"); Shepsle & Weingast, *When Do Rules of Procedure Matter?,* 46 J. POL. 206, 208 (1984) (considering the effect of institutional practices on majority coalitions).

24. *See* Easterbrook, *supra* note 6, at 547–48.

25. Riker may be correct that democratic procedures place a premium on the creativity and intelligence of leaders, but we doubt that many people share his view that this is somehow objectionable. W. RIKER, *supra* note 3, at 200.

26. *See* Fiorina & Plott, *Committee Decisions under Majority Rule: An Experimental Study,* 72 AM. POL. SCI. REV. 575, 590 (1978); Ferejohn, Fiorina, & Weisberg, *Toward a Theory of Legislative Decision,* in GAME THEORY AND POLITICAL SCIENCE 170–73 (P. Ordeshook ed. 1978). On the other hand, even where there is a single alternative that dominates all others, it is not always picked. *See* Hoffman & Packel, *A Stochastic Model of Committee Voting with Exogenous Costs: Theory and Experiments,* 27 BEHAVIORAL SCIENCE 43, 44–45 (1982) (note, by the way, how some of the participants cleverly evaded the experimental design to gather information and find a "mutually acceptable" solution, *id.* at 52–53).

27. For a brief summary of the literature, noting its relevance to the Riker thesis, see Coleman & Ferejohn, *Democracy and Social Choice,* 97 ETHICS 6, 23–24 (1986).

28. *See* Ferejohn, McKelvey, & Packel, *Limiting Distributions for Continuous State Markov Voting Models,* 1 SOCIAL CHOICE 45 (1984); Grofman, Owen, Noviello, & Glazer, *Stability and Centrality of Legislative Choice in the Spatial Context,* 81 AM. POL. SCI. REV. 539 (1987)

models involve a wide range of assumptions, ranging from strategic voting and open amendment processes[29] to a partially random amendment process involving coalitions of voters.[30] The models also use various mathematical tools to describe the focal area of legislative outcomes, variously defined as the "uncovered set," the "yolk," or the "strong point."

We will not attempt to discuss these highly technical mathematical models in any detail, but the reader is at least entitled to some idea of what these terms mean. Briefly, the uncovered set consists of outcomes that could survive sophisticated voting procedures by "dominating" other outcomes.[31] The yolk is the smallest sphere that intersects all of the median planes, where a median plane is one that divides the voters' ideal points (each voter's most preferred outcome) into groups of equal size. In a rough sense, the center of the yolk is the median of the various voters' ideal outcomes.[32] The strong point or Copeland winner is the one that beats the most alternatives in pairwise voting.[33]

Remarkably, these very different definitions all turn out to describe very similar outcomes.[34] These solutions also become more and more specific, the closer any single outcome comes to beating every other outcome (a Condorcet winner).[35] Small changes in preferences or agendas do not lead to big

---

[hereinafter cited as Grofman]; Miller, *A New Solution Set for Tournaments and Majority Voting: Further Graph-Theoretical Approaches to the Theory of Voting*, 24 Am. J. Pol. Sci. 68 (1980).

29. *See* McKelvey, *Covering, Dominance, and Institution-Free Properties of Social Choice*, 30 Am. J. Pol. Sci. 283, 297 (1986); Shepsle & Weingast, *Uncovered Sets and Sophisticated Voting Outcomes with Implications for Agenda Institutions*, 28 Am. J. Pol. Sci. 49, 69–71 (1984) (exploring the effects of different agenda formation rules).

30. *See* Ferejohn, McKelvey, & Packel, *supra* note 28, at 59. *See also* Banks, *Sophisticated Voting Outcomes and Agenda Control*, 1 Social Choice & Welfare 295 (1985) (similar results with exogenous agenda).

31. *See* McKelvey, *supra* note 29, at 288–89, 296–97. Equivalently, we can define the uncovered set as consisting of those alternatives that can beat all other alternatives in no more than two moves (either they beat any alternative X, or they can beat some alternative Y, which in turn can beat X.) *See id.* at 289. To see what this has to do with sophisticated agenda voting, the reader may find it helpful to work through the following hypothetical. Suppose A beats B and C, B beats C, C beats D, and D beats A and B. B is not part of the uncovered set, because it neither beats A directly nor beats anything else that can beat A. (Note, however, that B does cycle with A, but the cycle goes through both C and D before getting to A.) A little fiddling with pencil and paper will show that B cannot be the winner, regardless of the agenda order, if voters are sophisticated. On the final vote, they will vote for B only if it is paired with C, but since they prefer A to both choices, they will always pick it when it appears earlier on the agenda.

32. Ferejohn, McKelvey, & Packel, *supra* note 28, at 59.

33. *See* Grofman, *supra* note 28, at 541.

34. This point is developed at length in the Grofman article, which also summarizes the prior literature. *See* Grofman, at 547–49; *see also* McKelvey, *supra* note 29, at 304–5 (uncovered set centers around yolk).

35. *See* Cox, *The Uncovered Set and the Core*, 31 Am. J. Pol. Sci. 408, 417–20 (1987) (uncovered set shrinks to the core).

outcome swings. These models limit voting outcomes to relatively small subsets of all those possible. Even in the presence of massive cycling possibilities, these models predict stability of a kind missing from earlier models.[36]

Another source of stability consists of behavioral norms such as fairness.[37] Consider a very simple voting situation[38] in which three children—Andy, Betsy, and Carol—must vote over how to divide three dollars among themselves.[39] Assuming they seek to maximize their own gains, any proposal can always be upset by another proposal preferred by two of the players. For example, if Andy and Betsy vote to divide the money equally between themselves, Carol can make a motion to give Andy two-thirds and one-third to herself. This makes Andy and Carol both better off, so the amendment wins, leaving Betsy with nothing. But then Betsy can offer Carol a 50-50 split, making the two girls both better off, with Andy out in the cold. This process has no ending point: in technical terms, this game has no "core."[40] Yet there is a natural solution point: an equal three-way split (technically, the "value solution" of the game[41]). Any of the children *could* offer an amendment that would beat this outcome—but what would be the point of doing so, since this would simply set off a round of endless cycling? In a sense, the existence of massive cycling provides the basis for a new form of equilibrium, adopted precisely in order to avoid the cycles.[42]

Such norms should emerge even more strongly in voting situations that already have a certain stability, because of procedural rules or reasonably small "uncovered sets." The incentive to move away from these "natural"

36. For a general description of the results, see Panning, *supra* note 15, at 681.

37. Indeed, one common problem in designing voting experiments is the risk that participants will vote for "fair" rather than individually rational outcomes. *See* Wilson, *Results on the Condorcet Winner: A Committee Experiment on Time Constraints,* 17 SIMULATION & GAMES 217, 222–25 (1986); Fiorina & Plott, *supra* note 26, at 582 (describing pilot experiments).

38. As we will see, this simple model captures the essence of the "chaos" results on majority voting: "One common interpretation of those results is that institutions that use majority rule ought not to work: since choices are cyclical, losers should always be able to find some alternative they like better that could defeat the present status quos, and so on ad infinitum. Thus, all legislatures should be in constant turmoil as losers try to reverse decisions they do not like." Grofman, *supra* note 28, at 539. The simple voting game in the text has the same attribute, inasmuch as a loser can always propose a new split that will win a majority over the status quo, whatever the status quo might be.

39. For a general discussion of such "fair division" games, see M. SHUBIK, GAME THEORY IN THE SOCIAL SCIENCES: CONCEPTS AND SOLUTIONS 306–11 (1982).

40. *See* Wiley, *Antitrust and Core Theory,* 54 U. CHI. L. REV. 556, 559–61 (1987).

41. *See* M. SHUBIK, *supra* note 39, at 183–84; *see also id.* at 178—79, 413 (noting relevance of value solution to fair division games).

42. One of the hopes of game theorists is that the "solutions" to games will provide a deeper understanding of social norms and institutions, rather than simply identifying clever strategies for individual players. *See id.* at 2–3, 7.

equilibria is small, because the ensuing cycling is likely to send the outcome back into the equilibrium area anyway. Rational behavior calls for quickly finding and sticking with the equilibrium area. Successful institutions will have such norms, thus reinforcing any tendency toward equilibrium that is already present. The norms need not be explicit, but can be based on implicit understandings and sanctions, which are especially likely to arise in situations like legislatures where participants have long-term, ongoing interactions.[43]

"Natural selection" would eliminate any legislature that failed to develop defenses to cycling and instability. What purpose is served by a legislature whose outcomes are entirely unpredictable and fortuitous? One might as well have legislation chosen by lot from lists of proposals. Obviously, a totally unstable legislature cannot further any version of the public good, or even advance the welfare of any interest group. It cannot even further the self-interest of the legislators themselves; because the outcome of the legislative process is fortuitous, no one has any incentive to reward individual legislators.

In short, we have very strong reasons for believing that actual legislatures do not suffer greatly from instability and incoherence. Apart from this negative conclusion, can we draw any positive implications from this segment of the public choice literature? We believe that at least some tentative conclusions can be drawn from this evolving body of theory. We stress, however, the need for tentativeness: first, because of the inherent difficulties of translating tidy formal models to an untidy legal world; second, because the models are themselves still evolving; and third, because of the risk that outsiders such as law professors will misinterpret technical mathematical models. With these caveats in mind, however, we do think public choice has some useful guidance to offer.

Let us begin with the easy case of unipeaked preferences. Suppose that the legislative history shows that the vote on a crucial provision was ideological, so that all legislators "Left" of a certain point voted one way and those to the "Right" voted another. The outcome represents the majority will in a very straightforward sense.

Unipeakedness also simplifies the task of interpretation if the application of the provision to a given situation is unclear. Public choice theory suggests that the legislation represents the outcome most preferred by the median leg-

---

43. For discussions of how such implicit understandings can arise in long-term interactions, even though the parties are entirely self-interested and no external enforcement of agreements is possible, see R. AXELROD, THE EVOLUTION OF COOPERATION 73–108 (1984). For an example of such cooperative behavior in an actual legislative setting, see Krehbiel, *Unanimous Consent Agreements: Going Along in the Senate*, 48 J. POL. 541 (1986). Noncooperative bargains are explored in Baron & Ferejohn, *Bargaining in Legislatures*, 83 AM. POL. SCI. REV. 1181 (1989).

islator.[44] Given two possible interpretations of the provision, one may seem much closer than the other to this median position. A court can then say with some assurance that if the two interpretations had been offered for a vote, the one closer to the median legislator's views would have won.[45]

Actual legislative situations may be messier because of deviations from unipeakedness or because preferences fall on more than one dimension.[46] Nevertheless, an analogue to the "median legislator" may still exist. The "sense of the legislature" or legislative center of gravity corresponds to the solution sets (yolk, strong point, uncovered set or whatever) of recent formal models. These solutions tend to be close together. Some of them explicitly combine the views of all legislators but give less weight to those with extreme preferences, just like the "median" of a one-dimensional distribution.[47] Given the preferences of the legislators, these models identify a centrist position which represents the likely outcome of legislation. We can think of this as either representing the views of a "typical" centrist legislator, or we can think of it as the target the legislature was trying to hit. Either way, we can identify which outcomes are closest to this centrist position. Thus, we can generalize the idea of a "median legislator" to a much wider range of conditions.

Judges are in no position to perform the elaborate calculations involved in these mathematical models. Many judges, however, may have a good intuitive sense of the legislative center of gravity.[48] (When political parties are strong, party members tend to vote as if they had identical preferences, making the center of gravity easier to find.) Knowing the location of the legislative center, a judge may often be able to see that one reading of a provision places it much closer to the legislative center than another. As we suggest in chapter 4, statutory interpretation is a complex process, not necessarily limited to considerations of original intent. When original intent is relevant, however, finding the legislature's center of gravity may be a very useful way of thinking about intent. In any event, there is no reason to give way to the cynicism about legislative stability and coherence advocated by Riker and Easterbrook.

44. *See* W. RIKER, *supra* note 3, at 62.

45. The idea that courts attempt to identify the position of the median legislator is suggested in Fiorina, *Legislator Uncertainty, Legislative Control, and the Delegation of Legislative Power,* 2 J.L. ECON. & ORG. 33, 39 (1986).

46. Also, the precise preferences may be hard to determine, so that as a practical matter we must replace the median voter with a fuzzier concept of legislative consensus.

47. *See* Grofman, *supra* note 28, at 541–43, 548–49.

48. After all, the subjects of voting experiments were ignorant of game theory, but their actions showed they were nevertheless able to identify a centrist solution. There is good reason to believe that legislators too are capable of finding stable centrist outcomes without knowing the mathematics of uncovered sets.

In a sense, the Riker/Easterbrook thesis proves too much. If chaos and incoherence are the inevitable outcomes of majority voting, then appellate courts (which invariably have multiple members and majority voting rules) and even the 1787 Constitutional Convention are equally bankrupt. As a result, the Riker/Easterbrook thesis is bereft of any implications for public law, since it tells us to be equally suspicious of *all* sources of law. If we accept the thesis as to legislatures, we are left with nowhere to turn.

Fortunately, as we have seen, the chaos theorem is not reflected in the actual behavior of legislatures. These findings make the concept of a coherent legislative intent tenable, but they do not dispel the normative anxiety expressed by Mashaw and others. Perhaps legislatures are not chaotic, but they may still be arbitrary. If structural features such as agenda rules rather than majority preferences determine outcomes, what becomes of the normative case for democracy? Knowing that outcomes are predictable and stable is of little comfort if they are also unconnected with anything that can plausibly be called the popular will or the public interest.

IV. Public Choice and Legislative Deliberation

At present, our understanding of the stabilizing features of legislatures is still primitive. Any effort to assess the normative implications of those features must be tentative. It is not too early, however, to attempt at least an initial assessment of the normative issues.

One of the basic rules of legislative procedure is that any proposal must win a majority vote when paired against the status quo. This helps induce stability by limiting the set of possible outcomes. It also makes independent normative sense: clearly, the legislature should not adopt a measure when a majority prefers the status quo. While this rule is so simple that we take it for granted, it is the major distinction between democracy and dictatorship.

Stability can also be increased by restricting votes to a single dimension of dispute. This can be done through a "single subject" rule, by requiring bills to fit within the jurisdiction of specialized committees, or by a germaneness rule for amendments. Essentially, each of these devices seeks to ensure a sort of rationality. A combined vote on two unrelated issues (say abortion funding and arms control) leads to irrational results because preferences about abortion funding have no relevance to arms control.

Single-dimensionality is strongest as a source of coherence when preferences are unipeaked—for example, when a legislator's preferences are determined by her location on a liberal-to-conservative ideological scale. The republican conception of community requires that at some level everyone share a single set of preferences. Unipeakedness is a weaker but more realistic form of community. People may disagree strongly about outcomes, but they share a common cultural perspective which makes their disagreements coherent and understandable to each other. Single-peakedness enables people to locate their own positions with respect to those of others, to identify the source of disputes, and to reach coherent and consistent decisions.

Another structural stabilizer involves the use of committees as gate-keepers. Again, this device has at least some normative appeal apart from its stabilizing effects. Committees may develop useful specialized knowledge, which may increase the value of legislation, and they also offer an opportunity for group deliberation that may be unmanageable on the floor of the legislature. Either on the floor or in committee, deliberation may also provide an opportunity for changes in preferences; not, presumably, by revamping basic individual values, but by providing additional information about how to implement those values most effectively and about the intensity with which preferences are held.

Moreover, committees may also give some degree of veto power to the constituencies most vitally affected by certain legislation, giving them a form of insurance against adverse government actions. Suppose that most individuals have a particular vital interest that could be impaired by legislation. The committee system has two effects on them. If they control the relevant committee, they can veto legislation that affects their own crucial interest. On the other hand, other committees will veto legislation that might benefit that particular group, depriving the group of possible gains. Those lost gains are like the premiums paid for insurance against catastrophic loss. If individuals are "risk averse," they may find this an attractive tradeoff.[49]

The norm of fair division, which also supports stability, has obvious ethical underpinnings. It limits the extent to which losses are disproportionately imposed on subgroups. Like the committee system, this has an insurance-like aspect. It may also reflect more fundamental ethical concerns because of its egalitarian tinge. It can also reinforce concepts of community, by functioning as an acknowledgment of mutual concern and respect.

As we saw earlier, strong political parties can also help limit cycling. Probabilistic models of two-party systems also suggest that the resulting outcomes may have desirable normative properties. In fact, the "invisible hand" of political competition may lead to party platforms that optimize voters' utilities, a result utilitarians like Bentham and Mill would surely applaud.[50] This is a somewhat idealized picture of party politics, but it does

49. The normative benefits and risks of the committee system are explored in Shepsle, *Representation and Governance: The Great Legislative Trade-off*, 103 POL. SCI. Q. 461 (1988).

50. *See* D. MUELLER, *supra* note 1, at 201–2. Rather than electing legislators, the parties can be thought of as nominating presidential candidates, who garner votes based on their platforms. The presidential platforms will then converge on the utility maximizing outcome. If party discipline is weak in Congress, but presidential voting operates in the postulated fashion, then the President may be a truer representative of the public's preferences than Congress. (Note, however, that if voters differ in their responsiveness to changes in platforms, say because

have its appeal. Other work by more empirically inclined political scientists suggests that strong parties may serve an important role in constraining special interest groups.[51] Thus, the party system can have some normative attraction.

These anti-cycling devices[52] are not, of course, wholly beneficent in effect. Each device has potential side effects. Committees can given special interests the power to manipulate agendas or kill beneficial legislation. Ideology can take the place of thought or turn into fanaticism.[53] Issue-by-issue voting on expenditures can lead to runaway deficits, since those favoring individual programs are not forced to set priorities. Compromise based on norms of fair division can erode principled commitments. Political parties can quash debate and suppress important issues. Nevertheless, despite the possibilities of abuse, these stabilizers have important normative virtues. They are not just arbitrary methods for avoiding cycling and instability. Rather, they have independent normative appeal as fair procedures for making decisions.

Of all the implications of public choice theory, this may be the most profound, and yet it is insufficiently appreciated in the public choice literature. Much of the scholarship inspired by public choice exhibits enormous sophistication in its efforts to describe the political process, but at the same time applies less sophisticated normative standards. This mismatch can lead to an unduly pessimistic view of the political process. Public choice does reveal the inadequacies of simple "majority rule" as a method of government. It is tempting to equate democracy with pure majority rule, with unhappy consequences for the scholar's appraisal of democracy. But another way of reading the lessons of public choice is to make our normative vision more sophisticated. We can still use "democracy" as a normative standard for assessing actual government institutions, but we need to realize that democracy involves more than simply majority rule.

Public choice theory thus has an unexpected connection with republican-

---

some voters are better informed than others, then the more responsive voters will have a greater impact on the optimum platform, which will then maximize the sum of individual utilities weighted by individual responsiveness.)

51. Recent work by Michael Fitts reviewing this literature has stressed the normative attractiveness of strong political parties as components of the political system. *See* Fitts, *Can Ignorance Be Bliss? Imperfect Information as a Positive Influence in Political Institutions,* 88 MICH. L. REV. 917 (1990). *See also* M. FIORINA, CONGRESS: KEYSTONE OF THE WASHINGTON ESTABLISHMENT 162 n.6 (2d ed. 1989).

52. One other source of stability should also be mentioned. The range of possible outcomes can be sharply limited by strategic voting. *See* P. ORDESHOOK, *supra* note 2, at 266–81. Strategic voting means that voters look ahead on the agenda, frustrating the efforts of agenda setters to manipulate outcomes. This intelligent action by voters can prevent perverse outcomes in which voters would be led to undesired results. This seems to increase the rationality of the process.

53. *See* Rose-Ackerman, Book Review, 6 YALE L. & POL. REV. 505, 512 (1988).

ism. At first sight, the two seem irreconcilable: one seemingly based on a glumly pessimistic appraisal of politics while the other seems nearly utopian in its aspiration for the political process. But republicanism is basically a protest against the view that the political process is a purely passive reflection of preexisting preferences.[54] Public choice theory supports republicanism on this crucial point, because arbitrary preferences by themselves cannot generate coherent social choices.[55] Rather, preferences have to be processed through the legislative machinery, applying norms such as fairness and using committees and other stability-enhancing devices. Choice is considerably expedited if there is sufficient cultural consensus to generate unipeaked preferences along single dimensions of dispute. By undermining pluralism, public choice provides support for at least a weak form of republicanism, in which government is seen as not merely passive but instead as actively processing preferences.

Some of the stabilizing features identified by public choice are particularly evocative of republicanism. Unipeakedness reconciles the social diversity sought by traditional liberals with the cultural unity admired by republicans: a social consensus about the dimension on which policies will be assessed, combined with potentially unlimited diversity along that dimension. Devices such as the use of committees, germaneness rules, and preset agendas increase legislative deliberation, something much desired by republicans. Political parties can provide opportunities for political participation and communal discourse. Perhaps most strikingly, fairness norms involve a considerable degree of civic virtue—they call on individuals to moderate their own claims while respecting those of others.

In the work that originally gave rise to much modern public choice theory,[56] Arrow's concern was less with the political process than with how to measure social welfare.[57] His finding was that, in general, individual preferences cannot be reliably combined into a coherent societal preference. Thus, in some sense, the public interest cannot be an existing entity which is simply "out there" to be found, at least if the public interest is taken as the cumulative product of individual preferences. Such a value-neutral, nonpolitical definition of the public interest quite possibly does not exist. The legislature may also lack the ability to identify transcendent values through deliberation of the kind envisioned by some republicans. Nevertheless, leg-

---

54. *See* Sunstein, *Legal Interference with Private Preferences*, 53 U. CHI. L. REV. 1129, 1132–38, 1153–54 (1986).

55. *See* Frohock, *Rationality, Morality, and Impossibility Theorems*, 74 AM. POL. SCI. REV. 373, 382–83 (1980).

56. K. ARROW, SOCIAL CHOICE AND INDIVIDUAL VALUES (2d ed. 1963).

57. For an argument that Arrow's Theorem is only relevant to measurements of social welfare, as opposed to political choice, see Kadish, *Practice and Paradox: A Comment on Social Choice Theory*, 93 ETHICS 680, 691–94 (1983).

islation can still claim to represent the public interest when certain standards of fairness and stability are met.

A legislative decision has a good claim to represent the public interest when individual preferences on particular issues themselves generally fall into coherent ideological patterns; when decisions are made using techniques that embody society's understandings about relevance; when norms of fair division are respected; and when the end result is preferred by a majority to the status quo.[58] In short, perhaps we should not think of the public interest as something that the political process merely identifies. Rather, the public interest in some sense crystallizes as the political process goes to work on processing existing preferences.

The realities of the political process may sometimes realize the vices of these stability features rather than their virtues. On those occasions, the legislative process has a weaker claim to represent the public interest. But where the process operates properly, the resulting outcome has a good claim to represent "society's judgment"—not a mechanical combination of individual preferences of the kind Arrow showed to be a phantom, but rather a judgment created by and through the decisionmaking process. When we say that legislation is in the "public interest," we appear to be describing an inherent quality of the legislation. Perhaps we are better understood as meaning that the legislation has been or should be adopted by a properly functioning legislative process, given existing preferences as a starting point.

This proceduralist conception of the public interest needs to be applied with some degree of caution. First, the proceduralist conception may be ambiguous in the sense of being sometimes unable to decide which of two proposals is more in the public interest. Despite the presence of various stabilizing features, cycles may remain, though they will hopefully be infrequent or include alternatives that differ only in detail. Nevertheless, if there are any cycles, more than one outcome can be properly said to represent the public interest under the proceduralist conception. Moreover, at this point, we have no basis for claiming that there is a unique set of fair procedures that stabilize legislatures. If there is more than one such set, they could lead to different outcomes given the same preferences, so that more than one outcome could claim to represent the public interest.

Second, there are limits to how far one should press a proceduralist conception. At least in theory, there is no reason why a society cannot have absolutely dreadful individual preferences but extremely fair procedures. (We have some doubts that this is likely to happen in practice; the archetypical embodiment of depraved preferences, the Nazis, were not exactly

---

58. As Michael Fitts points out, attempts by courts to enforce these standards may be ineffective or even counterproductive. *See* Fitts, *supra* note 9, at 1625–42.

known for their attachment to due process.) Even short of extreme cases, procedures may not be able to improve very much on bad preferences. In sum, our proceduralist definition of the public interest judges outcomes relative to initial individual preferences. If those preferences are flawed, the resulting legislative outcome may correspond to the "public interest," so defined, but still be substantively unjust.

Even apart from flaws in preferences, a well-structured process does not guarantee good legislation. Practical reason must play an important role in the judicial process,[59] but its role is no less crucial in the legislative process. Well-designed institutions, like fair trial procedures, can provide a setting in which intelligent, principled decisions can be made. Legislative structures, like trial procedures, make good decisions possible by narrowing the context of decision. Out of all the possible mixes of social policy, only a few are presented to the legislator for a vote, providing a structure in which political discourse can proceed. But the best conceivable set of legislative procedures could not dictate good results, any more than the best trial procedures can guarantee justice. The ultimate responsibility for the quality of the decisions belongs to the participants—lawyers and judges in adjudication, legislators and citizens in legislation. Because the legislative structure allows but does not guarantee desirable outcomes, there are no substitutes for good judgment and political leadership.

This perspective cannot obviate Arrow's Theorem. Popular preferences may often contain cycles that make majority voting incoherent. Because of these cycles, the results of the political process cannot satisfy all of Arrow's postulates (transitivity, independence of irrelevant alternatives, etc.). No decision method can do so. But if we were to think of politics as an active reworking of the public's preferences, these postulates might seem less compelling. Arrow's postulates concern the relationship between the input and output of social decisions. Since we can never fashion a procedure that will fit his postulates, there may be little point in judging decisionmaking process by this standard: they *all* flunk. Our standards might do better to look within the legislative black box to inquire into the inherent quality of political procedures.[60]

We don't argue, of course, that chaos and arbitrariness are unheard of in

59. *See* Farber & Frickey, *Practical Reason and the First Amendment,* 34 UCLA L. Rev. 1615 (1987).

60. Nozick has proposed that we should judge the fairness of an existing wealth distribution by the fairness of the process by which it evolved, rather than on its intrinsic ethical appeal. R. Nozick, Anarchy, State and Utopia 153–55 (1974). Perhaps we should at least in part assess the validity of political outcomes on the basis of process rather than substance. We do not mean, however, to endorse a purely procedural model of justice. Some things would remain evil even if adopted under perfectly fair procedures. No amount of "due process of lawmaking" can suffice to make some outcomes morally acceptable.

actual deliberative bodies. No one who has attended faculty meetings can doubt the reality of this possibility. But on the whole, natural selection will lead legislatures to reach coherent outcomes that are related in some reasonable way to legislators' preferences. In areas where the legislature seems to dither or reach random results, there is less incentive to invoke the legislative process. Such issues will be left to other institutions such as the executive branch, the courts, or the market. When agenda setters use their power to reach results that are systematically opposed to the preferences of the legislators, they are more likely to face challenges to their power. Consequently, legislative action will tend to take place in areas where there are coherent preferences and those preferences strongly influence results. In the academic setting, then, the administration is likely to take control on those issues where there is no coherent faculty majority. In those areas where such a majority exists, administrators will have only a limited (but still real) power to use agenda manipulation to thwart that majority.

To the extent that recent advocates of republicanism have rejected total pluralism, public choice supports them. Like Professor Mashaw,[61] we are skeptical of the more utopian strands in neo-republican thought. A careful reading of the public choice literature does support, however, a more modest version of republicanism,[62] in which concern about the public interest and legislative deliberation play a role in politics.

Although civic virtue and legislative deliberation do play some role in the political process, there is no reason to be naively optimistic about the extent of that role. We have criticized republicanism for romanticizing politics, and we have no desire to repeat that error. But if we throw up our hands in disgust at the flaws of the political process, we are unlikely to improve matters.

We began this chapter by noting the uncomfortable implications of Arrow's Theorem regarding legislatures. Arrow's model conceives of social choice as simply a device for combining group preferences. In the political context, this concept means that governments are simply mechanisms for implementing majority preferences. Thus, the fundamental assumption is "democracy = majority rule." If we stick to this concept of democracy, then Arrow's result is indeed disheartening, for it seems to preclude the possibility of meaningful democracy.

The alternative is to deepen our understanding of democracy. Democracy cannot be equated with pure majority rule, because pure majority rule is incoherent. Rather, a viable democracy requires that preferences be shaped by public discourse and processed by political institutions so that meaningful

---

61. Mashaw, *supra* note 8, at 129–30, 139–41.

62. *See* Sunstein, *Interest Groups in American Public Law*, 38 STAN. L. REV. 29, 38–48 (1985) (sketching a synthesis of pluralism and republicanism, which the author calls "deliberative democracy" and attributes to Madison).

decisions can emerge. Given this richer understanding of democracy, Arrow's Theorem holds fewer terrors.

When our institutions work properly, they have a valid claim to represent the public interest. But they are also prone to breakdowns. Special interests can capture the legislative process, or the process can lose its coherence. What should be the judicial response? Can courts help reinforce civic virtue and legislative deliberation, or limit rent-seeking? The remainder of the book will address these issues.

THREE

Economic Regulation and the Constitution

*T*he most dramatic proposals to apply public choice have involved basic principles of constitutional law. Since the New Deal, the Supreme Court has given Congress a free hand in economic regulation. Some public choice scholars, however, have argued that the Court should reverse course. They believe judges should sharply limit the scope of economic regulation by both the states and the federal government.[1] The doctrines formerly used to limit government regulation are now defunct. Advocates of "economic activism" seek to resurrect pre–New Deal constitutional rules dealing with economic liberty, restrictions on federal power, and limits on administrative agencies.[2]

Expanded judicial review would inevitably limit the power of the more democratically responsive branches of government in favor of the judiciary. In a society that values democracy—as ours does, despite the concerns of some public choice theorists about the defects of majority rule—any expansion of the power of the courts requires powerful justifications. The basic issue in this chapter is whether public choice can furnish such justifications. A great deal is at stake here. Economic activism could lead courts to strike down minimum wage laws as restrictions of economic freedom. It could prevent Congress from using the Environmental Protection Agency to write pollution regulations, on the ground that Congress cannot delegate "legislative" power. Finally, it could invalidate federal discrimination laws in both the name of states' rights and that of economic freedom.

As we will explain at some length, we strongly reject these radical proposals for revamping constitutional law on the basis of public choice theory. Some of our criticisms are directed at the underlying public choice theory, but we also present objections based on institutional concerns about the role of courts. These two kinds of objections are interrelated. For example, if regulatory statutes invariably involved rent-seeking, courts could adopt

---

1. At the risk of being unduly repetitious, we should note again that the definition of public choice is disputed; some political scientists would prefer not to apply the term, as we and other legal scholars do, to encompass concerns about rent-seeking.

2. Most of these proposals are discussed in PUBLIC CHOICE AND CONSTITUTIONAL ECONOMICS (J. Gwartney & R. Wagner eds. 1988). A brief summary of this viewpoint can be found in Epstein, *The Mistakes of 1937*, 11 GEO. MASON U. L. REV. 5 (1988). For an overview of the constitutional issues discussed in this chapter, see L. TRIBE, AMERICAN CONSTITUTIONAL LAW chs. 5 & 7 (2d ed. 1988).

sweeping (and easily applied) rules to invalidate them. Because the economic model of legislation has only limited validity, however, courts would have to distinguish rent-seeking from public interest statutes, and we argue that judges would find this an unmanageable distinction.

This chapter should not be read as suggesting that we view public choice theory as irrelevant to public law. Quite the contrary. In the final two chapters of the book, we will devote considerable space to developing some more supportable applications of public choice to law. Before discussing those proposals, however, we first need to consider the more radical alternatives.

I. Economic Rights and the Constitution

Because of the Warren Court, we have come to associate judicial activism with the zealous defense of civil rights and civil liberties. Until fifty years ago, however, one of the Supreme Court's main activities was protecting economic interests from government regulation. The most famous example of economic activism was the *Lochner* case, in which the Court struck down a maximum hour law for bakers.[3] The Court considered the law an unconstitutional infringement of the bakers' freedom of contract. The *Lochner* era culminated in the Court's abortive effort to halt the New Deal in the early 1930s.

After Roosevelt's court-packing threat, the Supreme Court retreated from its former role as the guardian of economic liberty. Economic regulations were given a very strong presumption of validity—so strong that in the early seventies scholars questioned whether economic rights still enjoyed any real constitutional protection. Since 1976, however, the tide seems to have turned again. Economic rights still receive much less judicial protection than freedom of speech or other traditional civil liberties. Yet, in the last ten years there has been something of a revival in the Court's activism in the economic area.[4]

Before 1937 the Court used the due process clause to protect economic rights. Today, when the Court strikes down an economic regulation, it usually relies on a different clause: the taking clause of the fifth amendment. (Although this clause directly applies only to the federal government, it has been applied to the states by way of the due process clause of the fourteenth amendment.) The taking clause prohibits the government from taking private property "for public use without just compensation." The clause was designed for condemnation cases in which the government seizes property

---

3. Lochner v. New York, 198 U.S. 45 (1905).

4. For a recent review of the history of judicial protection of property rights, see Schwartz, *Property Rights and the Constitution: Will the Ugly Duckling Become a Swan?*, 37 Am. U.L. Rev. 9 (1987). The recent cases under the taking clause are insightfully summarized in Michelman, *Takings, 1987*, 88 Colum. L. Rev. 1600 (1988).

for roads and the like. In Justice Holmes's famous opinion in *Pennsylvania Coal v. Mahon,*[5] however, the Court held that a taking could exist if the government "went too far" in regulating private property. In *Mahon* the Court struck down a Pennsylvania law that effectively destroyed the economic value of certain mineral rights. Until 1975, however, the Court infrequently decided taking cases.

In recent years, the Court has applied the taking clause to a variety of government regulations, blocking these regulations in the absence of compensation to property owners. In one case, the federal government demanded that a developer give access to use a private marina, which the developer had connected with a public waterway. The Supreme Court held that requiring public access to the marina would be an unconstitutional taking of the developer's property.[6] In another case, Congress was trying to help Indians manage their lands more effectively. Some Indian lands had so many owners that land management became impractical. To consolidate land holdings, a federal statute mandated that some of the tiniest interests would revert to the tribe on the owners' deaths. This, too, was an unconstitutional taking.[7] To take another example, the Court also found a taking when New York required landlords to give their tenants access to cable television. The reason was that a cable box would "take" some of the space on the building's roof.[8]

A 1987 case best exemplifies the Court's revived interest in protecting property rights.[9] The case involved a California couple, the Nollans, who wanted to build a larger beach house. As a condition for issuing a building permit, the California Coastal Commission required them to allow the public to walk along the beach. The Nollans apparently had no serious objection to pedestrian traffic. In fact, the portion of the beach in question was separated from their yard by a seawall. But they did object in principle to the permit condition. With the help of the Pacific Legal Foundation, a conservative "public interest" group, they took the case to the Supreme Court. The Court said that the permit condition was a taking.

The majority opinion was written by Justice Scalia, who has quickly emerged as the most activist conservative on the Rehnquist Court. Scalia was willing to concede, at least for purposes of argument, that California could have banned the Nollans' construction entirely to preserve the public's right to see the ocean from the street. California could also have required the Nollans to let people walk from the street to the back of their house, as another way to preserve the public's right to see the ocean. But because the government had chosen to give the public access along the beach, rather than

---

5. 260 U.S. 393 (1922).
6. Kaiser Aetna v. United States, 444 U.S. 164 (1979).
7. Hodel v. Irving, 481 U.S. 704 (1987).
8. Loretto v. Teleprompter Manhattan CATV Corp., 458 U.S. 419 (1982).
9. Nollan v. California Coastal Comm'n, 483 U.S. 825 (1987).

from the street, Justice Scalia held the permit condition unconstitutional. The reason was that lateral access wasn't closely enough related to the government's right to protect the view of the ocean.

Justice Scalia seemed quite suspicious of the government's motives in imposing the permit condition, at one point referring to similar permit conditions as a form of "extortion." This distrust of government regulators is, of course, reinforced by some strands of public choice scholarship.

The taking clause does not seem like a particularly apt method of controlling government regulation. It focuses on property, yet special interests are as likely to seek limitations on other economic activities. The taking clause would lead courts to strike down rent controls while upholding minimum wages, just because one involves property and the other involves labor. Moreover, the taking clause directs our attention solely to the effects of the government's action on the property owner. But the real concerns relate more to the motivations of the government. It might make more sense to focus more on the decisionmaking procedures used by the government, rather than the result.

Another problem confronts those who would use the taking clause as a vehicle for attacking government regulation. It is true that the Supreme Court has become somewhat more activist in recent taking cases. So far, however, this activism has taken place in only one category of cases. Government regulations of property most often limit the ways in which the owner can use the property. Although the Court has made it clear that such regulations potentially constitute takings, in recent years it has never actually found a regulation that "went too far." It has struck down only statutes belonging to another category: those in which the government gives somebody else the right to use the property. For example, in *Nollan* the public got the right to use the Nollans' beach; in the Indian case the tribe got the right to use the property after the owner's death; and in the cable case, the cable company got the right to use the landlord's roof. Indeed, even in the old Holmes opinion, the taking occurred because the owners of the surface land were given the right to use the underlying minerals for support.[10]

The current round of takings cases are only a toehold for economic activism. The cases could be readily confined to a discrete category. This does not mean that they cannot be read more broadly, and the opinions do contain broad language about property and government regulation. Later judges

---

10. Actually, these cases can be narrowed even further, because each of them involved the transfer of a classic property interest familiar to generations of lawyers. For example, *Nollan* and some of the other cases involved easements (the right to enter another person's property). It does not take too much of a stretch of the imagination to call the forced transfer of a recognized property right a "taking." But such a requirement is quite distinct from most forms of government regulation, which address the owner's activities rather than transferring a traditional legal interest to someone else.

may treat these cases as involving only a special category of government regulations, or they might read the language of the opinions as having much broader implications.

Public choice might well encourage judges not only to read these cases broadly, but even to apply them by analogy to areas in which no "property" was taken, when economic benefits have been allocated in ways that public choice theory finds suspicious. Some lower courts, for example, have used the taking doctrine to protect utilities from excessive regulation, with generally unfortunate results.[11] Skepticism about legislative motivations and outcomes, which is such a strong strand in public choice theory, makes judicial protection for such economic rights more attractive. Largely because of public choice theory, prominent scholars have recently argued for a renewed judicial activism in scrutinizing economic legislation. Although the most notable of these scholars is Richard Epstein, a prominent conservative,[12] others are centrists or liberals.[13]

The argument for renewed economic activism comes in two forms. One argues that legislation should be struck down unless it is at least arguably justified by some kind of market failure. Thus, all rent-seeking legislation should be struck down by the courts. A less activist approach would allow the legislature to promote some "public values" that extend beyond economic efficiency, with laws outside of this range being subject to invalidation.

Although this focus on rent-seeking might lead to results not unlike *Lochner*, there is an important difference. The *Lochner* Court considered maximum hours legislation to be a violation of the rights of the bakers and their employers. The rent-seeking theory accuses the legislation of raising the price of bread to the detriment of consumers. Thus, it protects freedom of

---

11. *See* Pierce, *Public Utility Regulatory Takings: Should the Judiciary Attempt to Police the Political Institutions?*, 77 GEO. L.J. 2031 (1989). As Pierce points out, maltreatment by state utility commissions has actually had an unexpected benefit because it has led the companies to support federal deregulation.

12. *See* R. EPSTEIN, TAKINGS: PRIVATE PROPERTY AND THE POWER OF EMINENT DOMAIN (1985); Epstein, *Toward a Revitalization of the Contract Clause*, 51 U. CHI. L. REV. 703 (1984). Professor Bernard Siegan is another outspoken libertarian advocate of *Lochnerism*. *See* B. SIEGAN, THE SUPREME COURT'S CONSTITUTION: AN INQUIRY INTO JUDICIAL REVIEW AND ITS IMPACT ON SOCIETY ch. 3 (1987); B. SIEGAN, ECONOMIC LIBERTIES AND THE CONSTITUTION (1985); Siegan, *Rehabilitating Lochner*, 22 SAN DIEGO L. REV. 453 (1985). Siegan was nominated for the U.S. Court of Appeals by President Reagan, but was not confirmed by the Senate. On the other hand, one outspoken critic of the attempt to resurrect *Lochner* is another prominent conservative. *See* Bork, *The Constitution, Original Intent, and Economic Rights*, 23 SAN DIEGO L. REV. 823 (1986).

13. *See* Sunstein, *Interest Groups in American Public Law*, 38 STAN. L. REV. 29, 68–85 (1985); Mashaw, *Constitutional Deregulation: Notes Toward a Public, Public Law*, 54 TUL. L. REV. 849 (1980).

contract for instrumental reasons, not because it views this freedom as an intrinsically important value.

There are three major flaws in the proposal to have courts stamp out rent-seeking. First, it is based on a simplistic model of the political process. We all know that special interest groups make a difference in the legislative process, but the idea that they are generally decisive is a caricature. As we saw in chapter 1, empirical studies by political scientists and economists have shown that legislators' views of the public interest do matter. Probably the most dramatic evidence against the rent-seeking model is found in recent legislation deregulating crucial industries. The passage of such legislation is difficult, though not completely impossible, to square with the model.[14] Moreover, arguments about the public interest, often deriving from the work of prominent economists, played a crucial role in obtaining these reforms.[15] Thus, in presuming that statutes are normally the result of self-serving influence, the rent-seeking model is too cynical about the legislative process.

Second, the rent-seeking model, if taken seriously, would require much broader judicial review than even the *Lochner* Court ever contemplated. To begin with, even in the *Lochner* era, most regulatory statutes were upheld. Moreover, regulatory legislation is far from being the only potential form of rent-seeking. Recognizing this, Epstein broadens his attack to include such matters as the progressive income tax, which he regards as a taking of private property without just compensation.[16] Many tax exemptions would also presumably be vulnerable to charges of rent-seeking.[17] But this is only the beginning. The risk of rent-seeking is also found in legislation involving tariffs, defense contracts, public works projects, direct subsidies, government loans, and a host of other activities.

For control of rent-seeking to be effective, *all* these diverse government activities would have to be subject to rigorous judicial scrutiny. Leaving some areas such as tariffs or the defense budget untouched would simply encourage special interest groups to concentrate their efforts there. If strict judicial scrutiny were limited to regulatory programs, the amount of rent-seeking in other government programs would increase, largely cancelling out the reduction in rent-seeking regulatory programs. Thus, courts would have to assume the task of supervising virtually everything the government

---

14. *See* Kelman, *Public Choice and Public Spirit*, PUB. INTEREST, Spring 1987, at 80. *See generally* Peltzman, *The Economic Theory of Regulation After a Decade of Deregulation*, in MICROECONOMICS 1989 (Brookings) at 1; *id.* at 48–58 (comment of Roger Noll).

15. *See* Nelson, *The Economics Profession and the Making of Public Policy*, 25 J. ECON. LITERATURE 49, 60–64 (1987).

16. *See* R. EPSTEIN, *supra* note 12, at 303. *See also id.* at 322–24 (tax and transfer programs unconstitutional).

17. *See* Doernberg & McChesney, *On the Accelerating Rate and Decreasing Durability of Tax Reform*, 71 MINN. L. REV. 913, 953–60 (1987) (giving examples).

does. They would have to pass on everything from international trade policy to tax reform. This would be judicial activism on a truly heroic scale.

Third, limiting government to the pursuit of economic efficiency unacceptably eliminates other valid public goals. Major government programs, many of them with broad popular support and deep historical roots, are premised on a variety of other goals. Besides economic efficiency, the government may promote environmentalism, racial equality, or redistribution of income.[18] The rent-seeking model would require radical shifts in our social institutions. It would thereby drastically alter existing expectations about government action.

The other variant of heightened judicial scrutiny, which focuses on "public values," is less radical. Rather than specifying economic efficiency as the exclusive legitimate goal of government regulation, this model would allow government to implement a broader range of values. Courts would only strike down rent-seeking laws that fell outside this range, so more scope would be left for government action. Nevertheless, this model, too, has its problems.

To begin with, the notion of public values is very far indeed from being self-explanatory. For example, classic rent-seeking legislation is often supported by reference to noneconomic values. Restrictions on advertising by lawyers, for example, were said to rest on the values of professionalism.[19] Subsidies for farmers, which some consider a classic example of a "raid on the Treasury,"[20] are said by others to be justified by the inherent value of the family farm. If judges accept goals like these as public values, then the public value model will have little impact. On the other hand, judges might

18. As Frank Michelman explains: "To apply with any semblance of judicially principled rigor the economics-inspired, market failure condition on the validity of legislation—the rule that legislation is invalid unless it can somehow be seen as aimed at maximizing wealth by realizing potential gains from trade that the market may be failing to realize—would, as Justice Linde argued, be to rule out, or at any rate call into serious question, a great deal of legislation whose constitutionality many would not care to think the least bit questionable whatever we may think of its merits. Clouds of constitutional doubt would hang over legislation transferring wealth to the needy or to other favored groups such as veterans; over legislation aimed at ends lacking true economic exchange value such as preservation of endangered animal species, or of municipal sanctuaries for family values; over legislation expressing 'a sense of the fitness of things' as by forbidding ungrateful lawsuits by injured automobile guests, or inhumane treatment of animals, or consanguineous intermarriages; over legislation groping towards the redefinition of values in flux or ferment, a good example being laws which, by forbidding discrimination against the interests of women, or the handicapped, or racial minorities, inevitably seem to call for some form and degree of special solicitude for those interests." Michelman, *Politics and Values or What's Really Wrong with Rationality Review?*, 13 CREIGHTON L. REV. 487, 508 (1979).

19. *See* Bates v. State Bar, 433 U.S. 350, 368–72 (1977) (discussing this rationale).

20. *See* Bruff, *Legislative Formality, Administrative Rationality*, 63 TEX. L. REV. 207, 218 (1984) (dairy price supports are "a fairly stark payoff to a favored group").

attempt to give the model "bite" by narrowing the class of acceptable public values. If so, they may be unable to articulate any generally acceptable standards.[21] As we saw in the first chapter, one person's special interest is often another person's public value.[22]

The practical benefits of a public value approach are also dubious. Special interest groups often have the greatest effect, not on overall legislative programs, but on the details of statutes.[23] In one common situation, a "public interest" statute contains exemptions sought by powerful interest groups. For example, employment discrimination statutes may exempt seniority plans, or an environmental statute might exempt the steel industry. Judges have two choices, neither desirable, in applying the public value model to this situation. First, they could strike down the entire statute on the theory that it is tainted by the special interest provisions. This approach is unattractive. It would eliminate legislation that the court considers to have legitimate purposes overall, merely because some of the details were flawed. It would also allow groups to kill legislation by attaching special interest riders, inviting courts to strike down the entire statute.

Alternatively, the court could simply strike down the special interest provisions. This is also problematic. The special interest aspects of the legislation may involve changes in the basic statutory language rather than separate exemptions. If so, considerable judicial rewriting would be required. Moreover, this approach would make it more difficult to pass legislation with genuine public values.[24] If we approve of tax reform, civil rights legislation, deregulation, or other major legislative initiatives, we cannot afford to tie the political hands of the sponsors. An exemption for a

21. This point is discussed more extensively in Farber & Frickey, *The Jurisprudence of Public Choice,* 65 TEX. L. REV. 873, 909–11 (1987).

22. Although it is perhaps impossible to define public values, it might seem easier to describe a small category of "nonpublic values"—that is, judicially defined prohibited ends of legislation. Even here, though, any noncontroversial articulation is likely to be vacuous. For example, Cass Sunstein has suggested that a variety of constitutional provisions express a policy against "naked preferences" granted by the legislature on the basis of private political power. See Sunstein, *Naked Preferences and the Constitution,* 84 COLUM. L. REV. 1689 (1984). For us, problems of proof and fears about judicial capacity to make such evaluations render the "naked preferences" theory attractive largely at the aspirational level only. At most, this approach seems to identify an underenforced constitutional norm, see Sager, *Fair Measure: The Legal Status of Underenforced Constitutional Norms,* 91 HARV. L. REV. 1212 (1978), that may well be binding upon legislators, administrators, and judges, but because of institutional differences has far more practical relevance outside the judiciary.

23. *See* K. SCHLOZMAN & J. TIERNEY, ORGANIZED INTERESTS AND AMERICAN DEMOCRACY 8, 163–64, 311, 392, 394–95 (1986).

24. Whereas a politically powerful special interest can now be brought along by granting it a complete or partial exemption, this would become impossible if the exemptions were judicially invalidated. Any adversely affected special interest group would have only one choice: fight the entire legislation.

special interest, even if unprincipled, may be the necessary political price of a valuable reform.

The "public values" approach requires heightened judicial scrutiny of the reasonableness of a broad range of legislation to insure that the purported public value is indeed plausibly related to the legislation. Essentially all legislation would be subjected to this reasonableness test. This is a vast quantitative increase in the scope of judicial review, because serious judicial scrutiny is currently limited to discrete categories of statutes.[25] The framers of the Constitution rejected the idea of making federal judges part of a Council of Revision with veto power over new legislation. Allowing judges to decide the reasonableness of *all* legislation seems uncomfortably close to a Council of Revision. What is at stake here is more than an arcane historical detail. The Supreme Court should not duplicate the presidential veto power. Giving the Supreme Court a general veto power violates our basic constitutional scheme.

Thus, a revival of *Lochner* is an unappealing prospect. In its Chicago School, "rent-seeking" form, serious implementation would involve a revolutionary restructuring of both our government and our economy. In its milder form, the public values model, it would still significantly alter the institutional role of the judiciary, while probably achieving relatively little.[26]

Whatever its theoretical appeal, the idea of a return to *Lochner* is rejected by the overwhelming majority of lawyers, and seems to have no realistic prospect of judicial adoption. Indeed, this is itself consistent with public choice theory. It is not easy to imagine a public choice theory of judicial selection that would lead the Senate to pass regulations and the President to sign them—only for the President to nominate and the Senate to confirm judges inclined to strike all such laws down. Nor is a public choice theory of judicial behavior available that would explain why judges would be motivated to strike down most government regulations. (What's in it for the judges?)

Public choice does not provide an adequate basis for a broadscale judicial attack on special interest legislation. Can public choice provide any help with the narrower problems presented by traditional takings law? Virtually everyone agrees that the Court has never articulated a clear test for when a land-use regulation becomes a taking, and illumination from any source would certainly be welcome. Despite some preliminary work in the area, a

25. *See* Komesar, *Back to the Future—An Institutional View of Making and Interpreting Constitutions,* 81 Nw. U.L. Rev. 191, 215 (1987).

26. Our focus in this section has been on federal constitutional law. State courts have in fact been more activist on economic matters than the federal courts. Since state judges are often elected, and since state constitutions are more easily amended than the federal Constitution, this activism may be less objectionable.

general public choice theory of the subject is still far away.[27] A less ambitious use of public choice theory would be to establish some "safe harbors"—that is, to provide a test for establishing that some regulations are clearly not takings. As a preliminary step in that direction, we would like to suggest one possible safe harbor.

Public choice suggests that diffuse groups will generally find it difficult to obtain legislation that benefits them at the expense of more compact groups, even where the legislation creates much greater benefits than costs. We can assume that requiring compensation will make such legislation harder to pass (otherwise, the legislature would have provided the compensation voluntarily). Given the fact that diffuse beneficiary/concentrated cost legislation is already excessively hard to pass, applying taking law would only create an additional barrier to much-needed legislation. Thus, where the beneficiaries are substantially more diffuse than those regulated by a statute, a safe harbor might well be desirable.

Some examples might illustrate how this safe harbor would function. Consider *Loretto,* the cable TV case discussed earlier.[28] Superficially, the cable access rule benefits tenants (a relatively diffuse group) over landlords, so this rule would appear to fall within the safe harbor. But this assumes that when the cable company obtains free access, the entire saving is passed along to cable consumers, and there is no reason to expect this to happen. Realistically, at least part of the saving will be absorbed by the cable companies, who are a much more compact group than the landlords. So, the safe harbor does not apply. In contrast, consider the *Keystone* case.[29] *Keystone* was in many respects a 1987 replay of the 1922 *Pennsylvania Coal* decision that began the law of regulatory takings. *Keystone* involved another state law requiring coal mines to provide support for the land overhead, including homes, businesses, and public property such as schools. The statute benefitted a broad range of property owners. The burdened class consisted of coal-mining companies. This case falls squarely within the safe harbor, because the burdened class is far more compact than the beneficiaries of the regulation. Hence, as the Supreme Court concluded (albeit in a 5-4 vote), there was no taking.

The application of public choice theory to such problems of land-use regulation seems promising. Further work along these lines is more likely to be more productive than broad-ranging attacks on the general problem of rent-seeking.

27. Levmore, Just Compensation and Just Politics (VIRGINIA LAW & ECONOMICS WORKING PAPER # 89–3, 1989), makes a promising start on this project by linking taking law with concern about unprotected minorities, but does not provide a coherent test for political powerlessness.

28. Loretto v. Teleprompter Manhattan CATV Corp., 458 U.S. 419 (1982).

29. Keystone Bituminous Coal Assn. v. DeBenedictis, 480 U.S. 470 (1987).

If public choice theory is to make a contribution to the more general problem, its advocates will have to devise a less radical legal approach to controlling rent-seeking. One possibility, which we will discuss in chapter 5, is to approach the problem indirectly. Rather than scrutinizing the results of the legislative process for signs of taint, it may be better for the courts to police the process itself. An analogy may help explain the appeal of structural as opposed to substantive solutions. In the early 1960s, state legislatures were badly malapportioned in favor of rural districts. As a result, legislation tended to favor agricultural interests over urban interests. One way of dealing with the problem would have been heightened judicial review for statutes favoring rural interests. Judges could scrutinize such statutes in order to determine whether the discrimination against urban interests was clearly justified. Determining what statutes were guilty of this form of geographical discrimination would have been difficult, however, and assessing the justifications for the statutes would have involved courts in myriad policy decisions. A much simpler approach—and the one actually adopted by the Supreme Court—was to deal directly with the structural problem by ordering reapportionment. Similarly, rather than trying to apply special scrutiny to rent-seeking legislation, it may be more fruitful for courts to deal directly with some of the political conditions that foster rent-seeking.

II.   Federalism

The drive to repeal the New Deal has also sought to restrict the power of the federal government. Much of the argument has focused on the commerce clause, because today it is the most important source of legislative power for Congress.

Before the New Deal, the commerce clause was given a relatively narrow reading. Until around 1890, the clause mostly functioned as a restriction on the authority of the states. The Court's theory (roughly speaking) was that if interstate commerce was *within* congressional jurisdiction then it must be *outside* state jurisdiction. Under this so-called "dormant commerce clause" doctrine, even if Congress had not legislated, the states were forbidden to regulate interstate commerce. But drawing a rigid line between state and federal jurisdiction proved unworkable in practice. Today, although the basic doctrine survives, its application is much more pragmatic. State regulations are only struck down if they discriminate against or unreasonably burden out-of-state firms.[30] In many circumstances, the states and the federal government can now regulate the same transaction.

Most of the early judicial decisions involved the "dormant commerce clause" because Congress rarely exercised its authority over commerce.

---

30. For a brief survey and critique of current doctrine, see Farber, *State Regulation and the Dormant Commerce Clause*, 3 CONST. COMM. 395 (1986).

Most of the controversies involved situations in which Congress had been silent and states had stepped in to regulate. The Civil War began a trend toward greater congressional activity which has continued to the present.

The initial judicial reception to this new legislation was hostile. From 1890 until 1937, the Supreme Court adopted a restrictive view of congressional power under the commerce clause. For example, in *United States v. E.C. Knight Co.*,[31] the Court held that Congress lacked the power to stop the formation of a nationwide monopoly in sugar manufacturing. The rationale was that manufacturing sugar (unlike shipping it interstate) was an inherently local concern, reserved to the states under the tenth amendment. Any effect of the manufacturing monopoly on later sales across the nation was only "indirect" and therefore insufficient to give Congress jurisdiction. In an important later case, the Court ruled that Congress could not ban child labor in factories that sold goods in interstate commerce.[32] Even during this period, however, the Court did not consistently rule against Congress, leading some commentators to criticize its decisions as unprincipled.

In the first half of the 1930s, the Court applied its expansive view of the tenth amendment to strike down important portions of the New Deal, including labor legislation and agricultural price supports. These decisions led to a constitutional crisis in 1937. After the President threatened to pack the Court, a crucial Justice changed his views (perhaps coincidentally) and began to vote to uphold New Deal legislation. In key decisions in 1937, the Supreme Court upheld the National Labor Relations Act and the Social Security Act.[33]

Since 1937 the scope of congressional power under the commerce clause has steadily expanded. In *Wickard v. Filburn*,[34] the Court held that Congress could regulate the amount of wheat a farmer grew for his own use. The rationale was that when farmers divert grain for their own use, there is a cumulative effect on interstate commerce. In an even more striking application of the commerce clause, the Court held in *Heart of Atlanta Motel v. United States*[35] that Congress could use the commerce clause to prohibit racial discrimination by private businesses. The Court's theory was that racial discrimination has a significant cumulative effect on the national economy. Today, Congress regulates pollution, worker safety, discrimination, and virtually everything else imaginable, without serious constitutional challenge.

Since 1937 the Supreme Court has never struck down any federal regulation of private conduct as a violation of the tenth amendment or as exceeding congressional power under the commerce clause. But in one important case,

31. 156 U.S. 1 (1895).
32. Hammer v. Dagenhart, 247 U.S. 251 (1918).
33. This history is reviewed in L. TRIBE, *supra* note 2, at 297–310.
34. 317 U.S. 111 (1942).
35. 379 U.S. 241 (1964).

National League of Cities v. Usery,[36] the Court did hold that Congress lacked the power to impose minimum wage requirements on positions in state and local governments that perform "essential state functions." This federal legislation was held to be an undue intrusion on state sovereignty. In a series of later cases, the Court struggled to define the contours of this doctrine. It became increasingly obvious that the outcome in tenth amendment cases turned largely on the views of Justice Blackmun, who was usually the decisive swing vote. By 1985 he was apparently convinced that no principled way to apply *League of Cities* could be found. In another case involving the minimum wage, this time in the context of local transit workers, Justice Blackmun wrote the opinion overruling *League of Cities.*[37] The four dissenters protested vigorously and hinted that the *League of Cities* decision would be resurrected as soon as new appointments joined the Court.

The current law, then, is that Congress can regulate any conduct by private parties under the commerce clause, and almost any economic transactions by state governments. Inspired in part by public choice theory, however, some scholars have recently argued for a return to a much more restricted national role. They seek to reactivate the Court as a guardian of federalism.

There are several traditional arguments for federalism. Federalism allows local communities to experiment with different approaches to social problems; it allows for communities to pursue their own social visions rather than homogeneous social norms; it disperses power and therefore makes abuse less likely.[38] These arguments can all be restated in economic jargon. Doing so may well be intellectually fruitful. Economic analysis might illuminate the interconnections between these arguments and clarify the conditions under which they hold.[39] But the basic lines of argument are old hat. If the traditional arguments themselves were insufficient to persuade the Court to limit federal power, it seems unlikely that dressing the same arguments up in economic language will have much effect.

Public choice theory has, however, added one distinctively new argument—or rather, has turned an old argument on its head. One traditional reason for federal intervention has been that interstate competition effectively limits the regulatory powers of the states. For example, suppose a state

36. 426 U.S. 833 (1976).

37. Garcia v. San Antonio Metro. Transit Auth., 469 U.S. 528 (1985).

38. These traditional arguments are summarized in Merritt, *The Guarantee Clause and State Autonomy: Federalism for a Third Century,* 88 COLUM. L. REV. 1, 3–10 (1988).

39. For a thoughtful review of the public choice literature as it bears on the traditional arguments for federalism, see McConnell, Book Review, 54 U. CHI. L. REV. 1484, 1491–1511 (1987) (reviewing R. BERGER, FEDERALISM: THE FOUNDERS' DESIGN (1987)). *See also* Shannon, *Competition: Federalism's 'Invisible Regulator,'* TAX NOTES, April 3, 1989 at 93; Wagner, *Morals, Interests, and Constitutional Order: A Public Choice Perspective,* 67 ORE. L. REV. 73, 90–91 (1988).

decided to raise the minimum wage. The higher minimum wage laws would raise the labor costs of local firms, putting them at a disadvantage in the national marketplace. This economic effect harms a state that takes the initiative in regulating business. Over time, local industry will dwindle, as existing firms either fail to thrive against unregulated out-of-state competitors or else relocate in less regulated jurisdictions. Thus, even if the state governments unanimously wish to impose a minimum wage, they may find themselves unable to do so, because of the difficulty of coordinating group action and the substantial competitive benefit to laggards.

It is obvious why this inability of the states to regulate interstate competition effectively has traditionally been an argument for federal intervention. Some public choice scholars have innovatively inverted this argument, using it as a justification for limiting federal authority. For example, regarding child labor regulation, Professor Richard Epstein argues:

> There is no obvious reason to approach the . . . question with the assumption that child labor laws are intrinsically good, if only we knew how to enact them. Their strength, far from being a given, should be tested in competition between states. Such competition would show the true importance of child labor laws to the state: Will a state impose the restriction even when local firms may be hampered in interstate competition?[40]

The basic idea is that interstate competition limits the ability of states to pass inefficient, rent-seeking statutes. This is a useful barrier since such statutes are undesirable, so it should be respected rather than circumvented by Congress.

Although clever, this argument ultimately cannot be sustained. Interstate competition hampers inefficient regulation, but it can also hamper efficient regulation as well. Consider an industry that creates a local pollution problem. Having the industry might be a net social benefit for the state, but the benefit would be even greater if pollution controls were imposed. If the harm done by the pollution exceeds the cost of control, pollution regulation is economically efficient. Nevertheless, state authorities may be unable to impose the controls, since the industry can always move elsewhere to avoid them.[41] Other flaws in the market can also justify government intervention, but such intervention may be frustrated if the regulated party can make a credible threat to relocate.

Interstate competition can also be harmful if there are differences in mobility. If some resources are relatively mobile (for example, financial

---

40. Epstein, *The Proper Scope of the Commerce Power,* 73 VA. L. REV. 1387, 1431 (1987).

41. In theory, the state could cope with this problem by taxing its citizens to finance the firm's pollution controls. But this is politically unrealistic and may be rejected for distributional reasons as well.

capital) while others are less mobile (individual workers) and some are fixed (land and other natural resources), governments will compete for the mobile resources at the expense of the interests of owners of less mobile resources. For example, a real property tax will be preferred over a corporate income tax, regardless of the true desirability of the two forms of taxation, because real property is comparatively immobile.

The market for local regulation is subject to the same flaws as other markets. Unrestrained regulatory competition among the states may not lead to efficient results if local regulations have appreciable effects elsewhere, if the information needed to regulate is costly, or if there are economies of scale in regulation.[42] And why should efficiency be the only permissible goal of government regulation? Redistribution of wealth is clearly handicapped by interstate competition: all things being equal, rich people will prefer not to live in states where they pay higher taxes for the benefit of the poor.

Ultimately, the interstate competition argument is little more than a sophisticated restatement of economic libertarianism. If government regulation is bad, anything that makes it more difficult is good; and interstate competition does hinder state regulation. Epstein, for example, makes no bones about the fact that his support for federalism is directly linked with his rejection of government regulation. By his own admission, he "looks with suspicion" on child labor restrictions,[43] while he explains the Court's acceptance of national regulation as being based on a naive faith in the virtue of legislatures.[44] If we put aside Epstein's "democracy bashing" and assume that democratic government is on balance benign—or at least that courts are institutionally barred from adopting the contrary conclusion—his argument for a return to nineteenth-century constitutionalism goes up in smoke.

Nevertheless, with regard to federalism concerns, public choice may have a useful impact on public law. While public choice may not add a great deal of substance to the argument for federalism, it does rephrase the stock arguments in a new and more appealing vocabulary. Even in modern garb, we do not believe that these arguments justify serious revisions in constitutional law. Federalism is also relevant, however, in nonconstitutional settings. For example, in statutory interpretation, the courts may sometimes construe a federal statute narrowly in an area of traditional state concern. Although the Court often pays lip service to federalism when construing federal statutes, federalism is more often honored in the breach as a factor in statutory in-

---

42. Sometimes these effects may be obvious: there is a clear externality when a state regulates interstate pollution. The existence of other impacts may be quite controversial. For example, if the states regulate the local level of borrowing, credit, consumption, or wages, different macroeconomic theories may have different implications about whether the national economy is affected. Courts are in a very poor position to assess such arguments.

43. Epstein, *supra* note 40, at 1430.

44. *Id.* at 1451–53.

terpretation. Public choice suggests that courts might do well to interpret ambiguous federal statutes so as to preserve these areas of state autonomy.

III. The Delegation Doctrine

In its abortive attack on the New Deal, one of the instruments used by the Court was the delegation doctrine. This doctrine finds its roots in article I of the Constitution, which vests "the legislative power" in Congress. Since the legislative power must reside in Congress, it is said, any attempt to vest that power elsewhere is unconstitutional. Thus, according to this theory, Congress cannot delegate its lawmaking powers to administrative agencies.[45] This sounds fine in theory, but in practice Congress is often forced to write broad guidelines, leaving it up to an administrative agency to issue detailed regulations.

The delegation question has a long history. As early as 1825, the Court was faced with (and rejected) a claim of unconstitutional delegation.[46] In later cases, the Court struggled to define the permissible limits of congressional delegation. A major 1928 case upheld a broad grant of power to the President to regulate tariffs.[47] The test emerging from these cases is that Congress need only provide an "intelligible principle" governing the administrator. Notably, although the delegation issue was often raised in the first 150 years of the Republic, the Court never struck down a statute on this basis. Most of the delegations involved international affairs, an area in which a congressional delegation merely augments the President's own inherent constitutional powers.

The bark of the delegation doctrine is much worse than its bite. The Court has struck down federal statutes as unconstitutional delegations only twice. Both cases were decided in 1935, so it is arguable that the delegation doctrine has actually only been in effect for one year in American history.

The first case was *Panama Refining Co. v. Ryan*,[48] better known as the "hot oil" case. The National Recovery Act, a key piece of early New Deal legislation, contained a provision authorizing the President to prohibit interstate shipment of "hot oil" (that is, petroleum products produced in violation of state law). The statute contained no explicit standards governing the President's exercise of this power. The Court struck down the statute as an unconstitutional delegation of legislative power. Later that year, the Court struck down other crucial provisions of the National Recovery Act,

45. For a thorough recent review of the literature on the delegation doctrine, see Farina, *Statutory Interpretation and the Balance of Power in the Administrative State*, 89 COLUM. L. REV. 452, 476–88 (1989).

46. The Brig Aurora, 23 U.S. 1 (1825).

47. J. W. Hampton, Jr. & Co. v. United States, 276 U.S. 394 (1928).

48. 293 U.S. 388 (1935).

which authorized the President to establish "codes of fair competition" for particular industries. The codes were actually adopted by trade associations and then reviewed by the President. In *Schechter Poultry Corp. v. United States,*[49] the famous "sick chicken" case—there seems to be something about these delegation cases that lends itself to amusing nicknames—the Court struck down the code established for the poultry industry. The Court could find no adequate statutory standard to restrain the rulemaking discretion of these private industry groups.

The Court quickly retreated from the rigidity of the 1935 cases. Less than ten years later, the Court upheld a very broad delegation of power to establish price controls during World War II. The Court still purported to be following the "intelligible principle" test, but seemed willing to settle for vague congressional platitudes about the public interest.[50] Since then, courts have invariably managed to discern an intelligible principle in every delegation, no matter how sweeping the congressional grant of power.

Yet, it would be a mistake to view the doctrine as wholly moribund. On occasion, it has served as a justification for narrowly construing a grant of authority to an administrative agency.[51] Moreover, at least two Justices have recently invoked the delegation doctrine. They argued that the toxic chemical provision of the Occupational Safety and Health Act (OSHA) was unconstitutional because Congress defaulted on the fundamental policy judgment, leaving it to the agency to decide how much industry should be required to spend to save lives. Chief Justice Rehnquist has been the leading judicial proponent of the delegation doctrine in recent times.[52]

Public choice scholars have strongly endorsed Rehnquist's effort to revive the delegation doctrine. Professor Jonathan Macey, for example, recently said that current legislative delegations to administrative agencies are "[p]erhaps the greatest departure from the system of government envisioned by the framers."[53] There are two lines of public choice arguments in favor of reviving the delegation doctrine. One line of argument is based on interest

49. 295 U.S. 495 (1935).

50. Yakus v. United States, 321 U.S. 414 (1944). The *Yakus* approach was recently re-affirmed in Skinner v. Mid-America Pipeline Co., 109 S. Ct. 1726 (1989), and Mistretta v. United States, 109 S. Ct. 647 (1989).

51. See, for example, our discussion in chapter 5 of *Kent v. Dulles,* the decision narrowly construing the State Department's authority to withhold passports on ideological grounds.

52. *See* now-Chief Justice Rehnquist's dissents in Industrial Union Dept. v. American Petroleum Institute, 448 U.S. 607 (1980), and in American Textile Mfrs. Inst., Inc., v. Donovan, 452 U.S. 490 (1981), where he was joined by then-Chief Justice Burger. An excellent review of the history of the delegation doctrine can be found in H. BRUFF & P. SHANE, PRESIDENTIAL POWER 64–88 (1988).

53. Macey, *Transaction Costs and the Normative Elements of the Public Choice Model: An Application to Constitutional Theory,* 74 VA. L. REV. 471, 513 (1988).

group theory; the other relies on the notion of "structure-induced equilib-rium."

The "interest group" analysis attributes a variety of nefarious motivations to congressional delegations.[54] One theory is that legislators dislike distrac-tions from their primary vote-getting activity, which consists of providing individual service to constituents. Hence, they prefer not to devote time to setting specific regulatory standards. Indeed, passing vague standards puts more of their constituents at risk of administrative action, thus creating more opportunities for members of Congress to earn their gratitude by intervening on their behalf.

It is true that legislators devote much of their time—probably too much—to constituent service.[55] But narrowly written statutes would not necessarily help. The Internal Revenue Code is more narrowly drafted (and correspon-dingly more complex) than most regulatory statutes. But legislators can still seek to influence the exercise of the IRS's discretion in the enforcement pro-cess. Moreover, as the 1986 Tax Reform Act shows, legislators can benefit specific constituents through exemptions and individually tailored "grand-father" provisions.[56]

Morris Fiorina suggested the constituent-service explanation for broad delegation some years ago, but he now believes that this motivation is proba-bly important only in the House, because Senators are more issue-oriented and less casework-oriented.[57] In any event, even if legislators do unduly del-egate power in order to free their time for constituent service, judicial revival of the delegation doctrine might do very little good. If constituent services are now at their desired level, legislators can be expected to counter efforts to limit the "market" for these services. For example, if the delegation doc-trine were seriously enforced, legislators could leave the actual drafting of detailed laws either to the executive or to congressional staff, then serve their constituents by intervening with the drafting body for exemptions. Like

54. The interest group theory is most extensively developed in Aranson, Gelhorn, & Robin-son, *A Theory of Legislative Delegation,* 68 Cornell L. Rev. 1, 55–63 (1982). *See also* Macey, *supra* note 53, at 513; Schoenbrod, *The Delegation Doctrine: Could the Court Give it Substance?*, 83 Mich. L. Rev. 1223, 1243–46 (1985). Although he does not argue for a revival of the delegation doctrine, a similar descriptive view of delegation is presented in Eskridge, *Politics Without Romance: Implications of Public Choice Theory for Statutory Interpretation,* 74 Va. L. Rev. 275, 285–301 (1988). The descriptive model is discussed at greater length and critiqued in Mashaw, *Prodelegation: Why Administrators Should Make Political Decisions,* 1 J.L. Econ. & Org. 81, 82–91 (1985); Pierce, *The Role of Constitutional and Political Theory in Administrative Law,* 64 Tex. L. Rev. 469, 489–504 (1985).

55. For extensive discussion, see B. Cain, J. Ferejohn, & M. Fiorina, The Personal Vote: Constituency Service and Electoral Independence (1987).

56. *See* Doernberg & McChesney, *supra* note 17, at 936–45, 953–59.

57. *See* M. Fiorina, Congress: Keystone of the Washington Establishment 116 (2d ed. 1989).

many efforts to prevent willing buyers and sellers from reaching mutually advantageous deals, enforcement of the nondelegation doctrine will be costly and of limited effectiveness. If the legislature is indeed a market, and if constituent service is the product, then conservative public choice scholars ought to be skeptical of the prospects of successful regulatory intervention. After all, what other markets do they believe the government can successfully regulate?

According to another variant of the interest group theory, members of Congress also prefer broad delegations so they can "pass the buck" and avoid taking responsibility for the consequences of legislation. If there is a conflict between important political groups, the last thing a legislator wants to do is to take sides, thereby making political enemies. If one of the two groups is in a better position than the other to monitor administrative action, the legislator can have the best of both worlds. The group with higher monitoring costs is pleased by the passage of apparently constructive legislation, but cannot monitor the ultimate administrative outcomes. The more observant group is mollified by the knowledge that the administrative action will actually work to its advantage. So everyone goes away happy.

It is not at all clear that broad delegations actually correlate with disparities in monitoring costs. The President has been delegated broad power regarding tariffs, for example. Yet, the industry groups who are likely to be hurt by actual presidential decisions are well organized, while the consumers who benefit from the presidential commitment to free trade are not. The National Labor Relations Board has a very broad delegation, but both of the affected groups (industry and labor unions) have similar monitoring costs.

There are also theoretical difficulties with the idea that delegations result from informational disparities. If consumers are rational, they should know they have poorer monitoring abilities than industry. (If, on the other hand, consumers aren't rational, economic theory won't work, and all bets are off.) Rational consumers will then predict that delegations will result in unfavorable administrative decisions. Hence, they shouldn't be fooled by congressional delegations. Instead, they should favor administrative mechanisms that lower their monitoring costs. One way of reducing monitoring costs would be to concentrate more authority in the White House, because it is cheaper to monitor the President than a multitude of agencies. Another possibility would be greater reliance on formalized administrative rules rather than ad hoc adjudicatory decisions. It is easier to monitor one rulemaking procedure than a host of adjudications. Admittedly, it may not be worthwhile for individual consumers to attend to the legal details of each individual statute, so we can expect the pressure from consumers to be intermittent. Nevertheless, over time, disparities in information costs should be eroded by such innovations in the "legal technology."

In short, as Donald Wittman has observed, "[a] model that assumes that voters or consumers are constantly fooled and that there are no entrepreneurs to clear them up in their confusion will, not surprisingly, predict that decision-making process will lead to inefficient results."[58] But economists should be chary of the underlying assumptions of voter stupidity and entrepreneurial laxity.

In our view, the "information cost" theory is not an adequate basis for revitalizing the nondelegation doctrine. Nevertheless, it may have some other important implications for the courts. As we have seen, changes in legal "technology" may be important in restraining undue delegation and in giving voters a better ability to control public policy. Courts can do a great deal to encourage such changes. For example, in reviewing administrative agency decisions, courts can foster procedures that make it less costly for the public to monitor the behavior of agencies. To the extent that voters have trouble monitoring the details of a statutory delegation, courts can help prevent legislators from misrepresenting themselves to voters. Judges can encourage honest statutes by putting less weight on the fine details of the language, and more weight on the announced overall purpose of a statute when they interpret it. Although, unlike Professor Susan Rose-Ackerman, we are not persuaded that courts should invalidate statutes that lack clear statements of purpose, we agree with her that well-drafted purpose provisions serve useful purposes and should be encouraged by the courts.[59] These changes in public law are not as striking as a revival of the nondelegation doctrine might be, but they probably have more potential for making Congress more responsible. Thus, public choice may have some useful implications for public law theory, but as a basis for fundamental constitutional changes, the "information cost" theory has too many problems to be viable.

A third theory of congressional motivation avoids some of those problems, but only by relying on a dubious assumption about the preferences of

58. Wittman, *Why Democracies Produce Efficient Results,* 97 J. POL. ECON. 1395, 1402 (1989).

59. *See* Rose-Ackerman, *Progressive Law and Economics—And the New Administrative Law,* 98 YALE L.J. 341, 352 (1988). One way that courts might encourage such purpose statements would be to refuse to consider unarticulated purposes when laws are subjected to "rational basis" review. Courts might also announce a policy of narrow construction of statutes that lack meaningful purpose sections.

Professor Rose-Ackerman also suggests that statutes should be reviewed for "budgetary" inconsistency by striking down statutes if Congress later failed to provide adequate funding. *Id.* at 353–54. Again, we are dubious about judicial enforcement. One beneficial result of Gramm-Rudman, however, may be to force greater accountability on Congress by requiring Congress to identify specific funding sources at the time a new program is passed. As the recent uproar over catastrophic care for the elderly indicates, requiring the use of identified tax sources can act as a serious discipline on Congress.

the contending groups. If interest groups are "risk accepting," they may like the idea of gambling on outcomes before the agency. Even if they are just as likely to lose as win, they may prefer to buy into an "administrative lottery" as opposed to having no legislative action at all. Legislators then make everyone happy by enacting a broad delegation of power.

The major problem with this theory is its dubious postulate. Why assume that interest groups are eager to gamble? Economists usually assume that consumers are risk averse. Risk aversion explains why people buy insurance: they are willing to pay additional premium to avoid the uncertain prospect of a severe financial loss. Consumer groups, being risk averse, should oppose broad delegations. Industry groups should be risk neutral. Stock prices should reflect a risk neutral appraisal of a firm's probable future earnings.[60] To the extent that corporations are managed to maximize the returns to shareholders, firms themselves will also behave as if they were risk free. All of this is a matter of elementary finance theory. If firms are risk neutral, and individuals are risk averse, where do the risk-seeking interest groups come from?[61]

These theories of delegation really come down to this: Most legislation is rent-seeking, therefore bad. If Congress isn't allowed to delegate, there will be less legislation, so society is better off.[62] As we saw in chapter 1, however, this is a questionable appraisal of the legislative process. The political process is not a simple contest between special interests to extract largess from the public at large. Instead, there is a significant public interest component. Moreover, the "rent-seeking" label is either purely descriptive or, if it is intended to carry normative weight, makes the questionable assumption that economic efficiency is the only standard for assessing legislation. In short, the arguments based on interest group theory merely rehash the general argument for enhanced judicial review of rent-seeking statutes.

Another line of argument against delegation is based on the other major strand of public choice theory. As we saw in chapter 2, legislative outcomes can be as much a product of legislative structures and procedures as of legis-

60. Any deviation from risk neutrality in the determination of share prices creates opportunities for arbitrage. For example, if a stock's price reflects risk acceptance by shareholders, they are paying a premium over the firm's probable earnings in order to gain the opportunity to gamble. On average, then, they will obtain a subnormal return on their investment; the stock's value will on average decline on the "morning after" when the gamble fails to pay off. Arbitragers can make a profit, then, by selling such stocks short. In an efficient capital market, such opportunities for arbitrage cannot endure.

61. *See* R. Posner, Economic Analysis of Law 405–13 (3d ed. 1986).

62. For a discussion of this strand of the delegation literature, see Pierce, *supra* note 54, at 497–99. Another argument for the delegation doctrine is that the framers designed the Constitution to "minimize the amount of lawmaking to which the public would be subjected." *See* Bruff, *Judicial Review and the President's Statutory Powers*, 68 Va. L. Rev. 1, 28 (1982). (Bruff is not, nevertheless, enthusiastic about rekindling the delegation doctrine.)

lators' preferences. Structural constraints play a crucial role in disciplining what might otherwise be an unstable and capricious process. When the legislature delegates authority to an agency, however, the agency can "make law" without complying with the Constitution's procedural rules (passage by both Houses and signature by the President). Hence, Professor Macey argues, "the very existence of such agencies is a glaring contradiction of the carefully constructed lawmaking procedures articulated in article I [of the Constitution]."[63]

Macey's argument gathers some force from the *Chadha* decision, in which the Supreme Court struck down the legislative veto because it circumvented the article I procedures.[64] But there is a crucial difference between delegation and the legislative veto. When Congress delegates power, it pays an institutional price because power is shifted from Congress to an agency. It is unthinkable, for instance, that Congress would attempt to delegate all of its legislative authority to the President, since to do so would leave Congress impotent. Whether legislators are dedicated public servants or rapacious political hacks, they cannot expect much benefit from their offices if they give all their power away.[65] In contrast, the legislative veto increases Congressional power, and unless checked from outside, would be used without restraint.

Any exercise of "lawmaking" must follow the proscribed procedures in article I. But what is lawmaking? If lawmaking means "anything within the constitutional power of Congress," then Macey's argument proves too much. Congress passes a wide range of private bills, offering citizenship to particular individuals, augmenting pension rights, and conferring other benefits. If these activities are "lawmaking," then presumably only Congress can engage in them. Do all grants of citizenship, government pensions, and other benefits have to be individually provided through the legislative process, rather than being left to administrative agencies? Obviously not. No one believes that Congress is required to administer the social security system on its own. Obviously, some actions Congress could take on its own can nevertheless be delegated.

Thus, the article I legislative procedures must be mandatory only for some

63. Macey, *supra* note 53, at 514. *See also* Schoenbrod, *supra* note 54, at 1245–56.

64. *See* Immigration & Naturalization Serv. v. Chadha, 462 U.S. 919 (1983). The literature on *Chadha* is summarized in Frickey, *The Constitutionality of Legislative Committee Suspension of Administrative Rules: The Case of Minnesota*, 70 MINN. L. REV. 1237 (1986). We do not find the Court's rationale in *Chadha* convincing. In chapter 5, we develop an alternative rationale, one that does not support Macey's thesis.

65. The distinction between self-aggrandizing congressional enactments and other statutes affecting the separation of power is stressed in the special prosecutor decision, Morrison v. Olson, 108 S. Ct. 2597, 2620–21 (1988), but was explored in earlier commentary. *See* Frickey, *supra* note 64, at 1273–76. *See also* Bowsher v. Synar, 478 U.S. 714, 753–59 (1986) (Stevens, J., concurring in the judgment).

narrower category of legislative activity, falling short of Congress's full legislative power. But where do we draw the line?

Public choice theory suggests no answer—or if anything, it suggests the wrong answer. Particularized decisions allow more permutations of results, thereby increasing the likelihood of cycling and the importance of institutional constraints. Generalized decisions, on the other hand, restrict the possible patterns of outcomes, so cycling is less likely and procedures are less important. Thus, the article I procedures would be most important for particularized decisions and the least so for basic policy determinations. On this theory, the more basic the policy decision, the less reason there is to worry about delegation!

Obviously, public choice theory gives us no help in distinguishing between proper and improper delegations. But this is the nub of the problem. Everyone can agree that Congress should not delegate excessive legislative power, but how much is excessive?

The most common example of improper delegation is the OSHA provision governing toxic chemicals in the workplace. This was the provision condemned by Chief Justice Rehnquist as a standardless delegation of authority.[66] But the statute actually sets rather clear standards. It does contain a general provision defining the agency's power to make rules "reasonably necessary or appropriate to provide safe or healthful employment or places of employment."[67] But the statute also contains a much more specific directive governing toxic chemicals. The toxics provision directs the agency to set the standard "which most adequately assures, to the extent feasible, that no employee will suffer material impairment of health or functional capacity."[68] Employee health is the first priority, with the burden on the employer a secondary consideration. True, the statute could have been even more specific in defining "feasibility," but Congress made an unmistakable policy decision to favor health over economics.

If this is too broad a delegation, as supporters of the delegation doctrine contend, the problem cannot be that Congress is ducking basic policy decisions. The critics must want Congress not only to make the basic policy decision, but also to draft detailed regulations providing numerical standards for various industries. Even assuming that this is feasible, it is hard to see why it would be more conducive to good government than the present legal framework. Once Congress has established a goal, the agency's rulemaking is constrained by the possibility of review in the courts under the Administrative Procedure Act. The agency is required to give a reasoned explanation for its decision based on an evidentiary record. Congress, on the

---

66. *See* text accompanying note 52 *supra*.
67. 29 U.S.C. § 652(8).
68. 29 U.S.C. § 655(b) (5).

other hand, need give no explanation at all. How would having Congress provide the numerical standards lead to more principled or deliberative decisionmaking, or reduce illicit rent-seeking? As we mentioned in chapter 1, a classic example of rent-seeking was the Smoot-Hawley tariff, in which the statute provided enough numerical certainty to satisfy the most dedicated opponent of delegation. The arduous task of developing the numbers was largely left to the industries themselves, which had a field day writing the statute.

Much of modern government is designed around the administrative agency. A world with a strong delegation doctrine would be a world that differed in many other respects from our own. Congress would be organized differently. States would have taken on different regulatory powers where the inability to delegate prevented congressional involvement. Congress might also have adopted nonregulatory methods such as tax incentives where the inability to delegate made direct regulation impractical. This hypothetical world might have been better than the one in which we actually live. But the transition costs of developing a new legal framework would be large, and the benefits uncertain.

In this chapter, we have seen several efforts, partially inspired by public choice theory, to dismantle the modern regulatory state. By protecting economic liberty, resurrecting states' rights, and banning broad administrative delegation, some scholars seek to undo much of the New Deal. Perhaps the New Deal was a bad idea, but there are severe limits on our ability to unscramble eggs.

Science fiction stories have been written on the "what if Lee had won at Gettysburg" theme; if more lawyers were science fiction fans, we might see novels about hypothetical worlds in which the 1937 "switch in time that saved Nine" never took place. What would such a world look like? Would there have been a constitutional amendment to validate the New Deal? Would the free market, left unmolested by government intervention, have turned the Great Depression into the Great Boom? Would alternate institutions have developed to deal with the nation's problems within the confines of the pre–New Deal judicial doctrines? For that matter, would the government have survived at all, and how would World War II have come out?

The one thing we do know is that none of these events took place. There *was* a "switch in time," and our governmental system has grown up around it. If public choice is ultimately the application of economic reasoning to politics, its ultimate counsel should be to avoid the pursuit of abstractions without a sharp eye on the resulting costs. The long-run effects of undoing the New Deal might be beneficial, but the transition costs would be enormous—and as Keynes said, in the long run we are all dead anyway.

We do not wish to be misunderstood as devaluing the contribution of public choice theory to public law. We think public choice can make a real, if less dramatic, contribution to the legal system—not at the level of revolutionary new constitutional doctrines, but more modestly, by improving the implementation of existing statutes and the process for enacting future legislation. These form the topics of our final two chapters.

F O U R

Statutory Interpretation

*T*he Supreme Court is best known as a constitutional tribunal. But the Court has another crucial function. Important statutes like the Sherman Antitrust Act or the 1964 Civil Rights Act do not interpret themselves. The Court frequently must decide the tough questions arising under these statutes, often setting national policy on issues such as corporate mergers or affirmative action. As the role of statutes in American law has grown, statutory interpretation has become an increasingly crucial part of the Court's workload. Today, federal statutes protect the environment, regulate safety in the workplace, prohibit employment discrimination, and ban insider trading—and the courts have played a key role in implementing each of these statutes. And yet, statutory interpretation has never received scholarly (let alone, public) attention equal to its practical importance. Instead, legal scholars typically have focused on constitutional law or nonstatutory areas like tort law.

To a nonlawyer, statutory interpretation may seem like a pretty easy exercise: just read the statute and do what it says. Yet interpreting a statute is often a dauntingly difficult task. The language of the applicable section of the statute may simply be unclear, or worse yet, we may be unable to determine just which provision is the most relevant to the issue at hand. The legislative history may give us clues about the intentions of the legislators, but these clues may be unclear if not misleading. The general purpose of the statute may suggest an answer different than a literal reading of the language, which itself may not jibe with the legislative history. Moreover, at least some interpretations suggested by these sources may seem absurd or obsolescent in light of the broader legal landscape.

Trying to decide on the best interpretation of the statute in light of all these considerations calls for the highest level of judicial ability. No general theory of interpretation can hope to make statutory interpretation an easy job, but an interpretative theory might at least help determine just what considerations are relevant to interpretation and give some guidance about their relative weights. For many years, however, legal scholars wrote about statutory interpretation only in the context of specific statutes, without making serious consideration of the more general issues.

Public choice has helped revitalize scholarship about statutory interpretation.[1] Justice Antonin Scalia and Judge Frank Easterbrook have led a vigorous campaign against the conventional method of interpreting statutes. Traditionally, courts have seen statutory interpretation largely as a search for the legislature's intent. To find out what the legislature intended, judges have considered both a statute's language and its legislative history—a legal term that encompasses hearings, the reports of congressional committees, and floor debates.[2] Scalia, Easterbrook, and other pubic choice scholars have argued that the whole idea of legislative intent should be scrapped.

On the whole, we believe these scholars have been too impatient with conventional legal doctrines. We do think, however, that public choice theory can illuminate the task of statutory interpretation. In the first half of this chapter, we will critique the attacks on existing judicial methods. We will then explore some more promising applications of public choice theory.

I. Legislative Intent

Justice Antonin Scalia and Judge Frank Easterbrook have led the assault on the concept and utility of legislative intent. We will present a composite overview of their major lines of argument rather than exploring their individual positions in detail.[3]

1. Much of this recent scholarship is collected in W. Eskridge & P. Frickey, Cases and Materials on Legislation: Statutes and the Creation of Public Policy ch. 7 (1988).

2. For a historical overview of methods of statutory interpretation from Blackstone to the present, see Blatt, *The History of Statutory Interpretation: A Study in Form and Substance,* 6 Cardozo L. Rev. 799 (1985).

3. In presenting their position, we have relied upon Pittston Coal Group v. Sebben, 109 S. Ct. 414 (1988) (Scalia, J.); Puerto Rico Department of Consumer Affairs v. Isla Petroleum Corp., 108 S. Ct. 1350 (1988) (Scalia, J.); Sable Communications v. FCC, 109 S. Ct. 2829, 2840 (1989) (Scalia, J., concurring); Jett v. Dallas Independent School District, 109 S. Ct. 2702, 2724 (1989) (Scalia, J., concurring in part and concurring in the judgment); Green v. Bock Laundry Machine Co., 109 S. Ct. 1981, 1994–95 (1989) (Scalia, J., concurring in the judgment); United States v. Stuart, 109 S. Ct. 1183, 1193–97 (1989) (Scalia, J., concurring in the judgment); Blanchard v. Bergeron, 109 S. Ct. 939, 946–47 (1989) (Scalia, J., concurring in part and concurring in the judgment); United States v. Taylor, 108 S. Ct. 2413, 2423–24 (1988) (Scalia, J., concurring in part); INS v. Cardoza-Fonseca, 480 U.S. 421, 452–53 (1987) (Scalia, J., concurring in the judgment); Citicorp Indus. Credit, Inc. v. Brock, 483 U.S. 27, 40 (1987) (Scalia, J., concurring); Hirschey v. Federal Energy Regulatory Commission, 777 F.2d 1, 7–8 (1985) (Scalia, J., concurring); Address by Judge Antonin Scalia on Use of Legislative History (delivered at various law schools in 1985–86), discussed in Farber & Frickey, *Legislative Intent and Public Choice,* 74 Va. L. Rev. 423, 442–60 (1988); Judges and Legislators: Toward Institutional Comity 170–75 (R. Katzmann ed. 1988) (summarizing comments by Justice Scalia); *Hearings on the Nomination of Judge Antonin Scalia, To Be Associate Justice of the Supreme Court of the United States Before the Senate Comm. on the Judiciary,* 99th Cong., 2d Sess. 65–68, 74, 75, 105–7 (1986); Premier Elect. Const. Co. v. NECA, Inc., 814 F.2d 358, 365 (7th Cir. 1987) (Easterbrook, J.); Easterbrook, *The Role of Original Intent in Statutory Construction,* 11 Harv. J.L. & Pub. Pol'y. 59 (1988); Easterbrook, *Statutes' Domain,* 50 U.

If one were writing on a clean slate, Scalia and Easterbrook suggest, the traditional focus on the intentions of the legislature should be rejected. Instead, they say, interpretation should be based upon the meaning of the statutory words to a normal reader of the English language.

To begin with, these judges ask, how can legislative intent be found? How can we know the views of hundreds of legislators? How likely is it that legislators familiarize themselves with (and correct errors in) legislative history, which is often produced by congressional staff rather than legislators? Isn't reliance on legislative history an open invitation to plant strategic remarks designed to skew interpretation of the statute? Are judges institutionally well situated and skilled enough to make these kinds of inquiries?

Moreover, the argument continues, even if legislative intent can sometimes be discerned, it should carry no interpretive weight. Ours is a government of laws, not of persons, so law should be based on the objective import of statutory language rather than the unenacted intent of legislators. Once enacted, a statute becomes the domain of the executive officers and judges charged with its enforcement and application, rather than remaining somehow tethered to the unenacted intentions of legislators. Furthermore, giving effect to unenacted legislative intentions undermines the constitutional requirement that each bill pass both Houses. The difficult process of amending a bill to change its meaning should not be undermined by allowing manufactured legislative history to serve as a functional equivalent. Finally, judicial resort to legislative history also undermines the veto power of the President. How could a President become aware of, evaluate, and decide whether to veto a congressional intention that isn't expressed in statutory language? Only confusion, then, can be expected if judges stray outside the "four corners" of the document in their search for statutory meaning.

Not surprisingly, in their judicial opinions, Scalia and Easterbrook have been less radical than in their scholarly commentary. Their opinions do stress, however, that "clear" statutory language should not be impeached by legislative history. For example, in a case in which he agreed with the majority's construction of a statute but refused to endorse its use of legislative history, Justice Scalia wrote: "Judges interpret laws rather than reconstruct legislators' intentions. Where the language of those laws is clear, we are not free to replace it with an unenacted legislative intent."[4]

CHI. L. REV. 533 (1983). In a recent opinion, Judge Easterbrook seems to have softened his position somewhat, by conceding that legislative history can be used to explain ambiguous language or even to show "that a text 'plain' at first reading has a strikingly different meaning." *In re* Sinclair, 870 F.2d 1340, 1344–45 (7th Cir. 1989). For more discussion of the Scalia/Easterbrook approach, see Eskridge, *The New Textualism*, 37 UCLA L. REV. 621 (1990).

4. INS v. Cardoza-Fonseca, 480 U.S. 421, 452–53 (1987) (Scalia, J., concurring in the judgment). More recently, Justice Scalia stated: "The text is so unambiguous on these points that it

The Scalia-Easterbrook argument is based on a dichotomy between clear statutory language and "unenacted" (and therefore legally impotent) legislative intent. Most judges have been less doctrinaire on this score. In numerous cases, courts have discarded the most "natural" reading of statutory language, often because of a statute's historical setting and legislative history.[5] Even seemingly crystal-clear statutory language does not always prevail. For example, courts do not hesitate to correct inadvertent errors in statutes, such as omitted words.[6] The are also reluctant to follow statutory language when the result would be absurd or contrary to a statute's obvious purpose.[7]

---

must be assumed that what the Members of the House and the Senators thought they were voting for, and what the President thought he was approving when he signed the bill, was what the text plainly said, rather than what a few Representatives, or even a Committee Report, said it said. Where we are not prepared to be governed by what the legislative history says—to take, as it were, the bad with the good—we should not look at legislative history at all. This text is eminently clear, and we should leave it at that.

"It should not be thought that, simply because adverting to the legislative history produces the same result we would reach anyway, no harm is done. By perpetuating the view that legislative history *can* alter the meaning of even a clear statutory provision, we produce a legal culture in which the following statement could be made—taken from a portion of the floor debate alluded to in the Court's opinion: 'Mr. DENNIS . . . . "I have an amendment here in my hand which could be offered, but if we can make up some legislative history which would do the same thing, I am willing to do it." ' 120 CONG. REC. 41795 (1974). We should not make the equivalency between making legislative history and making an amendment so plausible. It should not be possible, or at least should not be easy, to be sure of obtaining a particular result in this Court without making the result apparent on the face of the bill which both Houses consider and vote upon, which the President approves, and which, if it becomes law, the people must obey. I think we have an obligation to conduct our exegesis in a fashion which fosters that democratic process." United States v. Taylor, 108 S. Ct. 2413, 2424 (1988) (Scalia, J., concurring in part). *See also* Citicorp Indus. Credit, Inc. v. Brock, 483 U.S. 27, 40 (1987) (Scalia, J., concurring) (plain meaning of statute controls notwithstanding any legislative purpose inconsistent with it). A related idea, which Justice Scalia has worked into an opinion for a majority of the Supreme Court, is that statutory language may operate more broadly or narrowly than matters focused upon in the legislative history. *See* Pittston Coal Group v. Sebben, 109 S. Ct. 414, 420–21 (1988) ("It is not the law that a statute can have no effects which are not explicitly mentioned in its legislative history"). Justice Scalia has also written a majority opinion dealing with something of a converse situation, in which comments in the legislative history do not link up to any provision in the bill. See Puerto Rico Department of Consumer Affairs v. ISLA Petroleum Corp., 485 U.S. 495, 501 (1988) ("While we have frequently said that pre-emption analysis requires ascertaining congressional intent, . . . we have never meant that to signify congressional intent in a vacuum, unrelated to the giving of meaning to an enacted statutory text. . . . [U]nenacted approvals, beliefs, and desires are not laws").

5. Church of the Holy Trinity v. United States, 143 U.S. 457 (1892), is the case most frequently cited for this proposition.

6. For a recent example, see United States v. Colon-Ortiz, 866 F.2d 6, 10–11 (1st Cir. 1989).

7. The Supreme Court waffles on this point. *Compare, e.g.,* Offshore Logistics, Inc. v. Tallentire, 477 U.S. 207 (1986) *and* Church of the Holy Trinity v. United States, 143 U.S. 457 (1892) (both deviating from plain meaning of statutory language to reach an interpretation more

When statutory language is ambiguous, the Scalia-Easterbrook arguments misfire. The idea of "government by laws" is irrelevant, because the judge's problem is precisely that she doesn't know what the "laws" require. Similarly, those who enact statutes are on notice that more than one interpretation is possible. Since legislative history is available to Congress and the President, they can intelligently appraise a bill's legal effects when casting their votes. Hence, the Constitution's procedural requirements are satisfied.[8]

The Scalia-Easterbrook argument essentially assumes that statutes have a legal meaning *before* the process of statutory interpretation. This makes anything "added" in the process of construction an illicit change in the preexisting meaning, as if the legislative history were being used to amend the statutory language. But an ambiguous statute lacks any clear preexisting meaning. In any legal setting in which its meaning becomes relevant, that meaning is necessarily the result of the interpretative process. As Judge Posner has said, "We cannot escape interpretation."[9]

Public choice, with its emphasis on the purposeful nature of legislators' conduct, also suggests that the "four corners" rule would have undesirable practical consequences. Today, Congress can legislate with confidence that courts will attend to the legislative intent. If the Scalia-Easterbrook approach is adopted, Congress can be expected to respond to a less hospitable judicial environment, with several resulting social costs.

A four corners rule raises the costs of drafting legislation by increasing the penalties for ambiguities. Congress will have to invest additional resources in drafting to eliminate some of these ambiguities. Realistically, however, even careful drafting cannot eliminate all ambiguities. As anyone who has ever done any drafting can attest, perfect clarity is a chimera. Since some ambiguity is inevitable, Congress will then be forced to devote additional

consistent with apparent statutory purpose and also more harmonious with overall legal landscape) *with* United States v. Locke, 471 U.S. 84 (1985) *and* Griffin v. Oceanic Contractors, Inc., 458 U.S. 564 (1982) (refusing to deviate from plain meaning). The issue is discussed at length in Public Citizen v. United States Dept. of Justice, 109 S. Ct. 2558 (1989). An important concurring opinion in *Public Citizen* argues for a narrower application of the "absurd result" rule. *See id.* at 2574–75 (Kennedy, J., concurring). *See generally* Note, *Intent, Clear Statements, and the Common Law: Statutory Interpretation in the Supreme Court*, 95 HARV. L. REV. 892 (1982).

8. Moreover, consulting legislative history does not improperly expand the power of legislators at the expense of judges and administrators, as Scalia and Easterbrook contend. It is true that courts and agencies rather than legislators are in charge of implementing the statute. Their practices must be consistent, however, with the meaning of the statute, and it is precisely that meaning which is at issue.

9. Posner, *Legal Formalism, Legal Realism, and the Interpretation of Statutes and the Constitution*, 37 CASE W. RES. L. REV. 179, 193 (1986–87). Judge Posner's views are explained more fully in chapters 9 and 10 of a forthcoming book, THE PROBLEMS OF JURISPRUDENCE.

resources to monitoring administrative agencies and pressuring them to interpret ambiguous statutes in conformity with legislative intent.[10] Because courts will more often contravene legislative intent, Congress will be required to pass more corrective laws. Finally, by increasing the need for detailed, unambiguous drafting, as well as the risk that legislation will be applied in unintended ways, a four corners rule would tend to discourage major reform legislation. This is not necessarily desirable even from the view of conservatives, since one effect would be to freeze current regulatory schemes in place.

The four corners approach suffers from another flaw. It assumes that statutory language can be interpreted in a vacuum. Often, however, statutory language is maddeningly elusive. As Justice Scalia admits, legislative history and other indicia of legislative intent can provide a simple way of answering otherwise intractable questions of statutory construction.[11]

Courts long ago realized the need to resolve ambiguous contract language with evidence about how the agreement was drafted.[12] If contract law is to serve the practical economic needs of society, courts cannot afford to be too rigid in interpreting contracts. Similarly, the Scalia-Easterbrook approach to statutory interpretation would only serve to hinder the practical business of government.

Even apart from its practical flaws, the four corners rule should be rejected for more fundamental reasons. As Judge Easterbrook has said on other occasions, in construing statutes a large part of the judicial role is to act as "honest agents of the political branches," engaged in "faithfully executing decisions made by others."[13] Literalism is not an attractive strategy for a faithful agent. Consider a staff member who receives an ambiguous presidential order. The staff member can adopt two methods of interpretation. The first is to take into account what the President said at lunch about what he had in mind. The second is to pick the interpretation of the language that would seem most plausible to the "reasonable citizen" who knew nothing about the President's actual desires. An honest and faithful agent of the Pres-

---

10. *See* R. POSNER, THE FEDERAL COURTS: CRISIS AND REFORM 292–93 (1985). Justice Scalia points out that the four corners rule is in use in England. *See* Scalia speech, *supra* note 3, at 1–2. The costs discussed in the text are much lower in a parliamentary system, particularly an effectively unicameral one with strict party discipline. For instance, passing corrective legislation is much easier.

11. Scalia speech, *supra* note 3, at 18. Justice Scalia also points out that extensive research into legislative history can be time-consuming and expensive. *Id.* at 14–15. We agree that this is a problem. Our response would be to deemphasize the use of materials other than committee reports, which are much more accessible and compact than other sources of legislative history.

12. *See* E. FARNSWORTH, CONTRACTS § 7.12 (1982).

13. Easterbrook, *Foreword: The Supreme Court and the Economic System*, 98 HARV. L. REV. 4, 60 (1984).

ident surely would not apply Scalia's four corners approach. Indeed, this approach would be far more appealing to an obstructive bureaucrat eager to sabotage a Presidential program than to a loyal staff member.

This example also suggests another objection to the four corners rule. The President's legitimacy derives from his election by the people. If a staff member knowingly interprets an ambiguous directive contrary to the President's actual intent, then the action he takes does not truly stem from the President's choice, and hence cannot claim legitimacy as a decision by the people's delegate. The unelected staff member is simply taking advantage of poor drafting to implement a policy that is only fortuitously related to any actual decision by the President. Thus, knowingly ignoring the intent of the elected drafter strains the chain of legitimacy from the electorate to the drafter and then to the implementor. Similarly, when a court ignores congressional intent in implementing a statute, it weakens the legitimacy of the statute by detaching the implementation from the actual purposes of the electorate's representatives.[14]

What, then, of unambiguous statutory language? Scalia contends that if legislative intent were crucial, we would allow it to override even clear statutory language. While overriding clear language is not unheard of, it is certainly exceptional.[15] Courts generally won't use legislative history to trump statutory language that seems plain on its face, at least when the plain meaning is not absurd. This approach is consistent with regard for legislative intent. Because unambiguous language is very strong evidence of intent, it should normally outweigh less reliable evidence such as legislative history.[16] In the long run, if courts were to make a frequent practice of going against clear statutory language, Congress would lose its best tool for communicating its intentions. Thus, a presumptive "plain language" rule, which limits the use of legislative history when the statutory language is clear, can actually serve to implement legislative intent. Similarly, in contract law, judges seek to implement the intentions of the parties, but judges are also reluctant to consider oral testimony about what the parties intended when the contract language is clear.[17] In both fields of law, a "plain meaning" approach sometimes frustrates the drafter's intent, but in the long run may implement that intent more often and more efficiently.

14. *See* Smith, *Law Without Mind,* 88 MICH. L. REV. 104 (1989).

15. On the current status of the "plain meaning" rule, see Wald, *Some Observations on the Use of Legislative History in the 1981 Supreme Court Term,* 68 IOWA L. REV. 195, 199 (1982); Note, *supra* note 7.

16. *See* Kay, *Original Intentions, Standard Meanings, and the Legal Character of the Constitution,* 6 CONST. COMM. 39, 45–47 (1989).

17. For an informative discussion of this area of contract law, see Goetz & Scott, *The Limits of Expanded Choice: An Analysis of the Interactions Between Express and Implied Contract Terms,* 73 CALIF. L. REV. 261 (1985).

Since legislatures have many members, they may sometimes lack a collective preference even regarding issues which have been directly considered. As we saw in chapter 2, this may happen with some frequency, although the incoherence of legislative preferences should not be exaggerated. Moreover, the issue before the court may not even have been foreseen by the legislators. Thus it is a mistake to make a shibboleth of legislative intent. But where an ascertainable legislative intention does exist, it should not be ignored.[18]

II. Legislative History

If legislative intent is important, how is it to be found? The language of the statute is obviously the starting point. Another time-honored source of legislative intent is the legislative history of the statute.[19] Statements made in the official committee reports on a bill, or by the sponsor of the bill during debates, are given particular weight by the courts.

Justice Scalia has roundly attacked the routine judicial consideration of legislative history.[20] His assault on legislative history is premised on a jaundiced view of its creation. He portrays legislative history as the product of legislators at their worst—promoting private interest deals, or strategically posturing to mislead judges, or abdicating all responsibility to their unelected staffs (who presumably either slant legislative history in their own self-interest or randomly run amok). The relationship between this jaundiced vision of the legislative process and the assumptions of public choice theory is obvious.

The Scalia attack began in *Hirschey v. FERC*,[21] which involved a federal statute governing the payment of attorney's fees by the government. When other portions of the statute were changed, the House committee report noted that courts disagreed about the interpretation of certain statutory language. The committee report then endorsed one of the competing

18. By legislative intent, we mean the collective purpose revealed by the public record. Sometimes these public statements may screen less creditable desires to aid special interests. We agree with Jonathan Macey that courts should attend to the public purpose, not the legislators' hidden agenda. *See* Macey, *Promoting Public-Regarding Legislation Through Statutory Interpretation: An Interest Group Model*, 86 COLUM. L. REV. 223 (1986).

19. *See, e.g.*, W. ESKRIDGE & P. FRICKEY, *supra* note 1, at 709–60. In recent manuscripts, William Eskridge and Nicholas Zeppos explore the proper use of legislative history in depth. See Eskridge, *Legislative History Values*, 66 CHI.-KENT L. REV. ** (1990) (Forthcoming); Zeppos, *Legislative History and the Interpretation of Statutes: Toward a Fact-Finding Model of Statutory Interpretation*, 76 VA. L. REV. 1295 (1990).

20. He has similarly attacked the use of Senate confirmation materials in construing treaties. *See* United States v. Stuart, 109 S. Ct. 647 (1989). For a powerful attack on Scalia's misuse of precedent in this regard, *see* Vagts, *Senate Materials and Treaty Interpretation: Some Research Hints for the Supreme Court*, 83 AM. J. INT'L LAW 546 (1989).

21. 777 F.2d 1 (D.C. Cir. 1985).

interpretations of this language (which was reenacted without change). Then-Judge Scalia was unimpressed:

> I frankly doubt that it is ever reasonable to assume that the details, as opposed to the broad outlines of purpose, set forth in a commit-tee report come to the attention of, much less are approved by, the house which enacts the committee's bill. And I think it time for courts to become concerned about the fact that routine deference to the detail of committee reports, and the predictable expansion in that detail which routine deference has produced, are converting a system of judicial construction into a system of committee-staff prescription.[22]

This is a rather stark judicial impeachment of the legislative process. Scalia was in effect asserting that legislators have abdicated important responsibilities to their staffs—who routinely connive to subvert the judicial function by planting their own political desires into committee reports, hop-ing that their distortions will blossom later in judicial opinions.

To support these assertions, Scalia attached a footnote presenting an anec-dote from the Senate floor.[23] This footnote contains the *only* evidence Scalia has ever given for his position about "committee-staff prescription." From his footnote, it would appear that Senator Dole, the committee chair who was managing floor consideration of a tax bill, made damaging admissions under sharp fire from Senator Armstrong: that Dole had not even read the entire committee report, much less written any of it; that the report was pre-pared wholly by staff; and that senators, including committee members, had little opportunity to object to the report's contents. From this footnote, it would appear that a serious breakdown of legislative responsibility had occurred.

The exchange between Armstrong and Dole was actually far more benign than Scalia's presentation suggests. Indeed, what Scalia portrayed as a gross malfunction of the legislative process turns out to have been, in Senator Armstrong's own evaluation, an admirable performance. The entirety of the colloquy demonstrates that even in the context of a complex tax bill, the committee reports were prepared responsibly and with careful attention to the views of the committee members. For example, after replying affirma-tively to Armstrong's question about whether the committee report should guide interpretation of the statute, Dole said that interpretation should also be guided by the floor debate on certain compliance provisions. (Thus, Dole, Armstrong, and everyone else understood that senators had other methods of creating legislative history, and of decreasing the au-thoritativeness of a committee report.) After reporting that he had "worked

22. *Id.* at 8 (Scalia, J., concurring) (footnote omitted).
23. *Id.* at 7 n.1.

carefully with the staff as they worked" on the report, Dole continued: "As I recall, during the July 4 recess week there were about five different working groups of staff from both parties, the joint committee, and the Treasury working on different provisions." The committee report was based on the legislative hearings (including statements at the hearings by the legislators), was prepared with the assistance of legislators, and was reviewed by members of the committee. Needless to say, these remarks rebut the suggestion that low-level, irresponsible staff concocted the report.

The Armstrong-Dole colloquy does confirm that staff draft committee reports, that legislators do not formally ratify language in reports, and that at least one senator hoped courts would not treat language in reports as equivalent to statutory language. The colloquy provides no support, however, for Scalia's claim of "committee-staff prescription."

Scalia's views on legislative history have received mixed reactions. During his confirmation hearing for the Supreme Court, Senator Charles Grassley criticized the *Hirschey* footnote, Senator Paul Simon seemed dubious, while Senator Howell Hefflin seemed somewhat supportive.[24] More enthusiastic have been several other Reagan appointees to the federal appellate bench, such as Judges James Buckley and Kenneth Starr.[25] Judge Alex Kozinski has embraced the Scalia viewpoint with particular enthusiasm:

> The fact of the matter is that legislative history can be cited to support almost any proposition, and frequently is. . . . Reports are usually written by staff or lobbyists, not legislators; few if any legislators read the reports; they are not voted on by the committee whose views they supposedly represent, much less by the full Senate or House of Representatives; they cannot be amended or modified on the floor by legislators who may disagree with the

24. *See Hearings on the Nomination of Judge Antonin Scalia, supra* note 3, at 65–68, 74, 75, 105–7.

25. For Buckley's views, see Overseas Education Assoc. v. FLRA, 876 F.2d 960, 974–76 (D.C. Cir. 1989) (Buckley, J., joined by Starr, J., concurring); International Brotherhood of Electrical Workers v. NLRB, 814 F.2d 697, 715–20 (D.C. Cir. 1987) (Buckley, J., concurring). Judge Starr's views are found in Ayuda, Inc. v. Attorney General, 848 F.2d 1297, 1299 & n.7 (D.C. Cir. 1988); American Mining Congress v. U.S. EPA, 824 F.2d 1177, 1190–92 (D.C. Cir. 1987); Natural Resources Defense Council v. EPA, 822 F.2d 104, 113 (D.C. Cir. 1987); Federal Election Comm'n v. Rose, 806 F.2d 1081, 1090 (D.C. Cir. 1986); International Brotherhood of Teamsters v. ICC, 801 F.2d 1423, 1428 n.4 (D.C. Cir. 1986); Starr, *Observations About the Use of Legislative History*, 1987 DUKE L.J. 371. In American Civil Liberties Union v. FCC, 823 F.2d 1554 (D.C. Cir. 1987), Judge Starr stated that "[w]e in the judiciary have become shamelessly profligate and unthinking in our use of legislative history." *Id.* at 1583 (Starr, J., dissenting in part). For instances in which federal judges appointed by other presidents have remarked favorably upon at least some of the elements of the Scalia approach, see International Brotherhood of Electrical Workers v. NLRB, 814 F.2d 697, 712–13 (D.C. Cir. 1987); Abourezk v. Reagan, 785 F.2d 1043, 1054 n.1 (D.C. Cir. 1986); Riddle v. Secretary of HHS, 817 F.2d 1238, 1247–48 (6th Cir. 1987) (Engel, J., dissenting).

views expressed therein. Committee reports that contradict statutory language or purport to explicate the meaning or applicability of particular statutory provisions can short-circuit the legislative process, leading to results never approved by Congress or the President. Of course, all this goes doubly for floor statements by individual legislators.[26]

Scalia himself, now as a Justice, has forcefully expressed continued skepticism about legislative history.[27]

In our view, Justice Scalia and his followers have indulged in some doubtful factual assumptions. For example, Judge Kozinski's statement that "few if any legislators read the reports" is mere unsupported assertion, if not flatly incorrect. To the contrary, it may well be that legislators outside the committee and their staffs primarily focus on the report, not the bill itself.[28] Moreover, because legislation today often involves numerous conflicting interest groups,[29] the possibility of "pulling a fast one" in the legislative history is somewhat remote. What one group smuggles into the history, other groups have an incentive to find and counter. Thus, competition between interest groups helps keep the system honest.

The critique that staff rather than legislators draft committee reports rings a bit hollow when coming from the federal judiciary, where law clerks routinely draft opinions. In both institutions, the important question is whether public officials have abdicated their decisionmaking responsibilities to staff. When Scalia's own example of committee report abuse is placed in proper context, it does not support his fear of "committee-staff prescription." No doubt, congressional staff sometimes exceed their appropriate role.[30] What

---

26. Wallace v. Christensen, 802 F.2d 1539, 1559–60 (9th Cir. 1986) (Kozinski, J., concurring in the judgment). In addition, see Kozinski, *Hunt for Laws' 'True' Meaning Subverts Justice,* Wall St. J., Jan. 31, 1989, at A14.

27. *See* cases cited in note 3, *supra.*

28. For example, Eric Redman, a former Senate aide, noted that committee reports provide information to courts and the executive branch about legislative intent. He then stated that "[w]ithin the Senate itself, reports are important chiefly because many Senators read nothing else before deciding how to vote on a particular bill. A good report, therefore, does more than explain—it also persuades." E. REDMAN, THE DANCE OF LEGISLATION 140 (1973). For additional background on the role of committee reports in Congress, see JUDGES AND LEGISLATORS: TOWARD INSTITUTIONAL COMITY, *supra* note 3, at 106–8, 172–75; W. OLESZEK, CONGRESSIONAL PROCEDURES AND THE POLICY PROCESS 104–6, 269–71 (3d ed. 1989). When administrative agencies interpret statutes, there may be additional reasons to encourage them to rely on committee reports. *See* Strauss, *Legislative Theory and the Rule of Law,* 89 COLUM. L. REV. 427, 438 (1989).

29. *See* M. FIORINA, CONGRESS: KEYSTONE OF THE WASHINGTON ESTABLISHMENT 122 (2d ed. 1989).

30. *See generally* M. MALBIN, UNELECTED REPRESENTATIVES: CONGRESSIONAL STAFF AND THE FUTURE OF REPRESENTATIVE GOVERNMENT (1980) (discussing tension between democratic theory and reality of large staff role). For an overview of political science studies about

that role should be is, however, surely the primary concern of the legislative rather than the judicial branch. In short, Scalia and others have not demonstrated pervasive abuse of legislative history by legislators or congressional staff. They have also failed to show that change in judicial use of legislative history will necessarily "reform" congressional processes.

Admittedly, legislative history does require careful handling. Legislative history is not some simple transmission of legislative intent, but this is hardly news to legislation scholars. The real problem is how to sort the wheat from the chaff. This problem has received serious attention from advocates of more traditional approaches to legislative interpretation.

In his classic writings about "the legal process," the late Henry Hart developed a thoughtful "tentative restatement of the law" of legislative history usage. He suggested that courts carefully evaluate the contextual relevance, competence, and probative value of legislative history.[31] The probative value of the legislative history depends upon how much light it sheds upon the overall purposes of the statute.[32] Thus, "[e]vidence in the internal legislative history of a statute concerning a specific application envisaged by individual legislators should be given weight only to the extent that the application envisaged fits rationally with other indicia of general purpose."[33] According to Professor Hart, this approach "should go a long way to take care of the manipulation problem."[34]

Judge Henry Friendly, who is commonly considered to have been one of the ablest federal judges ever to sit, took a similar position. He contended that if the committee reports are clear and consistent with the statutory language, a court "does pretty well to read the statute to mean what the few legislators having the greatest concern with it [*i.e.*, the committee] said it meant to them."[35] Friendly, too, thought courts capable of identifying cate-

---

legislative staff, see Hammond, *Legislative Staffs*, in HANDBOOK OF LEGISLATIVE RESEARCH 273–319 (1985).

31. *See* H. HART & A. SACKS, THE LEGAL PROCESS 1284–86 (tent. ed. 1958). These materials indicate that "one of the editors" developed the tentative restatement, *id.* at 1284. F. NEWMAN & S. SURREY, LEGISLATION—CASES AND MATERIALS 669–71 (1955), attributes this work to Hart.

32. This is consistent with the general approach to statutory interpretation adopted in the Hart and Sacks materials, under which the interpreter attributes an organizing purpose to the statute. *See* H. HART & A. SACKS, *supra* note 31, at 1410–17 (summary of their approach). *Cf.* Martin v. Comm'r of Internal Revenue, 783 F.2d 81, 83 (7th Cir. 1986) (Posner, J.): "As for the general danger that a committee report might not reflect the understanding of a majority of the members of Congress—might, indeed, not even be known to them, [citing the Scalia concurrence in *Hirschey*]—it is enough to say that we do not rest our decision entirely on the legislative history, nor use it to reach a result inconsistent with the language of the statute and with the purpose that can be inferred from that language without recourse to legislative history."

33. H. HART & A. SACKS, *supra* note 31, at 1285–86.

34. *Id.* at 1286.

35. Friendly, *Mr. Justice Frankfurter and the Reading of Statutes*, in H. FRIENDLY, BENCHMARKS 216 (1967).

gories of reliable legislative history and suggested that courts go slow in interfering with the conduct of committees and legislative sponsors.[36]

In sum, American public law has quite properly recognized that statutory meaning is greatly colored by statutory context. Legislative history is part of that context, and some aspects of it—frequently, for example, a committee report—will often represent the most intelligent exposition available of what the statute is all about. Legislative history should not be either the starting point or the end of the interpretive process, but it is a legitimate part of that process. In short, as Senator Orrin Hatch (an ideological ally of Scalia's) has said, "We all know that legislative history, like the law itself, can be misused. But it can also provide reliable context for the text of the law."[37]

We find nothing in the new attack led by Scalia to justify jettisoning this traditional approach. To the extent that the specific findings of public choice theory—rather than simply its general rejection of the public interest theory of legislation—have anything to say regarding Scalia's suggestions, they probably cut against him. Political scientists have long stressed the influence of committees on legislative outcomes.[38] Traditionally, committee power was attributed to the committee's roles as legislative "gatekeeper" and "policy incubator," to its expertise and agenda control, and to reciprocal deference among committees. Recently, public choice scholars have suggested that another critical element is often the existence of an ex post committee veto.[39] Even though the committee's proposal can be modified on the floor of the legislature, the committee can still control the final outcome if (1) a conference committee on the bill is necessary because it did not pass both houses of Congress in identical form, and (2) the standing committee essentially populates and controls the conference committee. Both contingencies apparently occur for nearly all major bills in Congress. The ex

36. "There is, of course, the fear that the 'intention' expressed even in committee reports and sponsors' statements may have been manufactured—perhaps, indeed, placed there for the very reason that it was known that the language could *not* be placed in the act itself. But is it not going too far to ask the courts to police such abdication of legislative responsibility?

This problem is quite different from the smuggling of 'intention' into hearing materials, which the legislators cannot prevent. The Justices [have] protested against undue reliance on such materials." *Id.* at 216 n.114.

37. Hatch, *Legislative History: Tool of Construction or Destruction,* 11 HARV. J.L. & PUB. POL'Y 43, 45 (1988).

38. For an overview of the political science literature, see Eulau & McCluggage, *Standing Committees in Legislatures,* in HANDBOOK OF LEGISLATIVE RESEARCH, *supra* note 30, at 395–470.

39. *See* Shepsle & Weingast, *The Institutional Foundations of Committee Power,* 81 AM. POL. SCI. REV. 85, 85 (1987). *See also* Baron & Ferejohn, *The Power to Propose,* in MODELS OF STRATEGIC CHOICE IN POLITICS (P. Ordeshook ed. 1989) (alternative explanation of committee power); Smith, *An Essay on Sequence, Position, Goals, and Committee Power,* 13 LEGIS. STUD. Q. 151 (1988); *Why Are Congressional Committees Powerful?,* 81 AM. POL. SCI. REV. 929–45 (1987).

post veto strengthens the committee's gatekeeping and proposal powers. For example, it makes little sense to use a discharge petition to dislodge a bill from committee if that committee's members will control the conference committee down the road. In the House, the committee also has the power to counter floor amendments with "perfecting" amendments, which allow the committee to protect itself against being "rolled."[40]

Although recent public choice scholarship has not addressed committee reports as such,[41] it does indicate that a coherent understanding of a statute must carefully attend to the work of the relevant committees. That work will be reflected, albeit imperfectly, in its report, which legislators and staff are likely to read far more carefully than the bill itself. Thus, recent public choice scholarship (like the long-standing views of political scientists) supports the traditional American public law presumption that "very likely most [members of Congress] knew only of the general purpose [of a bill], relied for the details on members who sat on the committees particularly concerned, and were quite willing to adopt these committees' will on subordinate points as their own."[42]

A fundamental finding of public choice—that legislative outcomes often are the result of "structure-induced equilibrium"—does counsel some caution in using legislative history as an interpretive source. Because legislative equilibrium can result from a combination of different legislative structures and rules, one bit or fragment of legislative history may have little to do with the final product. But when a fundamental aspect of legislative history, like a committee report, is unimpeached by other sources and is consistent with the apparent political equilibrium, it should be an important interpretive source.

---

40. Weingast, *Floor Behavior in the U.S. Congress: Committee Power Under the Open Rule*, 83 AM. POL. SCI. REV. 795 (1989).

41. Morris Fiorina has suggested that congressional committees may sometimes constitute handfuls of "unrepresentative members," and that courts "in reconstructing legislative intent may rely too heavily on the committee reports" prepared by such members and their staffs. Fiorina, *Legislator Uncertainty, Legislative Control, and the Delegation of Legislative Power*, 2 J.L. ECON. & ORG. 33, 49 & n.22 (1986). *See also* Eskridge, *Politics Without Romance: Implications of Public Choice Theory for Statutory Interpretation*, 74 VA. L. REV. 275 (1988) (problem of cycling majorities is not that "anything can happen," but that what does happen may be the result of agenda control and committee bias). We agree with Fiorina that committees may sometimes be unrepresentative of the legislative body as a whole, and that this may sometimes be reflected in committee reports. *But see* Krehbiel, *Are Congressional Committees Composed of Preference Outliers?*, 84 AM. POL. SCI. REV. 149 (1990). This is one of the many reasons why courts should not treat committee reports as sacrosanct. It does not, however, justify Justice Scalia's suggestion that we ignore such reports or systematically devalue them as compared to other aspects of legislative history. Courts will have great difficulty identifying "unrepresentative" committee reports in all but the baldest circumstances; in those instances, the reports ought to be considered less weighty.

42. Friendly, *supra* note 35, at 216. *See also* Maltz, *Statutory Interpretation and Legislative Power: The Case for a Modified Intentionalist Approach*, 63 TUL. L. REV. 1, 24–27 (1988).

That judges *can* make effective use of legislative history does not ensure that they always will do so successfully. The Court's opinions sometimes seemingly do misuse legislative history, exalting it as more important than the statute itself. Judicial opinions also sometimes appear more mechanical than reflective.[43] The Supreme Court's standard statutory opinion brooks little uncertainty: it argues with a straight face that all relevant sources of meaning unambiguously point in the same direction, while the dissenting Justices argue with equal conviction that the opposite meaning is just as clearly indicated.

These wrongheaded opinion-drafting techniques may occasionally mislead lower court judges or perhaps even the Justices themselves about the appropriate methodology of statutory interpretation. In addition, they are surely subject to criticism from members of Congress. The remedy is not, however, the replacement of some wooden rules with others (like Scalia's four corners rule). Rather, the appropriate reform is to draft opinions that candidly reflect the complexities of statutory interpretation.

III. Ambiguous Language and Rational Choice

Although we do not argue that legislative intent should always be controlling in statutory construction, we do believe that it plays a central role. Consequently, it is useful to develop a better model of intent-based interpretation.

Judge Posner's "communication" theory of legislation is a useful starting point. Posner argues that in construing legislation, judges are attempting to decode communications from their legislative superiors. Making a military analogy, he suggests that the judge is like a military officer who is attempting to follow obscure directions from headquarters.[44] Thus, in Posner's view, the task of the judge is to ascertain the most likely intention of the drafters.

The idea of a statute as an unclear communication can be easily modeled. The ambiguous statute has a number of interpretations (each of which is unambiguous), but the judge is unsure of which interpretation was intended. This is simply an instance of the general problem of decoding a "noisy" signal. The general question is this: if you have received a message that has more than one possible interpretation, which one should you adopt? Posner's answer would seem to be that you should always adopt the most probable interpretation.

This is not the best method of decoding a signal. Suppose, for example,

43. Consider Joseph Vining's view of the opinions produced by the current Supreme Court: "They are too much things of patchwork, things which seem, on their face, to express more the institutional process of their making than the thinking, feeling, and reasoning of the author and those persuaded with him." Vining, *Justice, Bureaucracy, and Legal Method*, 80 MICH. L. REV. 248, 251 (1981).

44. Posner, *supra* note 9, at 189–90.

that there are two possible interpretations, with one having a probability of 51% and the other 49%. One is slightly more probable than the other, and in the absence of any other information would be chosen. But suppose that we also know that the consequences are much different. Then we should take those consequences into account in choosing between risky alternatives, just as in buying a lottery ticket, we should consider not only the odds of winning but also the size of the prize in relation to the cost.[45] For example, in interpreting a partner's bid in bridge, a player would take into account not only how likely the partner is to have various possible hands, but also the consequences of adopting each interpretation: some mistakes may be much more costly than others.

To return to the military analogy, suppose that because of radio static the platoon leader is unsure whether he has been ordered to attack or retreat. The order sounded a little more like "attack," but the effect of an attack might be to wipe out his unit, while a retreat would seem more sensible. A responsible officer would not, we think, decide which course to take without considering the consequences. Within the constraints of his orders, the officer does bear the responsibility for the consequences of his decision. On the other hand, if the order had been clear, the officer would presumably have to obey even if the consequences seemed undesirable.

In effect, the judge is betting on the legislature's actual intention, and must take into account both the odds of being right and the consequences of being wrong. We might think of the various interpretations as being like different locations on a faded treasure map. The treasure seeker has some information about the location of the treasure, which he can translate into a list of probabilities. He also knows that the value of the treasure may depend on the location. If the treasure is in deep water, its economic value may be lowered by the expense of retrieving it. All things considered, which location is the most promising?

---

45. *See* Kaplan, *Decision Theory and the Factfinding Process,* 20 STAN. L. REV. 1065, 1066–71 (1968). As a general matter, decision theory indicates that the rational choice under uncertainty is to maximize the expected value of the utility of the outcome. *See* M. SHUBIK, GAME THEORY IN THE SOCIAL SCIENCES: CONCEPTS AND SOLUTIONS 417–24 (1987); E. STOKEY & R. ZECKHAUSER, A PRIMER FOR POLICY ANALYSIS 237–54 (1978). Here, the outcomes are that the chosen interpretation either upholds or violates the actual legislative intent. If judges value fidelity to legislative intent, the judicial payoff must be higher when the interpretation is actually correct, but the exact way in which the payoff should be modeled as a function of outcomes and correctness is unclear. In the text, we assume that the judge's payoff is zero when she chooses the wrong alternative, and that when she is correct the payoff varies depending on the alternative in question. This has the advantage that the judge will never choose an interpretation which is known to be directly opposed to legislative intent. For another method of modeling the costs of incorrect interpretations, see Rizzo & Arnold, *An Economic Framework for Statutory Interpretation,* 50 LAW & CONTEMP. PROBS. 165 (1987).

Decision theory suggests the following approach: multiply the probability of a given location by the economic value the treasure would have in that location. For example, if one location has a 75% chance of having the treasure, with a $100,000 profit if the treasure is there, then the "expected value" of that location is $75,000. (If you were lucky enough to have a lottery ticket with a 75% chance of paying $100, in the long run you would expect to win three-quarters of the time, making on average $75.) Another location might have only a 25% probability of being correct, but might also be much cheaper to explore. If the treasure is in the second location, the finder might earn a $400,000 profit. The expected value of exploring the second location is $100,000 (25% of $400,000). The second location is a better bet even though the probability is lower. You win less often this way, but bigger.

This model of statutory interpretation places a very high importance on correctly identifying original intent. No matter what benefits an interpretation might produce, these benefits count for nothing unless the interpretation is true to the actual original intent.[46] In case of a tie in likelihood, however, the judge picks the most beneficial interpretation of the statute, which seems reasonable.[47] In intermediate cases, the outcome is determined both by the likelihood that an interpretation corresponds with the drafter's intent and by the consequences of adopting the interpretation. With a new statute, these two factors may overlap, since the judge can reasonably presume that the drafters shared his assessments of the statute's consequences. For an older statute, however, this presumption may be quite unrealistic. It is simply unrealistic for judges to presume that the drafters of a century-old statute had any particular view on policy issues that have arisen in the meantime.

By letting the judge consider some of the consequences of an interpretation, this model allows some degree of judicial flexibility.[48] How much flexibility depends on how we define the "payoff." We could include the full social effects of adopting an interpretation, so the judge would consider the same range of consequences that a legislature would consider. On the other hand, the payoff could be defined much more narrowly to include only

---

46. There is a strong normative argument for this result. *See* Redish, *Federal Common Law, Political Legitimacy, and the Interpretative Process: An "Institutionalist" Perspective*, 83 Nw. U.L. Rev. 761, 768, 784–85, 801 (1989).

47. For an example of something like this situation, see Standard Office Bldg. Corp. v. United States, 819 F.2d 1371, 1379 (7th Cir. 1987) (Posner, J.).

48. The model also has the advantage of greater candor, since, as Judge Posner points out, the legislative intent is often unknown and decision must actually turn on other factors. We agree with him that judicial opinions more candidly acknowledging this would be desirable. *See* Posner, *The Decline of Law as an Autonomous Discipline: 1962–1987*, 100 Harv. L. Rev. 761, 777–78 (1987).

"legal process" costs of various kinds, such as litigation expenses or impact on the implementation of other statutes.[49]

Anyway, no matter how the payoff is defined, under this model the court will never disobey a clear directive from the legislature. The judge's actual decision is always constrained by the "probability factor," which brings into play whatever is known about the legislature's actual intentions. Thus, the model introduces a certain degree of flexibility while maintaining the principle that the legislature's will is supreme.[50]

This elementary model has at least heuristic value. It captures some—but we hasten to emphasize, not all—of the complex judgments that must be made in interpreting statutes. While building on Judge Posner's useful communication model of statutory construction, it gives more realistic insight into statutory interpretations, and ties statutory construction to the general problem of decoding unclear messages. When deciding between various interpretations of an unclear message, both the probability of a given interpretation and its consequences should be considered.

This model also reveals why statutory interpretation is such a complex process. The basic reason is that several distinct goals are involved. Giving effect to the legislature's intent is a goal with roots in basic democratic theory (as we saw in our earlier discussion of the relevance of legislative history). Another part of democratic theory, however, emphasizes the importance of the statutory language, both because of its unique formal status as the outcome of the legislative process and because of its special role in giving notice to citizens about the demands of the legal system. Finally, as the "noisy signal" model suggests, the judge also needs to consider the effect of a given interpretation on other public policies. When a judge is lucky, all of these norms will point toward the same decision in a given case. Often, however, they will have conflicting implications, and deciding on the right

---

49. An intermediate possibility would be for judges to consider broadly shared substantive values. *See* Eskridge, *Public Values in Statutory Interpretation*, 137 U. PA. L. REV. 1007 (1989). For an important effort to elaborate a coherent set of public values for use in interpreting statutes, see Sunstein, *Interpreting Statutes in the Regulatory State*, 103 HARV. L. REV. 405 (1989). For a critique of Sunstein, see Mashaw, *As If Republican Interpretation*, 97 YALE L.J. 1685 (1988).

50. This model could be usefully elaborated in several directions. It would be interesting to couple this model of judicial interpretation to various models of legislation, so as to determine how rational legislators would respond to the model. Another option would be to construct a Bayesian analysis in which legislative history modifies a prior estimate of probability based solely on statutory language. The whole topic of judicial interpretation has received very little attention from formal modelers. We can imagine (but have not attempted to construct) more elaborate models of cooperative games between judges and legislatures, or perhaps the application of communication theory to the problem. We encourage those with greater technical expertise to pursue these options.

interpretation will require an exercise of the judge's "practical reason." As legal pragmatists, we do not believe that legal theory can eliminate the need for judicial exercise of practical reason. Theory can, however, help illuminate and clarify the judge's task.

IV. Statutory Evolution

Even when a statute is drafted clearly, later events may raise questions about the viability of the original legislative intent. After a statute is passed, various unexpected events may take place. Public opinion may turn against the view of public policy underlying the statute. Changes in social conditions may frustrate the statute's ability to accomplish its original purpose. Or judicial precedents may misconstrue the statute. The degree to which courts should consider these later events is one of the most vexing problems in the theory of statutory interpretation. Public choice helps clarify the relevance of postenactment events.

Let us begin with the problem of the outmoded legislative policy. Statutes are difficult to pass, but they are also hard to amend or repeal. Consequently, a statute may stay on the books indefinitely even though it has become out of step with current public policy. If a court believes that a statute is obsolete, enforcing the legislative command may be rather distasteful. Yet, if the legislative intent is clear, the court may feel obligated to implement that intent.

There are accepted methods for dealing with statutory obsolescence, but only under certain limited circumstances. If later legislation on the same subject reflects more palatable views of public policy, the court can declare that the earlier statute has suffered a repeal by implication. Alternatively, if the statute touches upon some constitutionally sensitive area like gender discrimination, the age of the statute may be relevant to its constitutionality.[51] Usually, however, neither of these accepted approaches is applicable.

A somewhat radical solution to the problem of the outmoded statute is to declare the statute defunct. In support of this approach, Dean Guido Calabresi argues that the legitimacy of an old statute rests only on the facts "it has gone unrepealed; and it once commanded a majoritarian basis."[52] The first fact, he observes, is equally true of old common law decisions, while the second fact lacks significance if majority support for the statute has evaporated. Hence, Calabresi says, an old statute is no more (though also no less) entitled to the court's respect than an old judicial precedent.

Public choice theory illuminates a fundamental flaw in this argument. Calabresi treats inertia as simply an incidental aspect of the political system,

51. These conventional approaches are discussed in W. ESKRIDGE & P. FRICKEY, *supra* note 1, at 870–80.

52. G. CALABRESI, A COMMON LAW FOR THE AGE OF STATUTES 101–2 (1982); *see also* Mississippi Univ. for Women v. Hogan, 458 U.S. 717, 725, 730 n.16 (1982).

as if an ideal democratic system would instantly reflect changes of majority sentiment. On the contrary, the agenda rules and institutional structures that create legislative inertia are themselves crucial to the workings of legislatures. Without them, legislatures would be plagued by instability and could not function as deliberative bodies. In a real sense, the system is *designed* so that laws will outlive the political coalitions that enacted them.[53] Thus, it would be a mistake to adopt the rule that courts need not enforce a statute if the latest Gallup poll shows that it has lost majority support. Calabresi is not this simplistic, for he would allow courts to update statutes only when they are patently out of sync with the overall "legal landscape," as well as having lost majority support.[54] But the judgment Calabresi would have courts undertake is a slippery one, and the burden of legislative inertia that he would have courts reallocate is not simply an impediment to needed law reform. Rather, it is a vital attribute of the legislative process. It would be a mistake, then, to consider old statutes as equivalent to old precedents.

This is not to say, however, that courts must always ignore postenactment developments. An argument to the contrary can be based on the presumed intent of the enacting legislators themselves. Allowing courts to consider some kinds of later events may advance the goals of enacting legislators. These legislators would presumably endorse a rule allowing judges to consider such events; such a rule can be considered an "implied term" in the statute, much like the implied terms courts read into contracts and other legal documents. As we shall see, this argument is valid in some contexts. It cannot, however, save Calabresi's theory.

Consider a possible rule under which statutory directives could be nullified by courts if they are contrary to the judges' view of public policy and have lost majority support. Such a rule would not be favored by enacting legislators because it would substantially decrease the value of legislation to its supporters. Knowing that majority coalitions are unstable, the members of the coalition have good reason to want their legislation to survive the coalition itself.[55] Allowing courts to nullify statutes that have lost majority support would bring courts into conflict not only with the statutes themselves but also with the legislature's own "meta-intent" about how courts should apply statutes.

Changes in majority opinion are not the only reasons why a court might hesitate to follow a statute's original meaning. Other intervening events may also make the "original intent" seem questionable. The perspective of the

---

53. The importance of legal stability receives particular stress in *The Federalist No. 62*. See also *The Federalist Nos. 10 & 71*.

54. *See* G. CALABRESI, *supra* note 52, at 163–66.

55. *See* McCubbins, Noll, & Weingast, *Administrative Procedures as Instruments of Social Control*, 3 J.L. ECON. & ORG. 243 (1987).

enacting legislator again gives useful guidance. As courts have recognized in analogous situations, rational individuals would favor a rule that allowed a court to disregard their directives because of some kinds of "changed circumstances."

Several legal analogies exist. In contract law, for example, it is well established that performance of a contract is excused if it becomes impractical or if changed circumstances frustrate the basic purpose of the contract.[56] Similarly, under the cy pres doctrine, provisions of a trust may be nullified or rewritten by a court when changed circumstances prevent the original provisions from attaining the donor's goals.[57] To a literalist, these doctrines might seem to involve judicial disobedience to the directions of the contracting parties or the donor. But this criticism is misguided, because the rules are in fact those that rational parties would choose, and the actual parties have not manifested any specific inconsistent intentions. For the same reason, a statutory cy pres doctrine would only superficially conflict with legislative intent.[58] For example, technological change might render a statute passed for safety reasons an actual source of increased danger. Under such circumstances, serious doubt exists about whether the enacting legislators would intend it to apply, so disregarding the statute should not be considered improper. Like individuals entering into contracts, legislators who enact statutes could benefit from a cy pres rule, which would give courts some flexibility in dealing with unforeseen circumstances. If the cy pres doctrine is one that rational legislators themselves would favor, courts can properly claim to be implementing rather than frustrating the legislators' design.

A recent case prompted an intriguing debate about the effect of changed circumstances on statutory directives. *K Mart Corp. v. Cartier, Inc.*[59] involved an obscure customs regulation governing the importation of trademarked goods. The Tariff Act prohibits importation of such goods if the

---

56. *See* U.C.C. § 2–615; E. FARNSWORTH, CONTRACTS, §§ 9.1, 9.6, 9.7. Also, there are growing arguments in favor of allowing judicial modification of long-term contracts in light of changed circumstances. *See* Hillman, *Court Adjustment of Long-Term Contracts: An Analysis Under Modern Contract Law,* 1987 DUKE L.J. 1.

57. According to section 399 of the *Second Restatement of Trusts:* "If property is given in trust to be applied to a particular charitable purpose, and it becomes impossible or impracticable or illegal to carry out the particular purpose, and if the settlor manifested a more general intention to devote the property to charitable purposes, the trust will not fail but the court will direct the application of the property to some charitable purpose which falls within the general charitable intention of the settlor."

58. Although the concept of statutory cy pres has not found explicit recognition in American law, cases can be found that seem to reach somewhat similar results. *See* Li v. Yellow Cab Co., 12 Cal. 3d 804, 119 Cal. Rptr. 858, 532 P.2d 1226 (1975); Selders v. Armentrout, 190 Neb. 275, 207 N.W.2d 686 (1973) (both cases "interpreting" provisions in state tort statutes out of existence).

59. 486 U.S. 281 (1988).

trademark is owned by an American citizen or corporation. The case involved "gray market" goods, that is, goods bearing American trademarks but imported without the consent of the trademark holder. The Customs Service's regulation allowed gray market goods to be imported under certain circumstances. One of these regulatory exceptions allowed importation when the American owner had authorized the use of the trademark (but not the importation). Justice Kennedy's opinion for the Court rather brusquely held this exception to be inconsistent with the plain statutory language.

For present purposes, the more interesting discussion is contained in the separate opinions of Justices Brennan and Scalia, each of whom represented a faction of four Justices. Justice Brennan all but conceded that the plain language of the statute was against him. He argued, however, that trademark law had changed radically in the fifty years since the statute was passed. When Congress imposed the import restriction, he suggested, trademarks served only to identify the origin of goods, and any attempt to license a trademark could nullify it. Hence, legislators could not have imagined how the statute would apply in a world in which trademarks are readily transferable property interests. Justice Brennan drew an analogy to a nineteenth-century statute requiring ovens to be inspected for their propensity to spew flames; such a statute, he maintained, need not be applied to microwave or electric ovens.[60]

Justice Scalia vigorously attacked Brennan's analysis. While he agreed that a microwave might not really be an "oven," he could see no reason to exempt electric ovens from flame testing.[61] More generally, he argued that courts should not "rewrite the United States Code to accord with the unenacted purposes of Congresses long since called home." Rather, it is "the prerogative of each currently elected Congress to allow those laws which change has rendered nugatory to die an unobserved death if it no longer thinks their purposes worthwhile; and to allow those laws whose effects have been expanded by change to remain alive if it favors the new effects."[62]

Justice Scalia's argument has several flaws. First, Congress does not have the luxury of "allowing statutes to die an unobserved death"; rather, it must engage in active euthanasia. As Justice Scalia himself has noted, the fact that a statute has not been repealed often reflects nothing more than inertia.[63] So the fact that a statute has survived does not necessarily mean that Congress believes it has current social value. In *K Mart*, Scalia's argument is particularly weak because Congress might well have assumed that the customs

---

60. *Id.* at 312–17.
61. *Id.* at 324 n.2.
62. *Id.* at 325.
63. *See, e.g.,* Johnson v. Transportation Agency, 480 U.S. 616, 672 (1987) (Scalia, J., dissenting) ("vindication by congressional inaction is a canard").

regulations were valid, making legislative action to update the statute unnecessary. The very existence of the regulations could well have led Congress to believe that no amendment to the statute was needed to bring it in line with modern conditions.

Second, Justice Scalia's reference to rewriting statutes to accord with the "unenacted purposes" of past Congresses is puzzling, since it is precisely the enacted purpose of the statute whose application was in question. Brennan's argument in *K Mart* is that Congress had actually never made any decision about how to apply the statute to assignable trademarks, because such things did not exist at the time of enactment. Such an argument respects rather than flouts the legislature's prerogatives.

Third, Justice Scalia's reference to "ambiguity" is question-begging. If we doubt that a reasonable speaker in a particular context would mean an order to be applied in a certain situation, then the order cannot be considered wholly unambiguous. Of course, as Justice Scalia suggests, the legislature could have included an express provision about unforeseen circumstances. It is a commonplace in private law, however, that courts serve a useful function by providing "off the rack" terms that most people would agree to, since by doing so courts reduce the cost and difficulty of negotiating contracts. A similar rationale would support the use of "off the rack" statutory terms.

Thus, Justice Scalia is on weak ground in arguing for a complete rejection of the Brennan approach. He is on stronger ground, however, when he suggests that the approach should only be used cautiously. Between its passage and the time a statute is construed by the Supreme Court, some societal change will always occur because of the inevitable delays of litigation. If applied too broadly, the Brennan rule could give judges carte blanche to rewrite statutes, which enacting legislators would certainly find objectionable. As Justice Scalia suggests, statutory cy pres must ordinarily be limited to cases in which "(1) it is clear that the alleged changed circumstances were unknown to, and unenvisioned by, the enacting legislature, and (2) it is clear that they cause the challenged application of the statute to exceed its original purpose."[64] A similar analysis should apply, of course, when a statute's application falls short of its intended purpose.

Sometimes, the changed circumstances consist of actions by the judges themselves. Courts have been known to misapprehend the legislative intent, sometimes egregiously. Once the mistake has been made, however, respect for precedent makes the court reluctant to overturn its prior decision.[65] The result may be that judges in later cases will continue to interpret the statute in violation of a clear legislative directive. At first blush, this seems improper.

---

64. 486 U.S. at 325.

65. The Court strongly endorsed the importance of precedent in statutory cases in a recent, highly publicized case, Patterson v. McLean Credit Union, 109 S. Ct. 2363 (1989).

Since the court is not authorized to amend the statute, how can a previous erroneous decision suspend the court's continuing obligation to obey the legislature's command?

Several writers have recently argued that following an erroneous statutory precedent is questionable because it upsets the original legislative bargain.[66] As Judge Easterbrook says, "If courts become instruments by which packages are undone, laws will be harder to pass. Bargains must be kept to be believed."[67] As a general matter, this observation is quite correct. It may not have as much force, however, when the issue is whether courts should enforce the "statutory bargain" even at the cost of overruling precedent.

It is important to recall that we are considering the rule legislators would approve at the time of enactment. At that time, legislators know that judges may make serious mistakes but do not know the direction of the mistakes. Supporters of the legislation have no way of knowing whether future judicial mistakes will favor them (giving them more than the original "bargain") or injure them (giving them less than they bargained for). This is not to say that legislators would be indifferent to the possibility of serious judicial errors. It does mean, however, that their interest in having the statute honored is somewhat offset by the possibility that honest mistakes might redound to their benefit. Legislators must also weigh the potentially serious social costs of legal instability, which would result if courts frequently overruled their past decisions.[68] Sometimes the balance will weigh in favor of stare decisis;

66. *See* Cooper, *Stare Decisis: Precedent and Principle in Constitutional Adjudication,* 73 CORNELL L. REV. 401 (1988) (arguing that the doctrine of stare decisis is undesirable because it only shields error from correction); Rees, *Cathedrals Without Walls: A View from the Outside,* 61 TEX. L. REV. 347, 373–78 (1982). At the opposite extreme is the view that statutory precedents should *never* be overruled. *See* Marshall, *"Let Congress Do It": The Case for an Absolute Rule of Statutory Stare Decisis,* 88 MICH. L. REV. 177 (1989). For a discussion avoiding both extremes, see Eskridge, *Overruling Statutory Precedents,* 76 GEO. L.J. 1361 (1988).

67. Easterbrook, *supra* note 13, at 9. The idea of viewing statutes as legislative deals entered the economics literature in Landes & Posner, *The Independent Judiciary in an Interest Group Perspective,* 18 J.L. & ECON. 875 (1976).

68. Although judicial error as such may not be objectionable to enacting legislators, they may have more subtle reasons to be concerned about prospective uncertainty in judicial interpretations. If the enacting legislators are risk averse, they may have some reluctance to gamble on the direction of judicial error. There also may be social costs associated with uncertainty about how statutes will be construed, such as increased litigation and difficulty in planning transactions. Jettisoning stare decisis, however, would do relatively little to reduce these various uncertainty costs. On the other hand, a rule allowing ready judicial correction of prior mistaken opinions creates a variety of deadweight social costs. In general, then, enacting legislators would prefer that courts give weight to stare decisis in statutory cases, even at the expense of fidelity to the original legislative deal.

Professor Marshall suggests that legislators may have varying views about the desirability of stare decisis, depending on how they feel about the renewed lobbying effort by the losing side. Marshall, *supra* note 66, at 199–200. Since they have no way of knowing ex ante which side this will be, they should be indifferent on this score at the time of enactment. Marshall essenin other cases, the interest in legal stability may not seem important enough to outweigh fidelity to their original intentions. Like other forms of statutory cy pres, respect for precedent allows the meaning of a statute to evolve over time.

An interesting example of statutory evolution is provided by *Steelworkers v. Weber*[69] and *Johnson v. Transportation Agency,*[70] which involved affirmative action, one of the most divisive issues in American politics. Title VII of the 1964 Civil Rights Act forbids employment discrimination based on race or gender. Under *Weber* and *Johnson,* title VII allows employers to engage in affirmative action in favor of minority groups when a "manifest racial imbalance" is present, provided that the affirmative action plan meets certain standards of reasonableness.[71] Notably, under *Weber,* it is not necessary that the racial imbalance result from even *arguably* illegal conduct by the employer or anyone else.[72] In *Weber,* for example, because blacks were a large percentage of the local population but only a tiny percentage of skilled craftsworkers, the Court upheld a program reserving for blacks half of all openings in a training program.[73]

As now-Chief Justice Rehnquist pointed out in dissent in *Weber,* this highly expansive approach to affirmative action seems at odds with both the plain language and the legislative history of the statute.[74] Section 703(a)(2), for example, prohibits employers from classifying employees "in any way which would deprive or tend to deprive any individual of employment opportunities or otherwise adversely affect his status as an employee, because of such individual's race, color, religion, sex or national origin."[75] The legislative history demonstrates that Congress was troubled about allowing preferential treatment even as a remedy for illegal discrimination. The Senate floor captains in charge of the bill, for example, said that even if an employer had discriminated in the past, his only "obligation would be simply to fill future vacancies on a nondiscriminatory basis. He would not be obliged—or indeed permitted . . . to prefer Negroes for future vacan-

---

tially is assessing costs ex post, where the proper perspective in designing legal rules is usually ex ante. In particular, under the norms of democratic legitimacy, the ex ante preferences of the enacting legislature are what counts, not the desire of their successors to be lobbied or left alone.

69. 443 U.S. 193 (1979).

70. 480 U.S. 616 (1987).

71. *See id.* at 630–42.

72. For an explanation of this aspect of *Weber,* see *id.* at 630.

73. *See Weber,* 443 U.S. at 197–200.

74. Arguments that the statute is ambiguous focus on the use of the word "discriminate" in some provisions, claiming that this term might not be applicable to affirmative action since in that context the use of race to classify persons is not invidious. *See* R. DWORKIN, A MATTER OF PRINCIPLE 318 (1985).

75. 42 U.S.C. § 2000e–2(a)(1). Similar language is found in section (d).

cies."[76] Despite these difficulties, some forms of affirmative action, used to remedy or prevent actual discrimination, might be permissible under the statute. Allowing employers to make free use of racial preferences to remedy imbalance, however, appears to fly in the face of the congressional mandate.[77]

In response to these criticisms, Justice Brennan's majority opinion pointed out that the supporters of the bill intended to improve the economic lot of minority groups. True, but Congress apparently chose to pursue this goal with a policy of color blindness. The Court is not free to displace that congressional decision merely because the Justices think that Congress made the wrong choice of strategy. To return to Posner's military analogy, the Court is in much the same position as a captain who violates a general's order but argues that he didn't really disobey, because his action was a better way of attaining the general's ultimate purpose of winning the war.[78]

The best arguments in favor of *Weber* and *Johnson* rely on postenactment developments. One argument is that informed opinion has shifted on the issue of affirmative action. As we have seen, however, enacting legislators have no reason to want statutory directives to be conditional on the future state of public opinion. Such changes might well be relevant if the meaning of the statute were subject to genuine doubt, but they cannot release the court from compliance with the statutory command. Here, the statutory command seems inconsistent with unrestricted affirmative action.

A second argument is that social conditions changed after the enactment of title VII. Later events unexpectedly showed that discrimination by employers was only one barrier to the congressional goal of giving blacks equal economic opportunities, so broad affirmative action is needed to reach the congressional goal. This argument seems to make unrealistic assumptions about congressional expectations. The 1964 Congress did believe that the Civil Rights Act would help blacks attain economic equality. It would have taken exceptional naïveté, however, to believe that an employment statute

76. 110 CONG. REC. 7213 (1964). As the Rehnquist dissent demonstrates, the record is replete with similar statements in favor of color blindedness. 443 U.S. at 235–51.

77. *See* Meltzer, *The Weber Case: The Judicial Abrogation of the Antidiscrimination Standard in Employment,* 47 U. CHI. L. REV. 423 (1980).

78. Justice Brennan's fallback argument was that another provision of the statute introduces some ambiguity. Section 703(j) states that nothing in the statute shall be construed to "require" any employer to give preferential treatment to remedy a racial imbalance. This provision was adopted in response to fears that the statute might not be truly color-blind. Ironically, Justice Brennan argued that this provision affirmatively authorizes preferential treatment. Otherwise, he suggested, Congress would have disclaimed any intent to "require or permit" preferential treatment (rather than just disclaiming any intent to "require" such treatment). Hence, he says, Congress must have meant to allow employers to give preferential treatment. As even those who support the result in *Weber* concede, this argument is weak and in any event inconsistent with Brennan's refusal to adhere to the seemingly plain meaning of the basic prohibitions of title VII.

would immediately overcome the effects of generations of bad schools and poverty. At least, this reality does not seem so clearly unforeseeable as to meet the test for applying statutory cy pres.

The third argument is based on stare decisis.[79] Following *Weber* not a single bill was introduced in Congress to overturn it, and it has now been the law for over ten years.[80] It is true, as Justice Scalia pointed out in his dissent in *Johnson*, that congressional silence may be due to causes other than congressional approval, but the absence of *any* effort to overturn *Weber* seems telling. *Weber* has been the subject of substantial reliance by employers and unions. Even if the Court were to immunize them from damage suits based on past affirmative action plans, abolishing the plans would upset large numbers of career plans, while granting remedies to white male "victims" would wreak havoc with seniority rights and pension plans. More fundamentally, judicial waffling on such a crucial issue could undermine public confidence in the stability of the legal system.

In our view, application of stare decisis to *Weber* is quite legitimate. If the main objection to the broad affirmative action rule of *Weber* is that it contravenes congressional intent, stare decisis is a sufficient answer. For those like Justice Scalia, who believe in addition that affirmative action violates basic requirements of justice, the stare decisis argument understandably is likely to be unpersuasive. These broader questions about affirmative action are, however, outside the scope of this book.

The debate over *Weber* and *Johnson* involves far-reaching questions about the nature of statutory interpretation.[81] These questions have sparked some of the most interesting recent theoretical work on statutory interpretation. In important recent articles, Professors Eskridge and Aleinikoff have argued that the meaning of a statute changes over time, rather than being fixed at the time of enactment.[82] As we have seen, public choice theory

---

79. *See* Johnson v. Transportation Agency, 480 U.S. at 644 (Stevens, J., concurring). In *Weber* itself, Justice Blackmun argued that prior judicial decisions themselves made it impractical to return to the original legislative understanding. *See Weber,* 443 U.S. at 209–11.

80. *Johnson,* 480 U.S. at 629 n.7. On the subject of legislative silence, see Eskridge, *Interpreting Legislative Inaction,* 87 MICH. L. REV. 67 (1988).

81. The problems in *Weber* and *Johnson* are a good deal more complicated than our brief discussion in the text suggests. For a fuller explication of our somewhat conflicting views, see Farber, *Legislative Supremacy and Statutory Interpretation,* 78 GEO. L.J. 281 (1989); and Eskridge & Frickey, *Statutory Interpretation as Practical Reasoning,* 42 STAN. L. REV. 321 (1990). For reasons explained in these other writings, we both find Justice Blackmun's concurring opinion in *Weber* to be the most persuasive argument for the outcome in that case. *Johnson* clearly extends *Weber* beyond the theory espoused by Blackmun in *Weber,* and we have serious doubts that this wide-ranging validation of affirmative action can be squared with title VII. However, the *Weber* majority opinion is clearly subject to the reading given it in *Johnson,* and the considerations of stare decisis discussed in the text counsel against overruling *Weber.*

82. *See* Aleinikoff, *Updating Statutory Interpretation,* 87 MICH. L. REV. 20 (1988); Eskridge, *Dynamic Statutory Interpretation,* 135 U. PA. L. REV. 1479 (1987).

lends some support to this evolutionary approach. Where the original intent is unclear, rational judges would consider other factors, including current social policy. And even where the original meaning *is* clear, a rational legislator might want judges to take into account some kinds of changed circumstances.

The interpretative process is often obscure. Public choice theory is by no means a panacea, but it does have considerable potential for clarifying statutory interpretation. Like any other theoretical framework, it cannot fully capture the complexity of the legal landscape. What it *can* do is to impose sufficient order on that complexity to allow meaningful analysis. As long as we remember that the map is not the territory and the theory is not the reality, such guidance can be extremely helpful.[83]

83. For a thoughtful endorsement of the combination of practical reason and public choice in statutory interpretation, see Mashaw, *The Economics of Politics and the Understanding of Public Law,* 65 CHI.-KENT L. REV. 123, 160 (1989).

F I V E

Integrating Public Choice and Public Law

One conclusion to be drawn from chapters 1 and 2 is that knowledge about the legislative process is far more limited than some legal scholars seem to suspect. Easy generalizations and reductionist models have not fared well empirically. If nothing else, we hope to have persuaded the reader of the need for caution in relying on this literature when propounding grand theories of public law. What we do know about the legislative process is that ideology, economic interest, and legislative structures all play roles.[1] Their relative importance is unclear and probably quite variable. Even though the legislative process does not exhibit the chaos to which it is theoretically prone, it is nonetheless too unruly for the sweeping empirical generalizations needed to support comprehensive legal theories. For this reason, in chapters 3 and 4 we rejected general theories that have been proposed to alter fundamentally contemporary judicial approaches to constitutional law and statutory interpretation.

Public law should not be seen, however, as posing a choice between ad hoc decisionmaking and grand theories designed to solve all cases by deductive reasoning from first principles. As it has evolved in Anglo-American law, legal reasoning has often taken a middle ground, that of situational practical reasoning. Legal reasoning frequently involves an analogical and inductive method, resolving new problems by reasoning from well-established, paradigmatic cases. This more modest approach to public law decisionmaking recognizes that decisions are stronger if supported by a range of considerations, rather than simply flowing automatically from first premises. Although "[a] supportable answer may sometimes descend from deductive analysis alone[,] [m]ore often such an answer will ascend from a combination of arguments, none of which standing alone would constitute a sufficient justification. Such 'supporting arguments' are 'rather like the legs of a chair and unlike the links of a chain.' "[2] In short, this pragmatic ap-

---

1. Political party is obviously another relevant factor that deserves further attention.

2. Farber & Frickey, *Practical Reason and the First Amendment*, 34 UCLA L. REV. 1615, 1645 (1987) (quoting R. SUMMERS, INSTRUMENTALISM AND AMERICAN LEGAL THEORY 156 (1982)). In addition to this article, our discussion of legal reasoning is based on Farber, *Legal Pragmatism and the Constitution*, 72 MINN. L. REV. 1331 (1988); Eskridge & Frickey, *Statutory Interpretation as Practical Reasoning*, 42 STAN. L. REV. 321 (1990). For citations to recent legal commentary moving away from grand theory, see Farber & Frickey, *supra*, at 1645 n.129.

proach recognizes that public law must accommodate itself to society's complex, situationally sensitive web of beliefs.

Legal pragmatism, rather than grand legal theory, is the appropriate vehicle through which the lessons of public choice should influence public law. Although public choice cannot support the sweeping empirical generalizations needed to justify grand theory, it does provide fruit for more particularized inquiries about the formulation of public policy. In this chapter, we explain how courts might reform some aspects of public law through practical reasoning informed by the insights of public choice. The goal would be to tip the legislative process toward ideology and structure—and thus, toward legislative ability to formulate public policy—and away from legislative capture by special interests or incoherence.

We do not propose a substantial expansion of substantive judicial review, for the reasons explained in chapter 3. Instead, public choice's emphasis on structure and procedure is congenial to expansion of another judicial function—enforcing structural and procedural constraints on those aspects of the democratic process that public choice suggests are most vulnerable to malfunction. Judicial sensitivity to the forces that warp political outcomes has greater promise to promote legislative deliberation than does stricter scrutiny of the substance of legislation.[3] Consistent with our belief in legal pragmatism rather than grand theory, our case for these reforms is constructed by supplementing current legal doctrines in light of the implications of public choice.

In what follows, it may be helpful to distinguish three different ways in which public choice theory enters the analysis. First, public choice very often highlights problems of the political system. Lawyers may then try to devise workable solutions to those problems, but the solutions themselves may have no direct link with public choice theory. They are lawyers' answers to public choice's questions. Second, on occasion, public choice can also be a source of possible solutions to those very problems. Usually, public choice will not be the only basis for advocating a particular legal doctrine, but it may provide support for some technique intended to reduce rent-seeking or increase legislative stability. In these instances, public choice highlights the problem and also gives clues about a possible solution. Third, when courts

---

3. Although we have expressed skepticism about Cass Sunstein's suggestions that courts review whether particular legislation is premised upon public values (see chapter 3), we endorse his suggestion that courts play a role in structuring the overall processes of representation to insulate representatives from pressures so that they can better deliberate in the public interest. *See* Sunstein, *Interest Groups in American Public Law*, 38 STAN. L. REV. 29, 31–35 (1985). Sunstein correctly emphasized that Madisonian notions of the importance of representational structure support this inquiry. *See id.* at 40–45. *See also id.* at 52–53 (noting Supreme Court decisions affecting the structure of representation); Macey, *Promoting Public-Regarding Legislation Through Statutory Interpretation: An Interest Group Model*, 86 COLUM. L. REV. 223, 247–50 (1986) (discussing constitutional structures designed to impede rent-seeking).

are pursuing other values, public choice may have some insights to contribute about the probable effectiveness of particular techniques. Here, public choice speaks (usually not decisively) to the means, rather than the end.

In any of these settings, we do not claim that public choice is either necessary or sufficient to generate the conclusions. It is possible to be concerned about interest groups or legislative fairness without regard to public choice theory. Public choice theory does, however, add impetus to these concerns. It is also possible to mold judicial remedies with an eye toward legislative structure, using common sense or conventional political science rather than public choice. Public choice may well provide additional insights into the efficacy of such remedies. In any of these guises, to use our earlier metaphor, public choice serves as one leg of a chair, not one link in a chain.

A formalist approach to applying public choice would be quite different. One would begin with a mathematical model of the legislative process, and then formally demonstrate the effect of changing a particular legal rule on legislative outcomes. Next, one would empirically test the theory. Finally, one would apply these validated conclusions to derive specific policy recommendations. We have some general doubts about whether this is the best way to formulate legal policy, but in any event, it is clear that public choice theory in its present state is far too undeveloped to make such applications feasible.

In short, we do not claim to be *deducing* legal doctrines from public choice theory. What we do claim is that public choice can be useful as part of the public lawyer's intellectual tool kit. It can provide insights or reinforce other perspectives. As legal pragmatists, this is as much as we think any theory can truly be expected to provide. But when dealing with problems as difficult as those confronting public law, any source of guidance, however incomplete, is always welcome.

We will begin with an examination of how legislative structure and procedure are treated in current public law. We will then turn to some structural and procedural reforms that seem to follow from public choice. We will also consider how public choice can show courts where to put the burden of legislative inertia in certain hard cases.

I. Existing Strands of "Due Process of Lawmaking"

Courts have sometimes attempted to foster legislative deliberation by more aggressively overseeing the legislative process. Other writers, using the terms "structural due process"[4] or "due process of lawmaking,"[5] have iden-

---

4. Tribe, *Structural Due Process*, 10 Harv. C.R.-C.L. L. Rev. 269 (1975). *See also* L. Tribe, American Constitutional Law 1673–87 (2d ed. 1988); Tribe, *Perspectives on Bakke: Equal Protection, Procedural Fairness, or Structural Justice?*, 92 Harv. L. Rev. 864 (1979); Tribe, *The Emerging Reconnection of Individual Rights and Institutional Design: Federalism, Bureaucracy, and Due Process of Lawmaking*, 10 Creighton L. Rev. 433 (1977).

5. Linde, *Due Process of Lawmaking*, 55 Neb. L. Rev. 197 (1976).

tified some of the judicial roles involved in this oversight.[6] They have urged attention to "the structures through which policies are both formed and applied"[7] and to the primacy of legislative processes.[8] We agree with Hans Linde that courts seem more capable of constructing "a blueprint for the due process of deliberative, democratically accountable government"[9] than of assessing, in all but exceptional cases, whether legislation properly promotes public values.

Some recent Supreme Court opinions reflect an increased concern with structure and process.[10] Perhaps the most notable example is *Hampton v. Mow Sun Wong.*[11] *Mow Sun Wong* involved a Civil Service Commission regulation dating back to the nineteenth century barring aliens from almost all federal jobs. Because aliens cannot vote and have a history of prejudice, the Supreme Court has considered statutes disadvantaging them as raising serious questions of discrimination.[12] The regulation in *Mow Sun Wong* would have been unconstitutional, as violating the equal protection clause of the fourteenth amendment, if adopted by a state.[13] But the federal govern-

---

6. In addition to the works of Tribe and Linde, others who have made relevant contributions include A. BICKEL, THE LEAST DANGEROUS BRANCH (1962); C. BLACK, STRUCTURE AND RE-LATIONSHIP IN CONSTITUTIONAL LAW (1969); Bickel & Wellington, *Legislative Purpose and the Judicial Process: The* Lincoln Mills *Case,* 71 HARV. L. REV. 1 (1957); Conkle, *Non-originalist Constitutional Rights and the Problem of Judicial Finality,* 13 HAST. CONST. L.Q. 9 (1985); Dimond, *Provisional Review: An Exploratory Essay on an Alternative Form of Judicial Review,* 12 HAST. CONST. L.Q. 201 (1985); Estreicher, *Judicial Nullification: Guido Calabresi's Uncommon Common Law for a Statutory Age,* 57 N.Y.U. L. REV. 1126, 1147–53 (1982); Komesar, *Taking Institutions Seriously: Introduction to a Strategy for Constitutional Analysis,* 51 U. CHI. L. REV. 366 (1984); Luneberg, *Justice Rehnquist, Statutory Interpretation, the Policies of Clear Statement, and Federal Jurisdiction,* 58 IND. L.J. 211 (1982); Monaghan, *Constitutional Common Law,* 89 HARV. L. REV. 1 (1975); Sandalow, *Judicial Protection of Minorities,* 75 MICH. L. REV. 1162 (1977); Wellington, *The Nature of Judicial Review,* 91 YALE L.J. 486, 509 (1982). For a thoughtful critique, see Tushnet, *Legal Realism, Structural Review, and Prophecy,* 8 U. DAYTON L. REV. 809 (1983).

7. Tribe, *Structural Due Process, supra* note 4, at 269.

8. Linde, *supra* note 5, at 255.

9. *Id.* at 253.

10. Structural review seems compatible with fundamental concerns involving the separation of powers. *See generally, e.g.,* Neuborne, *Judicial Review and Separation of Powers in France and the United States,* 57 N.Y.U. L. REV. 363, 410–21 (1982); Quint, *The Separation of Powers Under Nixon: Reflections on Constitutional Liberties and the Rule of Law,* 1981 DUKE L.J. 1, 54, 63–70. Consider the holding in Buckley v. Valeo, 424 U.S. 1 (1976), that invalidated a provision of the Federal Election Campaign Act that provided that several members of the Federal Election Commission would be appointed by congressional leadership. Whatever else might be said about other aspects of *Buckley,* in our view the Court there correctly recognized the fear "that the Legislative Branch of the National Government will aggrandize itself at the expense of the other two branches." *Id.* at 129.

11. 426 U.S. 88 (1976).

12. *See* Bernal v. Fainter, 467 U.S. 216 (1984); Graham v. Richardson, 403 U.S. 365 (1971).

13. *See* Sugarman v. Dougall, 413 U.S. 634 (1973).

ment has legitimate reasons to regulate aliens that states do not. In *Mow Sun Wong*, the federal government defended the regulation as a bargaining chip in negotiations with foreign countries, an incentive for aliens to become citizens, and a guarantee of undivided loyalty for employees in sensitive positions. In striking down the federal regulation, the Court relied upon a due process of lawmaking approach rather than a simple antidiscrimination rule. The Court thereby accommodated the unique federal interests in regulating aliens with the likelihood that the regulation was rooted simply in discrimination or administrative lethargy.

Justice Stevens wrote for the five-member majority in *Mow Sun Wong* that, "[w]hen the Federal Government asserts an overriding national interest as justification for a discriminatory rule which would violate the Equal Protection Clause if adopted by a State, due process requires that there be a legitimate basis for presuming that the rule was actually intended to serve that interest."[14] Justice Stevens dismissed the first two justifications for the rule in question—that it served as a bargaining chip and provided an incentive for citizenship—because neither reason could have influenced either the Civil Service Commission or the government departments where aliens had applied for jobs. These justifications might allow Congress or the President to adopt the rule, Justice Stevens concluded, but neither had required the Civil Service Commission to adopt the rule or explicitly sanctioned it. The third justification—conveniently excluding potentially disloyal employees—was related to the business of the Civil Service Commission, but Justice Stevens found that the Commission had not fairly balanced this goal against the regulation's costs.[15] Thus, even assuming that Congress or the President could have constitutionally adopted the rule, the Court found it violative of due process.

Mow Sun Wong in many ways fits the "remand to the legislature" theory espoused in one form or another by a variety of commentators.[16] In effect, the Court forced the President or the Congress to reconsider a sensitive issue of discrimination. To implement the legislative remand approach, the Court in *Mow Sun Wong*, as Justice Rehnquist's dissent noted, "meld[ed] together the concepts of equal protection and procedural and substantive due process," and used "a novel conception . . . of procedural due process . . . to

---

14. 426 U.S. at 103.

15. Justice Stevens reached this conclusion because (1) the Commission had never made "any considered evaluation of the relative desirability of a simple exclusionary rule on the one hand, or the value to the service of enlarging the pool of eligible employees on the other"; (2) there was no showing that a narrower exclusionary rule would be onerous to establish or administer; and (3) under "[a]ny fair balancing" the individual interests of the aliens and the public interest "in avoiding the wholesale deprivation of employment opportunities" outweighed the government's interest in administrative convenience. *Id.* at 115–16.

16. *See* the sources cited in note 6, *supra*, by Bickel, Wellington, and Sandalow.

evolve a doctrine of delegation of legislative authority."[17] Although the *Mow Sun Wong* opinion did not discuss the possible motivation behind the civil service rule, its author has recognized elsewhere that restrictions on the employment of aliens are often special interest legislation.[18] *Mow Sun Wong* is a notable judicial attempt to protect against governmental abuses, not by substantive judicial review but by improving the structure of decisionmaking.

Some other recent opinions share this appreciation for structural and procedural concerns. A number of American Indian law cases fit this mold. Long-standing precedent establishes a trust relationship between the federal government and the tribes.[19] The federal government has vast legislative power over Native Americans, but the states have little authority absent an express delegation of authority from Congress, and the tribal governments retain a right of self-determination consistent with federal law.[20] Although federal legislation relating to Indians is subjected to extraordinarily minimal scrutiny,[21] the Supreme Court has endorsed canons of interpretation that promote statutory and treaty interpretation favorable to the tribes.[22] In general, tribal sovereignty may be invaded only by Congress, not by the states, and only where Congress has clearly evidenced the intent to do so.

A particularly important example of structural review is provided by the Court's affirmative action opinions.[23] Justice Powell's pivotal opinion in *Regents of University of California v. Bakke*[24] concluded that the faculty is the wrong entity to decide the question whether past societal discrimination might justify reserving some seats in a medical school for minorities.[25] Next, the Court in the *Fullilove*[26] case agreed that Congress had special authority to enact a public works bill that set aside ten percent of the

17. 426 U.S. at 119, 117. For a useful analysis of *Mow Sun Wong*, see Sager, *Insular Majorities Unabated:* Warth v. Seldin *and* City of Eastlake v. Forest City Enterprises, 91 HARV. L. REV. 1373, 1411–24 (1978).

18. *See* Foley v. Connelie, 435 U.S. 291, 307–9 (1978) (dissenting opinion).

19. *See* Cherokee Nation v. Georgia, 30 U.S. (5 Pet.) 1 (1831).

20. *See generally* FELIX S. COHEN'S HANDBOOK ON AMERICAN INDIAN LAW 207–572 (R. Strickland et al. ed. 1982).

21. *See* Delaware Tribal Bus. Comm. v. Weeks, 430 U.S. 73 (1977).

22. *See, e.g.*, United States v. Dion, 476 U.S. 734, 737–40 (1986); Wilkinson & Volkman, *Judicial Review of Indian Treaty Abrogation: "As Long as Water Flows, or Grass Grows Upon the Earth"—How Long a Time Is That?*, 63 CALIF. L. REV. 601 (1975).

23. For a now somewhat dated, but still useful discussion, see Note, *Principles of Competence: The Ability of Public Institutions to Adopt Remedial Affirmative Action Plans*, 53 U. CHI. L. REV. 581 (1986).

24. 438 U.S. 265 (1978).

25. *See id.* at 307–10 (opinion of Powell, J.). On the aspects of Justice Powell's opinion related to due process of lawmaking, *see* McCormack, *Race and Politics in the Supreme Court: Bakke to Basics*, 1979 UTAH L. REV. 491; Tribe, *Perspectives on Bakke, supra* note 4.

26. Fullilove v. Klutznick, 448 U.S. 448 (1980).

appropriations in question for minority contractors.[27] Dissenting in *Fullilove,* Justice Stevens explicitly adopted even broader aspects of due process of lawmaking.[28] More recently, in *City of Richmond v. J. A. Croson Co.,*[29] the Court held that a municipality could not adopt a minority set-aside program similar to the one enacted by Congress that was upheld in *Fullilove.*[30] The Court also stressed the city's failure to conduct adequate hearings.

Despite their individual quirks, the cases do seem to fall into discernible categories. Of these, the best-established model involves a hierarchy of institutional legitimacy. Under this approach, a court may invalidate a particularly sensitive decision by an entity comparatively unsuited to render it—for example, the Civil Service Commission in *Mow Sun Wong*—leaving open the possibility that the same decision could be reimposed by a more legitimate entity. Another model, one of legislative deliberation, would require not only compliance with formal legislative rules, but also evidence that the legislature actually acted with sufficient deliberation.[31] Both models were present in the *Richmond* affirmative action case.

27. The lead opinion in *Fullilove,* by Chief Justice Burger, repeatedly contrasted Congress's authority to approve affirmative action with decisionmakers he apparently considered less legitimate for that task, such as the federal courts or a school board. *See* 448 U.S. at 472–73, 480, 483–84. Similarly, Justice Powell went to great pains to suggest why Congress has more authority to adopt affirmative action measures than other entities. *See id.* at 497–502, 508–10, 516 (Powell, J., concurring). Justice Powell hinted that state legislatures might completely lack this power. *See id.* at 515 n.14. Neither Justice overtly embraced these kinds of structural considerations in the next affirmative action decision, however. *See* Wygant v. Jackson Board of Education, 476 U.S. 267 (1986).

28. Justice Stevens's dissent in *Fullilove* clearly embraced the "suspensive veto" aspects of due process of lawmaking and apparently was influenced by Linde, *supra* note 5, and Sandalow, *supra* note 6. *See* 446 U.S. at 548–54 & nn.24, 26–28. Similarly, he stressed the procedural regularity of the adoption of the affirmative action plan at issue in *Wygant,* the next affirmative action decision, and accordingly voted to uphold it. *See* Wygant v. Jackson Board of Education, 476 U.S. 267, 317–18 (1986) (Stevens, J., dissenting). *See also* Justice Stevens's dissenting opinion in Delaware Tribal Bus. Comm. v. Weeks, 430 U.S. 73, 92–97 (1977).

29. 109 S. Ct. 706 (1989).

30. The essential difference between Congress and a city council in this context, according to Justice O'Connor's opinion in *Croson,* is provided by the language and structure of the fourteenth amendment. Section 1 of the fourteenth amendment provides that no state shall "deny to any person within its jurisdiction the equal protection of the laws." Justice O'Connor contrasted this explicit constraint on state power with the grant of legislative authority provided to Congress in section 5 of the amendment, which states that "Congress shall have the power to enforce, by appropriate legislation, the provisions of this article." Although both the Congress and a city council have a compelling interest in assuring that public funds "do not serve to finance the evil of private prejudice," Justice O'Connor said that a city has the authority to use racial quotas in allocating public contracting only when it has a solid basis for concluding that it "had essentially become a 'passive participant' in a system of racial exclusion practiced by elements of the local construction industry." 109 S. Ct. at 720. (After this book went to press, the Court decided Metro Broadcasting v. FCC, 110 S.Ct. 2997 (1990), which recognized an even broader power of Congress to adopt affirmative action measures than Justice O'Connor posited in *Croson.*)

31. This model is the most controversial. Justice Stevens has embraced it occasionally, how-

These two forms of structural review are innovative. Their limits, let alone their ultimate judicial acceptance, are highly unclear.[32] One obvious question is how to discern which decisionmakers are more legitimate than others. Here, *Mow Sun Wong,* the affirmative action cases, and the American Indian law cases provide some guidance. They suggest that Congress is at the peak of the legitimacy hierarchy, presumably because of its popular responsiveness as well as its central policy-making role in the constitutional scheme. Another question is whether the showing of deliberation in the second model should be a general requirement, or limited to decisions that are in some sense constitutionally sensitive, like discrimination against aliens. The cases again provide some guidance, and they suggest the narrower of these views.

Perhaps the most critical question remains whether either form of structural review has a sufficient constitutional basis. The suspensive veto at the heart of this theory may seem to flow from the absolute veto power established in *Marbury v. Madison.*[33] After all, if the Court can strike down a law entirely, why can't it send the law back to Congress for further consideration? Yet, simple arguments that "the greater includes the lesser" do not always work in constitutional law.[34] In our view, however, "due process of lawmaking" does have a sufficient basis in constitutional structure[35] and the Madisonian constitutional ideal of deliberative legislative policy-making,[36] with perhaps some added help from the federal common law.[37]

---

ever. *See* Fullilove v. Klutznick, 448 U.S. 448, 548–54 (1980) (Stevens, J., dissenting); Delaware Tribal Bus. Comm. v. Weeks, 430 U.S. 73, 91–98 (1977) (Stevens, J., dissenting). *See also* Comment, *The Emerging Jurisprudence of Justice Stevens,* 46 U. Chi. L. Rev. 155, 217–32 (1978).

This model of due process has also been suggested occasionally by other Justices. *See, e.g.,* Rostker v. Goldberg, 453 U.S. 57, 72–83 (1981) (upholding exclusion of women from military draft because, *inter alia,* Congress carefully deliberated on the issue); Fullilove v. Klutznick, 448 U.S. 448, 456–67, 477–78, 490 (1980) (opinion of Burger, C.J.) (noting similar rationale in upholding federal affirmative action legislation). *See also* Shapiro v. Thompson, 394 U.S. 618, 674 (1969) (Harlan, J., dissenting) (complaining that statute held unconstitutional had been the product of appropriate legislative deliberation). This approach is somewhat similar to the "articulated purpose" requirement proposed in Gunther, *In Search of Evolving Doctrine on a Changing Court: A Model for a Newer Equal Protection,* 86 Harv. L. Rev. 1 (1972). *See also* Sunstein, *supra* note 3, at 69–72. Trenchant criticisms of this suggestion include Linde, *supra* note 5, at 201–35; R. Posner, Economic Analysis of Law 586–87 (3d ed. 1986).

32. *See generally* Tushnet, *supra* note 6.

33. 5 U.S. (1 Cranch) 137 (1803).

34. *See, e.g.,* Frickey, *The Constitutionality of Legislative Committee Suspension of Administrative Rules: The Case of Minnesota,* 70 Minn. L. Rev. 1237, 1267–76 (1986) (form of legislative veto under which a legislature delegates to one of its committees the authority to suspend administrative rules cannot be considered constitutional merely because courts will not invalidate legislative delegation of essentially standardless rulemaking authority to executive agency).

35. *See* C. Black, *supra* note 6.

36. *See* Sunstein, *supra* note 3.

37. *See* Monaghan, *supra* note 6.

Much of constitutional law turns on the degree of deference to be given to various governmental actions.[38] We see no reason why, for example, the views of the Civil Service Commission on a matter of foreign policy should be given the same deference that a presidential or congressional decision would receive. The model of institutional hierarchy is an attractive way to force more legitimate reconsideration of sensitive decisions. Even so, thorny questions remain to be resolved, including those about the effects of the federal constitution upon the distribution of lawmaking power in a state.[39]

We have somewhat greater doubts about the utility of the model of legislative deliberation. This model may underestimate both the role of political compromise and the need for legislative flexibility and speed. For example, consider *Fullilove,* the case in which the Court upheld a Federal minority set-aside program. That set-aside could be seen as an effort to obtain spoils by inserting a last minute floor amendment in a pork barrel bill that was already "greased to go." Another plausible story, however, would explain the set-aside provision as an attempt to insure that the benefits of a Keynesian spending measure were fairly distributed.[40] A model of legislative deliberation might have required that Congress reopen committee hearings to consider the desirability of a set-aside provision. In addition to delaying legislation for which time was of the essence, this requirement might have enhanced legislative consideration only marginally. As Chief Justice Burger's opinion in *Fullilove* reveals, in the 1970s Congress had been presented with substantial information from which it could have reasonably concluded that some sort of set-aside was appropriate.[41] It seems pointless to require

38. *See* Sager, *Fair Measure: The Legal Status of Underenforced Constitutional Norms,* 91 HARV. L. REV. 1212 (1978).

39. For an interesting discussion, see United Beverage Co. v. Indiana Alcoholic Beverage Comm'n, 760 F.2d 155 (7th Cir. 1985) (Posner, J.).

40. *See* Brief for Respondent Secretary of Commerce at 26–51, *Fullilove v. Klutznick;* Amicus Brief of NAACP Legal Defense and Educ. Fund et al. at 15–30, *Fullilove v. Klutznick.* The provision at issue in *Fullilove* was adopted in 1977 amendments to a 1976 public works legislation. According to the briefs cited above, the 1976 act can be conceptualized not as mere pork barrel spoils, but as a curative measure attacking the recession of that era, which featured high unemployment in the construction industry. The 1977 amendments were initially proposed to pump additional money into the struggling economy, and from the outset supporters urged quick adoption of the amendments so that the money would be spent while the economy was stagnant, not later when, if the economy heated up, the appropriations would have the unintended effect of refueling inflation. The limited information available at the close of the committee consideration of the 1977 amendments suggested that, although unemployment was far higher for minorities than for whites, contracting under the 1976 program had been distributed in a manner disproportionally disadvantaging minorities. One black congressman, testifying on the last day of committee hearings, noted this newly documented problem, suggested its linkage to historical discrimination in the construction industry, and announced that he might introduce an amendment to attack it. The minority set-aside followed in due course.

41. *See* 448 U.S. at 456–72. *See also* Brief for Respondent Secretary of Commerce at 32–

Congress to go through the motions of deliberating again about the same issue.

Despite its weaknesses, the model of legislative deliberation may sometimes have a useful role to play. The prima facie unconstitutionality of some classes of legislation perhaps should be rebuttable, if at all, only by clear and persuasive congressional deliberation. Or at least, where the evidence shows that Congress did not make a deliberate choice, otherwise "suspect" legislation should receive even less judicial deference. Thus, at the constitutional margin, this model might have some utility. As an overall principle of judicial review, however, it may well be insufficiently sensitive to institutional reality. Legislative deliberation is important and should be encouraged by the courts, but indirect methods may work better than demanding evidence of deliberation about particular laws.

A third model of due process of lawmaking is also available, one focusing on procedural regularity rather than on institutional legitimacy or deliberation.[42] Under this approach, courts would merely require legislatures to follow their own rules. At the federal level, respect for a coordinate branch has inhibited judicial intrusion into legislative processes except in compelling circumstances. Yet the Court has occasionally required compliance with congressional procedural rules.[43] In addition, federal judges sometimes favor the construction of a statute most consistent with legislative procedural rules.[44]

The principal federal case enforcing legislative rules is *Powell v. McCor-*

43, *Fullilove v. Klutznick;* Amicus Brief for the Lawyers' Committee for Civil Rights Under Law at 27–69, *Fullilove v. Klutznick.* Would the model of legislative deliberation allow Congress to compile an adequate record merely by having committee staff aggregate this diverse collection of documents, or would planned colloquies in hearings and other boilerplate also be mandated? Neither requirement would make much sense.

42. This is what Hans Linde had in mind when he coined the phrase "due process of lawmaking." *See* Linde, *supra* note 5, at 235–55.

43. *See, e.g.,* Gojack v. United States, 384 U.S. 702 (1966) (subcommittee conducted legislative investigation unauthorized by congressional rules). Consider the views of Hans Linde: "Fear of legislative resentment at judicial interference is not borne out by experience where procedural review exists, any more than it was after the Supreme Court told Congress that it had used faulty procedure in unseating Adam Clayton Powell. It is far more cause for resentment to invalidate the substance of a policy that the politically accountable branches and their constituents support than to invalidate a lawmaking procedure that can be repeated correctly, yet we take substantive judicial review for granted." Linde, *supra* note 5, at 243 (discussing *Powell v. McCormack,* which is analyzed in the text shortly). *See also* Fullilove v. Klutznick, 448 U.S. at 548–54 (1980) (Stevens, J., dissenting).

44. An example is TVA v. Hill, 437 U.S. 153 (1978), in which the Court refused to find a repeal of substantive legislation by subsequent appropriations legislation. In reaching this result, the Court took account of House and Senate rules declaring out of order any provision of appropriations legislation that changes existing law. *See id.* at 190–91.

mack.[45] At the beginning of the 90th Congress in January 1967, the House established a special committee to inquire whether Adam Clayton Powell should be allowed to take his seat. The committee eventually recommended that he be sworn into office, seated as a member, and then sanctioned. After a floor debate, a motion to bring the committee's recommendation to a vote was defeated by 222 to 202. An amendment was then offered calling for the exclusion of Powell from the House. The Speaker ruled that a simple majority would be sufficient to pass the amended resolution, and the amendment was adopted by a vote of 248 to 176. The House then adopted the resolution, as amended, by a vote of 307 to 116.

The Constitution has some specific things to say about the qualifications of House members, the way in which the House may sanction misbehaving members, and the manner in which the House may terminate membership. The Constitution expressly requires only that House members be at least twenty-five years old, citizens for at least seven years, and inhabitants of the state from which they were elected.[46] Powell met each requirement. The Constitution also says that each House shall be the judge of the elections, returns, and qualifications of its own members,[47] and more generally that each House may determine the rules of its proceedings.[48] But the Court concluded that these were general grants of housekeeping authority, which did not allow the House to add to the qualifications expressly set forth in the Constitution.

Each House has the constitutional authority to punish members for disorderly behavior and to expel a member "with the concurrence of two thirds."[49] The final vote to exclude Powell exceeded that margin. But the Court refused to allow the House to rely on its expulsion power. Why? Because Powell had not been expelled, he had been denied a seat in the first place. The difference between exclusion and expulsion seems like the kind of technicality that only a lawyer could love. After all, Powell was "excluded" by a vote of 307 to 116, more than a two-thirds vote, so why make anything of the technical distinction between exclusion and expulsion?

Public choice, however, supports the Court's willingness to attach significance to this seemingly technical distinction. The two votes before the final vote showed that most members wanted to punish Powell but were deeply divided about how much punishment was appropriate. There were probably fewer than two-thirds whose first preference was keeping Powell out of his seat. The strongest evidence is the motion to amend the resolution to exclude

---

45. 395 U.S. 486 (1969).
46. *See* U.S. Constitution, art. I, § 2, cl. 2.
47. *See id.* art. I, § 5, cl. 1.
48. *See id.* art. I, § 5, cl. 2.
49. *See id.* art. I, § 5, cl. 2.

Powell, which passed by less than a two-thirds vote. As a member of the House himself put it:

> Only on the final vote, adopting the Resolution as amended, was more than a two-thirds vote obtained. . . . On this last vote, as a practical matter, members who would not have denied Powell a seat if they were given the choice to punish him had to cast an aye vote or else record themselves as opposed to the only punishment that was likely to come before the House. Had the matter come up through the processes of expulsion, it appears that the two-thirds vote would have failed, and then members would have been able to apply a lesser penalty.[50]

Powell v. McCormack demonstrates what public choice theorizes—that agendas and procedural rules can make an enormous difference.

The point is not that the Court should enforce procedural rules whenever it is unhappy with outcomes. Rather, we believe that uniform enforcement of procedural rules will tend to produce better results on the average.

The model of procedural regularity suggested by *Powell* is better established at the state than the federal level.[51] State constitutions routinely give detailed rules of legislative procedure. In reviewing whether laws were validly enacted, some state courts will not look beyond the enrolled bill, while others will also examine the legislative journals.[52] State constitutions commonly limit legislative sessions to specified periods,[53] and some state supreme courts invalidate legislation passed after the constitutional deadline, even if they have to rely on newspaper accounts and other unofficial sources for proof.[54]

One legislative rule that seems trivial, but whose significance is shown by public choice,[55] is the "single subject" rule—a common state constitutional requirement that legislation may embrace only one subject, which must be expressed in its title.[56] This rule has at least three purposes: (a) to limit logrolling, (b) to keep surprises from being hidden in bills, and (c) to prevent

---

50. Eckhardt, *The Adam Clayton Powell Case,* 45 Tex. L. Rev. 1205, 1209 (1967), quoted in Powell v. McCormack, 395 U.S. at 511. See also *Powell,* 395 U.S. at 511 n.32, for remarks of other members who felt boxed in by the procedures that were being followed.

51. *See generally* Williams, *The Politics of State Constitutional Limits On Legislative Procedure: Legislative Compliance and Judicial Enforcement,* 48 U. Pitt. L. Rev. 797 (1987).

52. *See generally* 1 Sutherland Stat. Const. §§ 15.01–.18 (N. Singer 4th ed. 1985); Comment, *Judicial Review of the Legislative Enactment Process: Louisiana's "Journal Entry" Rule,* 41 La. L. Rev. 1187 (1981).

53. *See, e.g.,* Minn. Const. art. IV, § 12.

54. *See, e.g.,* Dillon v. King, 87 N.M. 79, 459 P.2d 745 (1974); State *ex rel.* Heck's Discount Centers v. Winters, 147 W. Va. 861, 132 S.E.2d 374 (1963); 1 Sutherland Stat. Const., *supra* note 52, at § 14.10.

55. *See* chapter 2, part III.

56. For an overview, see Sutherland Stat. Const., *supra* note 52, at §§ 17.01–.06.

use of irrelevant riders to dilute the governor's veto power.[57] The problem of
the "Christmas tree" bill was recognized as long ago as Roman times, before Christmas trees themselves were invented. Beginning in 1818, state
constitutions began to include the single subject rule.[58] Many state courts
construe the rule flexibly to avoid interfering with legislative processes.[59]
Yet the purposes of the rule are worthy, and more vigorous enforcement may
well be in order. Enforcement of the rule is particularly attractive when substantive riders have been attached to appropriations legislation.[60]

Even under a single subject rule, the complexity of many bills leaves room
for legislative cycling. Nevertheless, if multiple, unrelated subjects are cov-
ered in the same bill, the possibility of cycling is greatly enhanced. Hence,
the single subject rule promotes stability.

Some commentators question whether any form of structural review can
affect the ultimate legislative decision.[61] Pluralists may well believe that the
legislative process is too mechanical for "legislative remands" to serve any
useful purpose. Yet, as chapters 1 and 2 demonstrated, Congress is not merely the reflection of private political power. Faith in congressional
deliberation about sensitive issues is not entirely misplaced, particularly
when courts stand ready to assist the deliberative process through structural
and procedural review. By requiring legislative reconsideration, courts can
shift the burden of inertia, highlight moral concerns about the decision,
and—because of the passage of time—often return the issue to a legislature
with changed membership. Considering the ease of killing legislation and
the difficulty of passing it,[62] these consequences should not be underesti-
mated.

Although the remand in *Mow Sun Wong* did not affect the ultimate outcome,[63] *Kent v. Dulles*[64] is a more successful example of a suspensive
judicial veto. In *Kent,* the Supreme Court held that the executive branch

57. *See* Simpson v. Tobin, 367 N.W.2d 757 (S.D. 1985); Ruud, *"No Law Shall Embrace
More Than One Subject,"* 42 Minn. L. Rev. 389 (1958).

58. *See* Ruud, *supra* note 57, at 389–90.

59. *See, e.g.,* Bernstein v. Comm'r of Public Safety, 351 N.W.2d 24, 25 (Minn. App. 1984),
suggesting that a "strict adherence to [the rule's] letter would seriously interfere with the practical business of legislation."

60. For a good discussion, see Department of Education v. Lewis, 416 So. 2d 455 (Fla.
1982). A related issue is whether the executive should have a line item veto in these circumstances. *See* Robinson, *Public Choice Speculations on the Item Veto,* 74 Va. L. Rev. 403
(1988).

61. *See, e.g.,* Tushnet, *supra* note 6, at 826.

62. *See* chapter 1, part II, text at note 28.

63. President Ford subsequently issued an executive order reinstating the rule, and the lower
courts upheld it. *See* Mow Sun Wong v. Hampton, 636 F.2d 739 (9th Cir. 1980), *cert. denied,*
450 U.S. 959 (1981).

64. 357 U.S. 116 (1958).

lacked the needed express statutory authority to deny passports to "subversives." President Eisenhower immediately sent an urgent message to Congress demanding legislative action. "It is essential," he said, that the government be given the power to deny passports to travelers whose actions threatened the national security. "Each day and week that passes" without such legislation "exposes us to great danger."[65] Nevertheless, despite continued pressure from the White House, Congress refused to enact even a limited form of the legislation the President sought. Thus, the Court's decision ended a widespread and pernicious government attempt to control foreign travel.[66]

These three models of due process of lawmaking—structural, deliberative, and procedural—are not mutually exclusive. Nor should they be, if they are to perform the kinds of pragmatic roles suggested at the beginning of this chapter. Indeed, the Court's landmark legislative veto decision, *Immigration & Naturalization Service v. Chadha*,[67] neatly demonstrates how these theories can combine to give a pretty clear answer to what might otherwise be a hard public law problem. For half a century, Congress had used a technique called the legislative veto. Under this scheme, Congress would delegate authority to the executive branch but reserve the right to veto—sometimes by both Houses, but other times by one House or even by a committee—later executive actions taken pursuant to the delegated power. Defenders of the legislative veto saw it as the only way to give sufficient authority to executive agencies to handle complex problems, without abdicating the legislative role to the executive. In fact, though, the legislative veto ran afoul of all the components of due process of lawmaking.

Even the deliberative model of due process of lawmaking, which has the weakest support in American law, is hard to brush aside in *Chadha*. Mr. Chadha was an East Indian who had been lawfully admitted to the United States but overstayed his student visa. An Immigration Judge had suspended his deportation, because Chadha had resided in the United States for over seven years, was of good moral character, and would suffer extreme hardship if deported. The federal statute under which the judge acted allowed one House of Congress to veto a suspension of deportation.[68] Eighteen months after the Immigration Judge acted in Chadha's case, the House of Representatives vetoed the suspension of deportation for Chadha and for five other aliens—but did not disturb 334 other suspensions of deportation. The resolution to this effect was introduced by the chair of the House subcommittee

---

65. 104 Cong. Rec. 13,046, 13,062 (1958).

66. The history is examined in detail in Farber, *National Security, The Right to Travel, and the Court*, 1981 Sup. Ct. Rev. 263, 278–82.

67. 462 U.S. 919 (1983). *See generally* B. Craig, Chadha (1988).

68. *See* 8 U.S.C. § 1254(c)(1).

just as the session of Congress was about to end. The resolution was introduced and adopted by the House in a matter of a few days, had not been printed, was not available to members when they voted, and was passed without debate or recorded vote. So far as we know, to this day no one has explained why Chadha and the other five were singled out. Whether or not Chadha deserved to be deported, he clearly did not get a fair hearing.

This is truly a lousy, arbitrary, and mean-spirited way to make a decision profoundly affecting the personal liberty of a human being.[69] By this we do not simply mean that we regard the outcome as unjust, although it may have been. More than that, we mean that even the rudiments of due process were lacking in a situation essentially involving adjudication rather than rulemaking. So far as the record shows, no one in Congress gave serious thought to Chadha's case. The Court did not rely on lack of legislative deliberation in *Chadha,* and neither need we do so, for the structural and procedural arguments are extremely strong. The total absence of legislative deliberation does, however, highlight the structural and procedural flaws of the legislative veto.

The Constitution says that laws are supposed to pass both Houses of Congress and go to the President for signature; the legislative veto, as exercised in *Chadha,* allowed subunits of Congress—the House, and in effect merely a subcommittee chair—to make law. If this deviation from the constitutional framework were truly necessary for meaningful legislative oversight, perhaps it could be justified. But, as public choice would predict, quite the contrary was true.[70] In a nutshell, the legislative veto allowed Congress to avoid hard questions of public policy. The legislative veto made it simultaneously easier to pass a controversial bill and harder to implement the bill. Members of Congress could vote in support of virtue and later veto any effort to be virtuous. In practice, the veto decision was controlled by the committees, which often cared more about their own current political interests than the original congressional intentions for the statute. Thus, the legislative veto encouraged "responsiveness to a changed legislative intent that may be

69. Indeed, in *Chadha* Justice Powell concurred in the judgment on the ground that the House had improperly assumed an adjudicatory function in making its own determination whether the six persons in question met the statutory criteria for suspension of deportation. He reasoned: "Unlike the judiciary or an administrative agency, Congress is not bound by established substantive rules. Nor is it subject to procedural safeguards, such as the right to counsel and a hearing before an impartial tribunal, that are present when a court or an agency adjudicates individual rights. The only effective constraint on Congress' power is political, but Congress is most accountable politically when it prescribes rules of general applicability." 462 U.S. at 966 (Powell, J., concurring in the judgment).

70. The legal literature on the legislative veto is legion. The analysis that follows is a summary based on Frickey, *supra* note 34, which in turn relied heavily upon Brubaker, *Slouching Toward Constitutional Duty: The Legislative Veto and the Delegation of Authority,* 1 CONST. COMM. 81 (1984).

prompted by nothing more profound than a momentary shift in the mood of the public, the proximity to an election, an altered composition of the overseeing committee, the rise of a new and committed interest group—a change of intent that would not be sufficient to stir the passage of a law, but that would be adequate to affect administrative rules under the threat of a legislative veto."[71]

The Court struck down the legislative veto in *Chadha*, largely justifying its decision with a rather wooden approach to the constitutional language requiring bicameral Congressional action and presentment of bills to the President. The Court did note, however, that bicameralism and the President's veto power protect against the "fear that special interests could be favored at the expense of public needs."[72] An elaboration of this perspective based on the insights of public choice,[73] rather than formalistic constitutional interpretation, could have strongly bolstered the Court's decision. The effect of the ruling was to require the observance of appropriate legislative procedures. Public choice theory suggests that strict adherence to a preordained lawmaking format can limit the opportunities for strategic behavior on the part of legislators, moderate the influence of interest groups, and reduce the possibility of arbitrary outcomes.[74]

71. Brubaker, *supra* note 70, at 94.

72. 462 U.S. at 950.

73. Professor Harold Bruff made the argument succinctly when he explained that the legislative veto "subverted primary controls on the fairness of legislation in two ways. The first is to vitiate the effectiveness of the bicameralism and presentment requirements in raising the size of coalitions needed for collective choice. Retention of veto authority systematically favored interest groups having advantages in one or both houses of Congress because of their distribution throughout the nation. Second, the veto device allowed Congress to select its decision rule at the operational stage of policymaking rather than at the constitutional stage. A check on the fairness of selecting decision rules is the difficulty of determining who will profit from their later use in specific cases. Yet at the operational stage it is much easier to predict the winners and losers from a change in the decision rules." Bruff, *Legislative Formality, Administrative Rationality*, 63 TEX. L. REV. 207, 221 (1984) (footnotes omitted).

74. For an example older than *Chadha* that is supported by a cumulative assessment of due process of lawmaking principles, consider United States v. Lovett, 328 U.S. 303 (1945). In an appropriations bill, Congress forbade the expenditure of federal funds for the salaries of three named employees of the executive branch who were suspected of being subversives. This provision violated all the norms of due process of lawmaking. Under our constitutional separation of powers, Congress is not the appropriate entity to fire executive branch employees (except through the mechanism of impeachment). Melding a substantive provision into an appropriations measure is bad legislative form. Indeed, the Senate refused to go along with the provision five times, until it became apparent that without it the House would not pass the appropriations measure. The President signed the bill reluctantly, stating that he did not consider the employees subversives and that he wanted to retain them. The President said: "The Senate yielded, as I have been forced to yield, to avoid delaying our conduct of the war. But I cannot so yield without placing on record my view that this provision is not only unwise and discriminatory, but unconstitutional." In summary, the procedures Congress followed in enacting the

II. Expanding the Influence of Public Choice in Public Law

What follows are several examples of how the insights of public choice could enrich public law. The illustrations are intended to show how a sensitivity to public choice can inform decisions in concrete cases. If enough cases are eventually decided this way, they may provide sufficient fodder for modifying public law theory in a more general fashion. Building general theory from the ground up, so to speak, is the most likely way in which public choice might influence broad areas of public law.

Although we have rejected the radical constitutional solutions proposed by Richard Epstein and others, we agree with them that the rising influence of special interests on the political process is very troubling. This influence is unfortunate in at least three respects. First, some people are not members of any organized interest group. Interest group politics redistributes wealth and political power away from these segments of the population. Second, apart from the distributional effect, there is also the "Pogo effect" ("We have met the enemy and he is us"). Even if everybody belonged to a "special interest" group, so that special interest politics did not affect the distribution of wealth, interest groups would still direct resources to socially unproductive programs. Some reason exists to blame our current problems in controlling the federal budget on the Pogo effect. More generally, the Pogo effect can potentially do substantial long-term economic damage. Third, and perhaps most important, the activities of special interest groups tend to undermine the democratic ethos. The successful functioning of a democracy requires voters and sometimes government officials to act in ways that are economically irrational. Because these behaviors are not reinforced by economic incentives, they depend on a somewhat fragile public adherence to a social code. Special interest groups, by creating the impression that government is simply an arena of self-interest, foster an atmosphere of cynicism that is incompatible with a healthy democracy.

Unfortunately, identifying the problems posed by special interests is easier than finding a solution. We do not claim to have discovered any "miracle cure," but we do have a few suggestions.

One way of reducing the power of special interest groups is to limit their role in the political process. We believe that a strong case can be made for

---

provision seemed more like a witch-hunt than a careful deliberation about the loyalties of the individuals involved.

The Court invalidated the provision on the ground that it was an unconstitutional bill of attainder, in that it constituted a legislative punishment of ascertainable persons without any judicial trial. Justice Frankfurter, in a separate opinion, more squarely invoked due process of lawmaking principles. He relied on the maxim that judges should interpret statutes to avoid constitutional issues if possible, and he interpreted the statute as simply saying that the named employees could not be paid out of certain specifically appropriated moneys.

limiting campaign expenditures by business and labor PACs. Contributions from these PACs are clearly linked to a legislator's performance on legislation favoring these groups. Eliminating such "economic" PACs would reduce the tendency of legislators to favor these special interests in gratitude for past contributions or in the hopes of future contributions. It would also help combat unhealthy public cynicism about government.[75]

Ironically, on those rare occasions when legislatures have attempted to curb special interests, the Supreme Court has intervened on behalf of the special interest groups themselves.[76] In particular, the Supreme Court has struck down limitations on campaign expenditures as violations of the first amendment.[77] Our proposal, however, is much narrower than those the Court has invalidated. The intrusion on free speech would be minimal, since individuals could divert their PAC contributions to noneconomic PACs.[78] A full discussion of the first amendment issues would take us far afield.[79] A

75. The argument for such a restriction is persuasively made in Sorauf, *Caught in a Political Thicket: The Supreme Court and Campaign Finance*, 3 CONST. COMM. 97 (1986). *See also* F. SORAUF, WHAT PRICE PACS? (1984). For a much more benign view of PACs, see A. MATASAR, CORPORATE PACS AND FEDERAL CAMPAIGN FINANCING LAWS (1986).

76. *See* FEC v. National Conservative Political Action Comm., 470 U.S. 480 (1985); First National Bank v. Bellotti, 435 U.S. 765 (1978); Buckley v. Valeo, 424 U.S. 1 (1976). A recent case, Austin v. Michigan Chamber of Commerce, 110 S.Ct. 1391 (1990), is a welcome break from this pattern.

77. FEC v. National Conservative Political Action Comm., 470 U.S. 480 (1985) [*NCPAC*], invalidated a federal statute limiting the amount of money a PAC group can spend supporting a candidate who is also receiving federal campaign financing. We believe that *NCPAC* is distinguishable from our proposal in several regards. First, the Court suggested that the outcome might have been different if the statute had not been so broad as to include even small neighborhood groups. *Id.* at 500–501. Second, combined with the limits on direct contributions to candidates and parties upheld in *Buckley,* the effect of the PAC restriction considered in *NCPAC* was to limit the total amount of campaign speech. Our proposal, however, would leave noneconomic PACs open, and thus would rechannel rather than limit speech.

78. As a result, the legislation we propose would be less likely to prevent challengers from raising enough money to successfully challenge incumbents.

79. For an introduction to the voluminous literature, see Sorauf, *supra* note 75; BeVier, *Money and Politics: A Perspective on the First Amendment and Campaign Finance Reform,* 73 CALIF. L. REV. 1045 (1985); Polsby, *Buckley v. Valeo: The Special Nature of Political Speech,* 1976 SUP. CT. REV. 1; *The Supreme Court—1985 Term,* 99 HARV. L. REV. 223 (1985). Much of the argument has focused on whether Congress may properly use restrictions on campaign financing as a means of equalizing political influence. *See, e.g.,* Wright, *Money and the Pollution of Politics: Is the First Amendment an Obstacle to Political Equality?,* 82 COLUM. L. REV. 609 (1982). In *Buckley,* the Court held this to be a constitutionally impermissible purpose, 424 U.S. at 48–49.

More recent information indicates that PAC contributors are more representative of the general population than campaign contributors in general, so that equality may not be as great a concern as some commentators feared. On the other hand, PACs are strongly skewed in terms of the types of interests they reflect. For example, of the nearly 3,000 PACs, only seventeen are concerned with environmental preservation and energy, and only one represents consumers.

carefully tailored ban on economic PACs could probably be defended, however, as a means of channeling (rather than limiting) speech.[80] The objection
to economic PACs is not based on the content of their speech, which would
be a highly suspect motivation under the first amendment. Rather, it is based
on the secondary effects of that speech on the legislative process and the
democratic ethos. Even if the same individuals gave the same amount of
money through other PACs, the contributions would be less clearly linked to
votes on specific issues. Hence, the ban on economic PACs seems valid under the Court's recently formulated *Renton* test.[81]

Unlike most proposals to limit campaign contributions, ours is not aimed
at limiting the role of money in politics as such. Rather, it is directed at a
much more limited problem: the collection and disbursement of campaign
money from groups defined by narrow economic interest rather than party or
ideology. When a PAC group of dairy farmers supports a candidate, the candidate is clearly on notice that future support depends on votes for dairy
subsidies. If the farmers gave the same amount of money through some other

---

See K. Schlozman & J. Tierney, Organized Interests and American Democracy 247–
52 (1986). Of course, the extent to which PAC contributions influence legislators is itself controversial. *See* Sorauf, *supra* note 75, at 109–12, for a review of the literature. In addition, as
Sorauf argues, *id.* at 112–19, economic PACs undermine the fragile set of values necessary for
a healthy democracy. Our own view is that economic PACs do raise serious concerns about the
health of the political process.

The Framers themselves seem to have been concerned about these matters, under the broad
rubric of what they called "corruption." (Their concept of corruption was obviously far broader
than even the "appearance of corruption" discussed in the Supreme Court opinions, for the
Court seems to have in mind bribery rather than the pursuit of private interests at the expense of
the public). *See* Sunstein, *supra* note 3, at 35–45. Thus, present-day concern about PACs can
lay claim to a tradition embodied in the Constitution itself.

80. Presumably, many of the same individuals would still make contributions to noneconomic PACs.

81. *See* City of Renton v. Playtime Theatres, Inc., 475 U.S. 41 (1986). *Renton* upheld a
severe zoning restriction on adult theatres, a context admittedly far removed from campaign
financing. For our purposes, the importance of *Renton* is that it refined the test for content neutrality. According to the Court, a statute is content-neutral if it is *"justified* without reference to
the content of the regulated speech." *Id.* at 48 (emphasis in original), quoting *Virginia Phar-
macy Bd. v. Virginia Citizens Consumers Council,* 425 U.S. 748, 771 (1976). This test is
satisfied, the Court said, if the government's justification relates to the secondary effect of the
speech on its surroundings, rather than any objection to the viewpoint expressed. *Id.* at 49–50.
Regulations of this kind may be upheld if they serve a substantial government purpose and do
not unreasonably restrict the available channels of communication. *Id.* at 46–50. In short,
Renton appears to adopt the view that the government may generally take the content of speech
into account when channeling speech, but only rarely when the purpose is censorship. We believe that in doing so *Renton* merely states explicitly what was implicit in a long line of prior
cases. *See* Farber & Nowak, *The Misleading Nature of Public Forum Analysis: Content and
Context in First Amendment Adjudication,* 70 Va. L. Rev. 1219 (1984). In restricting expenditures by economic PACs, the legislature is not objecting to the viewpoint expressed by the
PAC's speech, which is simply that a certain candidate should be elected.

PAC (an ideological group, for example), or directly to a political party, the linkage would be less clear. Moreover, if the successful candidate did vote for dairy subsidies, the effect on public confidence in the democratic process would be less, because there would be a smaller appearance of impropriety. Finally, because economic PACs exist to protect the special economic interests of their members, their effect on the legislative process is likely to be to promote rent-seeking rather than any arguable public interest. American political life would be improved without these economic PACs.

Admittedly, making economic PACs illegal would not by itself radically diminish the power of special interest groups. It would, however, be a step in the right direction. Certainly, a reduction in the number of PACs to which people may contribute seems far less radical than imposing new substantive limitations on legislation of the kind discussed in chapter 3. In any event, despite the potential first amendment problems, we believe that reforms of campaign financing and perhaps greater control of lobbying[82] can be useful means of controlling special interest groups.

The power of special interest groups, according to many political scientists, is also likely to be weakened by strong political parties. The party system has not been very strong in the last decade or so, but there has been a more recent tendency for campaign financing to be funneled increasingly through the party organization.[83] It would not be difficult to amend the tax laws so as to encourage this trend by giving preferred tax treatment to contributions to political parties. By providing a tax credit with a cap for large contributions, we could also encourage small donations by lower income individuals, thus fostering egalitarianism as well as undermining the special interests.

---

82. Although direct sanctions against the lobbyists themselves raise serious first amendment problems, *see* United States v. Harriss, 347 U.S. 612 (1954), the Court has indicated that the first amendment conveys no right to have an official listen to a speaker. In Minnesota State Board v. Knight, 465 U.S. 271 (1984), the Supreme Court held that the state could constitutionally prohibit administrators from listening to the views of dissident teachers. The Court's broad language seems to indicate that legislators could be prohibited from listening to lobbyists: "However wise or practicable various levels of public participation in various kinds of policy decisions may be, this Court has never held, and nothing in the Constitution suggests it should hold, that government must provide for such participation. . . . Nothing in the First Amendment or in this Court's case law interpreting it suggests that the rights to speak, associate, and petition require government policymakers to listen or respond to individuals' communications on public issues." *Id.* at 285. The Court also recognized that Congress was free to "enact bills on which no hearings have been held or on which testimony has been received from only a select group." *Id.* at 284. This suggests that the *Knight* holding is not limited to administrative officials, but also encompasses legislators. If so, then the first amendment would not bar legislation restricting contacts between legislators and lobbyists.

83. *See* M. FIORINA, CONGRESS: KEYSTONE OF THE WASHINGTON ESTABLISHMENT 144–55 (2d ed. 1989). On the desirability of strong political parties, see text accompanying notes 50–51 in chapter 2.

Special interests might also be better controlled if courts were to police covert delegations by legislatures. Although we have rejected attempts to police delegations of authority to administrative agencies,[84] other delegations of legislative authority might warrant increased judicial scrutiny. For example, in *Chadha* the legislative veto amounted to a delegation to a small coterie of legislators—those on the relevant committee or subcommittee—of the authority to thwart the implementation of legislation.[85] This delegation violated all the norms—structural, deliberative, and procedural—of due process of lawmaking. It is one thing to delegate power to administrators chosen by the President. It is another to delegate to a handful of legislators chosen on the basis of seniority or party loyalty.

Another troublesome form of covert delegation results when a legislature essentially cedes its authority to private interests. A good illustration is *U.S. Railroad Retirement Board v. Fritz.*[86] Retirement benefits for railroad workers come from the railroad retirement system, not the social security system. This causes problems in coordinating the two systems. To illustrate the issue in *Fritz,* assume that someone working for the railroad for ten years qualified for $300 in monthly railroad benefits, while someone with equivalent nonrailroad work likewise qualified for $300 in social security benefits. Twenty years of railroad work increased the benefits to $500, just as twenty years of nonrailroad work increased social security to $500. Many workers spend part of their employment years working for the railroad and another part working elsewhere. The formula used prior to 1974 gave some of these people a windfall; a worker with ten years inside and ten years outside the railroad industry received $600 ($300 railroad benefits, $300 in social security) rather than $500 in benefits.

In 1974 Congress restructured the retirement system to eliminate this windfall, but did not make the change effective across the board. Retirees who were already receiving the windfall continued to get it. For persons still working in 1974, Congress adopted complicated rules. To simplify, in general people working in the railroad industry would get the windfall if they had already had ten years of railroad work by 1974; people currently employed outside the industry, however, lost most or all of the retirement windfall unless they had already completed twenty-five years of railroad work by 1974.

At first glance, this seems like a strange compromise. To be sure, leaving intact the benefits of persons already retired seems fair, even if their pensions may be excessive compared to those of other retirees. But what about the favorable treatment of current railroad workers versus former railroaders

---

84. *See* chapter 3.
85. *See* notes 67–74, *supra,* and accompanying text.
86. 449 U.S. 166 (1980). *See* Sunstein, supra note 3, at 69–72.

holding other jobs? This odd distinction becomes explicable when we consider its source. The bill embodied a proposal from a joint labor-management negotiating committee, which had formed at the request of Congress. The members of this committee were not appointed by public officials, and no one on the committee represented the workers who bore the brunt of the bill—nonrailroaders who had earlier worked between ten and twenty-five years in the railroad industry.

The statute is also suspect for other reasons. It actually raised the benefits for current union members, apparently at the expense of the former railroaders. In addition, the House and Senate committee reports contained some false statements that no one would lose vested benefits under the bill (although other portions of the reports accurately reflected the bill's impact). Nowhere in the legislative history did any legislator note, much less justify, the potential unfairness of the bill. Moreover, members of the joint labor-management negotiating committee may have misled Congress at the hearings about the bill's effect on vested benefits. Not only did Congress fail to demonstrate any deliberation about the potential unfairness of the bill, there are some reasons to doubt whether Congress even understood what the bill would accomplish.

In *Fritz*, however, a majority of six Justices upheld the constitutionality of the statute by applying the weakest sort of rational basis inquiry. The Court asked only whether it was possible to imagine a plausible reason for what Congress did. The Court concluded that preferring those currently connected to the railroad industry was a sufficient reason. For the Court, it was constitutionally irrelevant " 'whether this reasoning in fact underlay the legislative decision.' "[87] The majority said:

> [W]e disagree with the District Court's conclusion that Congress was unaware of what it accomplished or that it was misled by the groups that appeared before it. If this test were applied literally to every member of any legislature that ever voted on a law, there would be very few laws which would survive it. The language of the statute is clear, and we have historically assumed that Congress intended what it enacted.[88]

Thus, the Court in *Fritz* strongly repudiated a deliberative model of due process of lawmaking. For reasons explained earlier, we agree that an inquiry about legislative deliberation, standing alone, is insufficient to justify invalidating the statute in *Fritz*. But, contrary to the Court, the absence of deliberation—indeed, the positive evidence of legislative confusion—in *Fritz* should not be constitutionally irrelevant, for it should reduce the degree of deference given the statute. When this concern about deliberation is

---

87. 449 U.S. at 179 (quoting Flemming v. Nestor, 363 U.S. 603, 612 (1960)).
88. 449 U.S. at 179.

woven together with a due process of lawmaking inquiry about structure and procedure, a strong argument can be made that *Fritz* is wrongly decided.

What Congress did in *Fritz* was to delegate the resolution of a public problem—the financial difficulties of the railroad retirement fund—to a committee made up only of private interests, indeed a committee that did not represent even all of the private groups that had an interest in the problem. The private committee decided to balance the retirement fund's budget by stripping an unrepresented group of vested benefits. Had Congress then articulated some justification for the resulting bill, that bill might have deserved judicial deference. As it was, however, Congress apparently simply deferred to the equilibrium of power in an unrepresentative committee made up solely of private interests. Striking down the bill in *Fritz* would have done no more than discipline Congress to avoid covert delegations to interest groups, or at least to deliberate about the proposals that come from such entities. Requiring some measure of legislative due process seems especially proper when Congress seeks to deprive individuals of vested benefits, which are not technically property rights but are very similar as a practical matter.

On the surface, the disadvantaged class in *Fritz* might seem to deserve little sympathy. They are left no worse off than persons who never worked in the railroad industry and must rely upon Social Security retirement benefits. Did the plaintiffs in *Fritz* deserve a windfall simply because Congress gave a windfall to others who were similarly situated? When vested benefits are involved, there is a real likelihood that workers have relied on those benefits in making career decisions and retirement plans. Even a "windfall" should not be too readily subject to retroactive destruction. More fundamentally, the essence of equal protection is that the government must treat similarly situated people similarly, not just out of fairness, but also to discipline the policy-making process against undue influence.[89] Similarly, the essence of due process goes beyond the opportunity to participate in a governmental process affecting one's interests.[90] The rest of us, who are not directly af-

---

89. The classic overall justification for equal protection scrutiny was written by Justice Jackson: "Invocation of the equal protection clause . . . does not disable any governmental body from dealing with the subject at hand. It merely means that the prohibition or regulation must have a broader impact. . . . The framers of the Constitution knew, and we should not forget today, that there is no more effective practical guaranty against arbitrary and unreasonable government than to require that the principles of law which officials would impose upon a minority must be imposed generally. Conversely, nothing opens the door to arbitrary action so effectively as to allow those officials to pick and choose only a few to whom they will apply legislation and thus to escape the political retribution that might be visited upon them if larger numbers were affected." Railway Express Agency, Inc. v. New York, 336 U.S. 106, 112–13 (1949) (Jackson, J., concurring).

90. The conventional context for this point is in adjudication or regulation, rather than the

fected by the statute, have a stake in whether retirement laws are the product of a fair process. These norms of equal protection and due process were flouted by the covert delegation of authority and the resulting discrimination in *Fritz*.

Covert delegations are probably not uncommon. Due process of lawmaking could attack only the most obvious errors of decisional structure or procedure, and might be limited to cases where vested benefits or other particularly important individual interests were at stake. Due process of lawmaking, like any other public law theory, cannot solve all public choice problems. But this is no reason not to do what can be done to improve the policy-making process.

Considerations related to public choice might also help encourage legal evolution. When most legal doctrines were of common law origin—that is, created by judges on a case-by-case basis—the law had the built-in capacity to evolve over time, as society changes and necessitates a rethinking of legal rules. In twentieth-century America, most important legal rules, particularly in public law, are rooted in statutes or administrative regulations. Because legislatures are not particularly good at updating statutes, contemporary American law is prone to obsolescence.[91]

We have already seen some illustrations of how due process of lawmaking can encourage legal evolution. In *Mow Sun Wong*, the Court threw out an old administrative regulation and prodded the other branches to consider the issue from a contemporary perspective. Similarly, in several gender discrimination cases, the Court has struck down statutes that purported to help women but seemed rooted in outdated sexist stereotypes.[92] In contrast, the Court

---

legislative process. Considering its virtues, however, should not at least some minimal aspect of it be applied in a context like *Fritz?* For a recent extended discussion of the value of due process, consider Marshall v. Jerrico, Inc., 446 U.S. 238, 242 (1980): "The Due Process Clause entitles a person to an impartial and disinterested tribunal in both civil and criminal cases. This requirement of neutrality in adjudicative proceedings safeguards the two central concerns of procedural due process, the prevention of unjustified or mistaken deprivations and the promotion of participation and dialogue by affected individuals in the decisionmaking process. . . . The neutrality requirement helps to guarantee that life, liberty, or property will not be taken on the basis of an erroneous or distorted conception of the facts or the law. . . . At the same time, it preserves both the appearance and reality of fairness, 'generating the feeling, so important to a popular government, that justice has been done,' . . . by ensuring that no person will be deprived of his interests in the absence of a proceeding in which he may present his case with assurance that the arbiter is not predisposed to find against him."

91. This theme is developed at length in G. CALABRESI, A COMMON LAW FOR THE AGE OF STATUTES (1982); Eskridge, *Dynamic Statutory Interpretation*, 135 U. PA. L. REV. 1479 (1987). We considered some aspects of the problem in chapter 4, part IV.

92. *See* Mississippi University for Women v. Hogan, 458 U.S. 718 (1982) (all-women's nursing college); Wengler v. Druggists Mutual Ins. Co., 446 U.S. 142 (1980) (widows, but not widowers, entitled to death benefits under worker's compensation statute without having to

has upheld newer statutes that granted women special benefits clearly designed to remedy gender discrimination.[93]

Public choice suggests some ways to sharpen this judicial interest in encouraging legal evolution. Public choice provides some rich insights into why legislatures, if left undisturbed, do not revisit obsolescent statutes, and how courts might stimulate appropriate legal evolution without invading legitimate legislative prerogatives. The doctrine of statutory *cy pres* discussed in the previous chapter is one way to do so. Another method is illustrated by *Moragne v. States Marine Lines, Inc.*[94]

Understanding *Moragne* requires a brief introduction to personal injury law. Historically, almost all the tort doctrines that govern personal injury cases were of common law origin—made by judges on a case-by-case basis. Under British tort law, transplanted to America, it was considerably better to kill people than to maim them. A maimed accident victim could recover hefty damages, but the family of a dead victim got nothing. The historical reasons for this idiotic rule are obscure. In the nineteenth century, American state legislatures abolished this rule by establishing a statutory right to sue for wrongful death. For wrongful deaths of seaworkers, Congress also enacted remedial legislation in 1920. The federal Jones Act[95] provides a cause of action for the negligent death of a seaman, and the federal Death on the High Seas Act[96] (DOHSA) establishes a cause of action for wrongful death of workers on the high seas—outside the territorial waters of the United States—"caused by wrongful act, neglect, or default."

The situation in *Moragne,* somewhat simplified, was that a widow attempted to bring an action for the wrongful death of her husband. He had died from injuries suffered in American territorial waters. The basis of the suit was that the vessel was "unseaworthy." Unseaworthiness does not fit the Jones Act (which is limited to negligence actions).[97] DOHSA does encompass the unseaworthiness theory but does not cover accidents in

---

demonstrate dependence upon deceased spouse); Califano v. Goldfarb, 430 U.S. 199 (1977) (widows, but not widowers, entitled to federal survivors' benefits without having to demonstrate dependence upon deceased spouse); Weinberger v. Wiesenfeld, 420 U.S. 636 (1975) (widowed mother, but not widowed father, entitled to social security benefits based on earnings of deceased spouse).

93. *See* Califano v. Webster, 430 U.S. 313 (1977) (retired women workers received higher monthly social security benefits than "similarly situated" men); Schlesinger v. Ballard, 419 U.S. 498 (1975) (women naval officers granted longer period in which to attain promotion than men).

94. 398 U.S. 375 (1970).

95. 46 U.S.C. § 688.

96. 46 U.S.C. §§ 761, 762.

97. Also, the Jones Act provides relief only for "seamen," and Mr. Moragne was a longshoreman.

American territorial waters. In short, the widow Moragne had fallen into a hole in the statutes. The only other law to apply, federal maritime common law, would preclude her action as well, because of the old rule that there can be no recovery for wrongful death.[98]

What was obviously needed in *Moragne* was some way to update federal law, either by reinterpreting the Jones Act to accommodate the modern tort of unseaworthiness, or by abandoning the old, draconian rule of the common law. We have some doubts about free reinterpretation of statutes, though,[99] and in this case the statutory language was not easily amenable to any construction that would allow her recovery. Perhaps statutory cy pres could have been used, since Congress had not foreseen the growth of the unseaworthiness doctrine. The more obvious solution is to abandon the old common law rule.

The Supreme Court, in a well-crafted opinion by Justice Harlan, changed the federal maritime law so that it embodied a general principle of recovery for wrongful death. The Court concluded that Congress in 1920 was simply fixing the problems squarely presented to it, not comprehensively addressing an area of law and freezing it from judicial creativity.

The *Moragne* setting illuminates how public choice can provide rich insights for the judicial role. The interest groups lobbying for statutes like the Jones Act and DOHSA are likely to focus on particular problems, not across-the-board inquiries that may complicate passage of legislation. Ms. Moragne and similarly situated persons have no idea that they are without remedy until they suffer the loss of a loved one; they have no incentive to organize before the fact to lobby for remedial legislation. Such large, diffuse, unorganized groups are, according to public choice, the least likely to lobby successfully for legislative action. Consider also the nature of the defendants in a case like *Moragne*. Shipping companies have the problem of compensating work-related injuries every day, in contrast to the one-shot tragedy suffered by Ms. Moragne. These companies are small in number, easily identified, and have the resources to lobby Congress—in short, public choice would predict that they can organize and protect themselves in the legislative arena. The industry, in short, is well positioned to obtain congressional relief from any harshness resulting from the application of *Moragne* to future injuries; the Ms. Moragnes of the world are unlikely to obtain legislative relief before their respective losses occur.

---

98. Note the obvious unfairness of denying her recovery. Had her husband survived his injuries, he could have brought an unseaworthiness action under federal common law. Had her husband's fatal injuries occurred a little further from shore, on the "high seas," she could have brought an unseaworthiness wrongful death action under DOHSA. But because of the combination of two factors—his death, and where he had been injured—all readily applicable sources of law were unavailing.

99. As we explained in chapter 4, part IV.

A more recent decision is less adept than *Moragne*. In *Boyle v. United Technologies Corp.*,[100] a military supplier was sued after a marine was killed in the crash of a defective helicopter. Over a strong dissent, the Court established a new defense for military contractors, freeing them from liability so long as they warned the government about product defects. As the dissent pointed out, government contractors had conducted a vigorous but unsuccessful lobbying campaign to get this exemption from Congress.[101] Public choice suggests that the burden of legislative inertia was properly placed on these firms, which are well-organized, politically powerful, and wealthy. Unfortunately, the Court instead placed the burden of seeking new legislation on the widows and orphans of soldiers.

Judges are not infallible, and encouraging legislatures to reconsider judicial holdings seems compatible with norms of legislative supremacy. As we explained in chapter 3, judges cannot simply discard statutes because they have lost majority support or are incompatible with the legal landscape. That would conflict too sharply with supremacy of the legislature in making public policy. Legislative supremacy is not, however, a barrier to judicial relief in situations like *Moragne*, where statutes do not address the precise problem before the judge. As we have seen, the appropriate reach of the congressional intent concerning a statute can be informed by public choice. Moreover, legislative silence about a problem under litigation can often be explained by public choice as well. Public choice, therefore, provides insights about the proper limits of legislative supremacy and about where the legislative burden of inertia should fairly be left in some cases.[102]

In this chapter, we have not tried to offer any grand design for revamping public law in light of public choice theory. In the previous two chapters, we have considered a number of unsuccessful attempts along those lines. As legal pragmatists, we are skeptical that any such grand design is feasible. There are many points at which public law depends on some conception of the political process. Beyond the topics we have considered in this book, for example, are questions such as the application of the antitrust laws to government bodies, the design of appropriate administrative procedures, judicial oversight of legislative districting, and the use of judicial review to protect politically powerless minorities. It seems inherently unlikely that any general theory can speak equally to such a diverse set of problems.

Public choice may have little relevance to some of these issues, while it may have varying lessons about others. Moreover, in redesigning legal doctrines, we need to keep in mind not only the teachings of public choice, but a

---

100. 108 S. Ct. 2510 (1988).

101. *Id.* at 2520 (Brennan, J., dissenting).

102. For another illustration similar to *Moragne*, see Selders v. Armentrout, 190 Neb. 275, 207 N.W.2d 686 (1973) (updating a nineteenth-century wrongful death statute to encompass modern tort principles).

multitude of other considerations relating to the legal process. Consequently, bringing public choice to bear on legal issues will require a long process of thoughtful reappraisal of existing doctrine. Our goal in this chapter has been only to initiate that process.

The major role of public choice in this process, as to some extent its role has been in political science, may be to reawaken the Madisonian interest in issues of institutional design and procedure. The "New Institutionalism" in public law probably will not take the form of directly translating public choice results into legal rules. Rather, public choice may be most important simply in sensitizing lawyers and judges to the kinds of institutional issues that so interested the Framers. Perhaps it should not have taken advanced mathematical models and econometric studies to remind us of the sage perspective of Madison & Company. In the twentieth century, however, wisdom comes much easier when it comes in technocratic garb—one reason being, of course, that we have painfully learned how important it is to be rigorous, both in empirical and theoretical work.

EPILOGUE

Beyond the Economic Sphere:
A Madisonian Perspective
on the Privacy Cases

*B*ecause of its connection with welfare economics, public choice has influenced public law mostly regarding economic legislation. Indeed, we have illustrated this book almost exclusively with examples of the intersection of public choice, public law, and economic regulation. Public choice's assumptions about the motivations of legislators and private groups were formulated largely with the "rent-seeking" paradigm in mind: the use of legislation by private interests to obtain an economic advantage beyond what the free market will bear.

We have been cautious in suggesting how public law might partially incorporate the public choice perspective. As chapter 5 indicates, public choice's focus on structure, procedure, and legislative inertia provides useful suggestions about the evolution of public law generally. Our prescriptions in chapter 5 for reforming public law in light of public choice—campaign finance reform, discouraging covert delegations, and encouraging legal evolution—were largely illustrated with economic examples. Legal controversies far removed from economic regulation could also profit, however, from increased attention to concrete political setting and legislative inertia. Public choice could perform a great service by increasing judicial sensitivity to those political dynamics.

On the surface, the Supreme Court's highly controversial decisions about contraception and abortion seem far removed from the appropriate sphere of public choice. To be sure, the behavior of reelection-minded legislators faced with the antiabortion lobby fits the public choice perspective. Beyond that obvious linkage, it may be hard to see how public choice adds anything to the contentious debate about the sexual privacy decisions. These decisions take on a new light, however, under a particularized focus on political setting and legislative inertia. A realistic understanding of politics requires Madison's awareness of factionalism, instability, and the role of institutions, as well as his aspirations for deliberative democracy. A Madisonian perspective may not justify going as far as the Court has gone in the privacy area. It does suggest a more modest judicial strategy, which might have had ultimately a better chance of success.

In most of what follows, we will be using public choice as a source of general inspiration, not as a specific body of knowledge or set of analytical tools. Public choice does, however, shed some interesting light on the political dynamics of privacy. We saw in chapter 2 that relatively compact groups are likely to exercise undue influence. This means that, as a general matter, producer groups (firms and unions) tend to exercise influence at the expense of consumer groups. In the sphere of moral behavior, religious organizations enjoy a similar organizational advantage; it was not for nothing that Madison's concern over factions extended to religious factions.

Moreover, beyond the normal disadvantages of organizing large, diffuse groups, opponents of "morals" legislation have a special disadvantage. The regulated conduct is usually considered otherwise private—and from an economist's point of view, privacy simply means that individuals regard the revelation of certain information as costly. It is consequently hard to organize individuals who would like to buy contraceptives, obtain abortions, or engage in homosexual activity—partly because it is hard to identify them in the first place, and partly because of their fear that political involvement will indirectly reveal their private conduct. For example, political action against antisodomy laws was limited until a significant number of people no longer found it desirable to "remain in the closet." It is hard enough to organize car buyers into an effective political force, but it would be much harder if most people were embarrassed to admit in public to owning a car.

Putting these factors together, we can conclude that the political process is apt to overrepresent the views of organized political groups and underrepresent their opponents. Because of the inertia created by legislative structures like the committee system, this imbalance will be all the more pronounced when the question is not whether to pass new morals legislation but to repeal old legislation. Knowledge of these political dynamics does not necessarily translate directly into new constitutional doctrine. Nevertheless, awareness of these dynamics may provide a basis for a more intelligent judicial response.

As the rejection of Robert Bork's nomination for the Supreme Court demonstrates, American society widely embraces *Griswold v. Connecticut*,[1] in which the Court held that married couples have a constitutional right to use birth control. What has been largely forgotten is the cautious path the Court took to reaching this decision. Over a period of two decades, the Court seemingly took political reality into account in attempting

1. 381 U.S. 479 (1965). Bork's refusal to find any legitimacy for the Court's sexual privacy opinions, most notably *Griswold,* was one of the most controversial aspects about his candidacy for the Court. For Bork's writings attacking *Griswold,* see Dronenburg v. Zech, 741 F.2d 1388, 1392 (D.C. Cir. 1984); Bork, *Neutral Principles and Some First Amendment Problems,* 47 IND. L.J. 1, 11 (1971).

to force the state legislature to resolve the issue itself. The Court stepped into the breach only when it had satisfied itself that no legislative resolution would be forthcoming.

The Connecticut statute struck down in the 1965 *Griswold* decision was before the Supreme Court as early as 1943. In the 1943 case, a physician argued that the statute prevented him from giving birth control advice to women whose health would be threatened by pregnancy and birth. The Court avoided the issue because, it said unanimously, the doctor did not have "standing" in this situation: he had alleged no injury to himself caused by the statute, and he could not get into court merely by asserting the rights of other persons, such as his patients.[2]

Not quite two decades later, a new lawsuit was brought. The plaintiffs included married women who allegedly had a medical need for birth control advice. The Court again ducked the issue, this time concluding that the lawsuit was not "ripe."[3] Apparently only one prosecution had been brought since the statute's adoption in 1879, and in that case the prosecutor eventually refused to proceed. Contraceptives were readily available in Connecticut drug stores, notwithstanding the statute. As Justice Frankfurter explained for four Justices, "[t]he undeviating policy of nullification by Connecticut of its anti-contraceptive laws throughout the long years that they have been on the statute books bespeaks more than prosecutorial paralysis. . . . 'Deeply embedded traditional ways of carrying out state policy . . . '—or not carrying it out—'are often tougher and truer law than the dead words of the written text.' "[4] Justice Brennan, who provided the crucial fifth vote not to hear the case, stated that he was not convinced that plaintiffs "as individuals are truly caught in an inescapable dilemma."[5]

As Justice Harlan pointed out in dissent, the Court's refusal to hear the 1961 case was dubious as a matter of the Court's precedents on ripeness. But the majority of the Court apparently concluded that its power of judicial review—the countermajoritarian authority to invalidate legislative pronouncements as inconsistent with the Constitution—should not be exercised except where truly necessary as a practical matter. Professor Alexander Bickel explained the majority's apparent sensitivity to legislative inertia:

> The point was that the office of the Court, even in a perfectly real, concrete, and fully developed controversy, is not necessarily to resolve issues on which the political branches are in deadlock; it may be wise to wait till the political institutions, breaking the deadlock,

2. Tileston v. Ullman, 318 U.S. 44 (1943) (per curiam).
3. Poe v. Ullman, 367 U.S. 497 (1961).
4. *Id.* at 502.
5. *Id.* at 509 (Brennan, J., concurring in the judgment).

> are able to make an initial decision, on which the Court may then
> pass judgment. . . . The influences that favor the objective of the
> [Connecticut] law cannot—or perhaps will not—summon suffi-
> cient political strength to cause it to be enforced. . . . The influ-
> ences that oppose the law cannot summon sufficient political
> strength to cause it to be repealed; attempts have been made from
> 1923 onward, and they have failed.[6]

The Court was properly hesitant, we think, to decide whether the legislature
of Connecticut had the power to forbid the use of contraceptives when such
great doubt existed about whether the people of Connecticut really wanted to
do so.

The Court seems influenced too rarely by this kind of Madisonian sensitivity to policy-making processes, a sensitivity that public choice can
sharpen. Public law is usually viewed as the application of general principles
in generalized fashion—uniformly, to all similar cases properly before the
Court. This conception of public law has merit, for it tries to prevent the
Court from being influenced by "politics" with a small "p," of the "Republicans versus Democrats" or "whose ox is being gored" variety.[7] But
particularized attention to political detail, coupled with the avoidance tactics
that Bickel termed "passive virtues," ought to be part of the judicial arsenal.
Returning to the 1961 case, public officials in Connecticut had essentially
"shift[ed] the decision to the Court," as Bickel wrote. What was needed was
a technique "to turn the thrust of forces favoring and opposing the present
objectives of the statute toward the Legislature, where the power of at least
initial decision belongs in our system."[8]

In chapter 5, we considered a recent effort by the Court to remand a sensitive issue to the appropriate decisionmaker in *Hampton v. Mow Sun Wong*.
The Court might have made effective use of a legislative remand in the 1961
case. Professor Bickel suggested one theory, "desuetude," a doctrine in
Continental law under which a statute may become unenforceable through
disuse.[9] Public choice theory, by sharpening our awareness of legislative
inertia, provides a rich source of insights for the use of such passive virtues.

Connecticut officials finally did bring a prosecution under the statute
against two doctors who provided birth control information to married persons at a large clinic. No controversy could have been riper, nor could the
doctors' standing have been clearer to challenge the constitutionality of
the statute. In 1965, when this case made its way to the Supreme Court, the
Justices held that married couples had the right to use birth control, and that

6. A. BICKEL, THE LEAST DANGEROUS BRANCH 146–47 (1962).

7. *See* Gunther, *The Subtle Vices of the "Passive Virtues"—A Comment on Principle and Expediency in Judicial Review*, 64 COLUM. L. REV. 1 (1964).

8. A. BICKEL, *supra* note 6, at 148.

9. *See id.* at 148–56.

doctors could not be prosecuted as accessories to the crime of birth control use by such persons.

The legitimacy of *Griswold* would have been undercut, as a practical matter, had the Court reached out to make this decision prematurely. The Court bought itself two decades of judicial delay—and societal evolution—before it found itself forced to tackle the difficult constitutional question in *Griswold.* Surely the public's ultimate acceptance of *Griswold* is attributable in some part to the Court's strategic restraint in this regard.

The Court's abortion decision in 1973, *Roe v. Wade,* could have profited from the practical lessons of the birth control cases. In 1962 the influential American Law Institute, in its Model Penal Code, proposed liberalizing criminal abortion statutes.[10] Beginning in 1968, thirteen states had softened their abortion statutes to allow abortions not only if the woman's life was threatened, but also if the pregnancy seriously endangered her physical or mental health, if the child would have major physical or mental abnormalities, or if the pregnancy resulted from rape. Four states allowed abortion on demand if performed early in the pregnancy. Both the American Bar Association and the American Medical Association had gone on record favoring liberalization of abortion laws.[11]

Although many states continued to have restrictive approaches to abortion in the early 1970s, the trend in the states, if left unimpeded, might well have led to much wider availability of abortion through state legislation. Indeed, immediately after *Roe,* 52% of those polled in a national survey said that they approved of *Roe*'s holding, which was described as "making abortions up to three months of pregnancy legal."[12] A prudent Court might well have allowed the issue to percolate further, rather than leaping into the fray in 1973.

Moreover, the Court in 1973 had little help in addressing the abortion issue. The question whether a woman has a constitutional right in this context had been seriously litigated for only a few years prior to *Roe.* Indeed, no federal court of appeals had even considered the issue.[13]

As with the birth control statute in *Griswold,* many of the abortion statutes on the books in the early 1970s were a century old, adopted in a different time and climate, both moral and political. The primary purpose of those statutes apparently was to protect the life and health of the mother from the

10. *See* MODEL PENAL CODE § 230.3 (Proposed Official Draft 1962).

11. For an overview, see Morgan, Roe v. Wade *and the Lessons of the Pre-*Roe *Case Law,* 77 MICH. L. REV. 1724, 1726–30 (1979).

12. *See* Uslander & Weber, *Public Support for Pro-Choice Abortion Policies in the Nation and States: Changes and Stability After the* Roe *and* Doe *Decisions,* 77 MICH. L. REV. 1772, 1775 (1979).

13. *See* Morgan, supra note 11, at 1727–29.

comparative danger of abortion instead of childbirth.[14] By 1973 the medical basis for the criminal statutes had evaporated: abortion in the early stages of pregnancy had become safer than carrying the fetus to term. Consequently, one lower court judge argued that the old abortion statutes should be invalidated because there was no longer any logical connection between the nineteenth-century legislature's purpose and the means chosen to effectuate that purpose.[15] He thus was able to avoid the enormously controversial question of whether a state legislature might constitutionally criminalize abortion for the purpose of preserving the life of the fetus.

Had the Supreme Court taken this limited tack in *Roe,* it would have disappointed many abortion advocates. Moreover, it would have invited the state legislatures to adopt new abortion statutes, and some of those might have been highly restrictive.[16] The Court would then have been required to address the ultimate question whether outlawing abortion could be squared with the sexual privacy right recognized in *Griswold.* At a minimum, however, the Court would have bought itself—and American society—some additional time to come to grips with this profoundly difficult question. It would have contributed to a national dialogue about women's rights. Furthermore, the doctrinal foundation of the opinion would have been strengthened, because it could have exploited post-1973 developments regarding women's rights. The Court could then have linked some protection for abortion to the Court's gender discrimination cases, which recognize that statutes discriminating against women may be rooted in outdated stereotypes. In any event, with the benefit of hindsight, a continuation of the politics of abortion of the early 1970s might well have been preferable to the political storm that looms with the possible overruling of *Roe* less than two decades later.

The Court missed a similar opportunity in its most recent sexual privacy case, *Bowers v. Hardwick.*[17] There the majority of the Justices said they were answering this question: "whether the Federal Constitution confers a fundamental right upon homosexuals to engage in sodomy and hence invalidates the laws of the many States that still make such conduct illegal and

14. *See* Means, *The Phoenix of Abortional Freedom: Is a Penumbral or Ninth-Amendment Right About to Arise from the Nineteenth-Century Legislative Ashes of a Fourteenth-Century Common Law Liberty?,* 17 N.Y.L.F. 335 (1971); Means, *The Law of New York Concerning Abortion and the Status of the Foetus 1664–1968: A Case of Cessation of Constitutionality,* 14 N.Y.L.F. 411 (1968).

15. *See* Abele v. Markle, 342 F. Supp. 800, 809 (D. Conn. 1972) (three-judge court) (Newman, J., concurring in the result).

16. Indeed, in response to *Abele v. Markle* (*see id.* and accompanying text) Connecticut quickly adopted a new statute allowing abortion only to save the mother's life. *See* Abele v. Markle, 351 F. Supp. 224 (D. Conn. 1972) (three-judge court), *vacated and remanded,* 410 U.S. 950 (1973).

17. 478 U.S. 186 (1986).

have done so for a very long time."[18] The Court, predictably, answered this leading question in the negative. But the statute before the Court did not single out homosexuals; it provided harsh penalties for all manner of sodomy. Thus, while the Court focused on the traditional social taboo against homosexuality, the Georgia legislature that adopted the statute in question (a version of which dates back to 1816) obviously had in mind a different justification: that all nonvaginal sex was immoral, whether homosexual or heterosexual. That purpose seems as obsolescent as the "maternal health" justification had become for abortion statutes. Moreover, the statute had not been enforced in Georgia for decades even in the context of private consensual homosexual sodomy, and many states have decriminalized sodomy.

Thus, leaving aside larger arguments about the possible inconsistency of the statute with the broad rights of sexual privacy recognized in *Griswold* and *Roe,* the Court had a solid basis for striking down the Georgia law. The statute no longer had a rational connection with any current state objective, and enforcement had become so sporadic and unpredictable as to violate the due process requirement of fair notice. Had the Court acted on these narrow grounds, the burden of inertia in the Georgia legislature would have been shifted. If that body overcame the inertia and passed a new sodomy statute, there would be no need to speculate about what motivated the legislation. Such a development would stand in sharp contrast to *Bowers,* where the majority of the Court lamely justified the statute by "the *presumed* belief of a majority of the electorate in Georgia that homosexual sodomy is immoral and unacceptable."[19] As Justice Stevens pointed out in dissent, "the Georgia electorate has expressed no such belief—instead, its representatives enacted a law that presumably reflects the belief that *all sodomy* is immoral and unacceptable."[20]

Public choice strongly supports Stevens's reluctance to infer public attitudes from legislative inaction. It is rank speculation to presume that the Georgia legislature would outlaw homosexual sodomy had the Court struck down the old general sodomy statute on obsolescence grounds. If Georgia did ban homosexual conduct, there would have been ample time for the Court to address the much larger, and more difficult, question about whether a ban on all homosexual activity violated sexual privacy rights or the equal protection of the laws.

The majority of the Court profoundly erred in *Bowers* because it saw the issue as being whether judges may invalidate the populace's moral judgment. Viewing constitutional law at this gross level of abstraction is, perhaps, the unhappy consequence of activist decisions like *Roe,* where the

18. *Id.* at 190.
19. *Id.* at 196 (emphasis added).
20. *Id.* at 219 (Stevens, J., joined by Brennan & Marshall, JJ., dissenting) (emphasis in original).

Court went out of its way to define privacy rights broadly in a detailed, legislative fashion. If, instead, the issue in *Bowers* becomes whether a state may selectively threaten to enforce an ancient, obsolescent statute only against a few members of an unpopular minority, a different answer naturally emerges. If that answer is inconsistent with the wishes of a motivated majority of the state legislature, it would be free to respond accordingly.

Our quick survey of the privacy cases shows that narrower, more Madisonian inquiries about public policy and legislative inertia would have helped reform birth control, abortion, and sodomy laws, while leaving room for the political institutions to respond. Our discussion has not used the technical jargon of public choice: terms like "rent-seeking," "free rider," and "incoherence" seem to have attenuated value when social legislation is examined. But awareness of public choice might have prevented the Court in *Bowers* from jumping to the ultimate constitutional issue of the limits of majority rule, thereby treating an obsolete 1816 statute as the equivalent of focused, carefully deliberated contemporary legislation. A sensitivity to public choice also suggests that a wide range of difficult public law issues, many of them far removed from socioeconomic regulation, can be analyzed profitably by "thinking small" rather than by generating broad theories of individual rights. Those theories have their place in constitutional law, but only after less intrusive strategies have failed. Moreover, the Court can profit from more extended public debate about rights. That debate is now needlessly truncated by premature judicial attempts to define the boundaries of legislative power.

Alexander Bickel once properly pointed out that to look to constitutional history for specific answers to specific legal issues is to ask the wrong question. "No answer is what the wrong question begets, for the excellent reason that the Constitution was not framed to be a catalogue of answers to such questions."[21] In our view, a similar poverty of answers flows from asking public choice to resolve public law controversies. But, as with constitutional language and history, even if public choice cannot provide a complete answer, it may well be a necessary component of analysis.

Although we doubt that judges and legal scholars were ever actually as naive as they sometimes appeared in their writings, much of public law has been characterized by a simplistic view of the political process. Too often, the leap is made from the existence of a statute to an inference about majority preferences. It does not take public choice theory to see that this leap is sometimes unjustified, but the teaching of public choice is that this problem must be taken very seriously.

---

21. A. BICKEL, *supra* note 6, at 103. Professor John Hart Ely later attempted to hoist Bickel on his own petard by quoting this language. *See* J. ELY, DEMOCRACY AND DISTRUST 43, 72 (1980).

Public choice has two main lessons in this regard. First, compact, easily organized groups are likely to have an undue influence on the legislative process. Second, legislative outcomes may be the product of the legislature's structure and procedures, rather than being any simple reflection of voter preferences.

Some of the earlier legal scholarship on public choice took these conclusions to extremes. For these writers, if legislation does not simply reflect the "majority will," then its legitimacy seemed to be very questionable. We have argued that this is an overreaction. The empirical news about special interests is not so bad, while a deeper understanding of legislative structure and procedures can rehabilitate the legislature's legitimacy. Because of our more guarded appraisal of the teachings of public choice, we have resisted the temptation to translate public choice theorems directly into legal doctrines. We have contended, however, that public choice used properly can be a useful tool in shaping public law.

Ambrose Bierce defined politics as "[a] strife of interests masquerading as a contest of principles. The conduct of public affairs for private advantage."[22] Seventy years later, enough academic merit was found in a sophisticated modeling of Bierce's epigram to justify a Nobel prize. We mean no disrespect to James Buchanan and other practitioners of the dismal science when we suggest that public choice provides no sure foundation for public law. As Oliver Wendell Holmes said, "[t]he law embodies the story of a nation's development through many centuries, and it cannot be dealt with as if it contained only the axioms and corollaries of a book of mathematics."[23] But if axiomatic theory cannot be incorporated directly into public law, it nonetheless can perform some valuable roles, which we have attempted to identify. To say that public choice has only this limited application in public law is not to defame it, but to put it in its appropriate place as a tool, not a talisman.

22. A. BIERCE, THE DEVIL'S DICTIONARY 103 (1979 ed. 1st publ. 1911).
23. O. HOLMES, THE COMMON LAW 5 (1963 ed.).

INDEX

Abortion, 9, 145–46, 149–50
Administrative agency. *See* Legislative
  power, delegation of
Affirmative action, 112–15, 121–25
Agenda, importance of, in legislature, 3,
  39–42, 49–50, 55, 58, 61. *See also*
  Single-subject (germaneness) rule
Aleinikoff, T. Alexander, 114
American Indians, federal law concerning,
  121, 123
Americans for Democratic Action, ratings of
  legislators, 29–32
Anti-Federalists, 44. *See also* Republicanism
Armstrong, William, 96–97
Arrow, Kenneth, 7, 38, 58. *See also* Arrow's
  Theorem
Arrow's Theorem, 7, 10, 38–42, 47–62;
  Condorcet winner and, 51; Copeland
  winner and, 51; core, game with, and, 52;
  Constitution of United States and, 55;
  fairness and, 52, 56–59; formal voting
  models and, 50–52; legislatures and, 39–
  42, 47–62; multimember courts and, 55;
  public interest and, 38–42, 58–62;
  political parties and, 49, 54, 56–58;
  procedural rules and, 39–42, 49–50, 52,
  55, 58; republicanism and, 44–47, 57–62;
  strategic voting and, 40–42, 57n.52;
  strong point and, 51, 54; value solution
  and, 52; voting experiments and, 50;
  uncovered set and, 51, 52, 54; uni-peaked
  preferences and, 48–49, 53–56, 58, 59;
  yolk and, 51, 54

Bickel, Alexander, 147–48, 152
Bierce, Ambrose, 153
Birth control, 145–49
Blackmun, Harry, 75
Bork, Robert, 146
Bowers v. Hardwick, 150–52
Boyle v. United Technologies Corp., 142
Brennan, Goeffrey, 26
Brennan, William, 109–10, 113, 147

Buchanan, James, 1–2, 26, 153
Buckley, James, 97
Budget deficit, U.S., 35–36
Burger, Warren, 124

Calabresi, Guido, 106–7
Campaign financing. *See* Election financing
Chaos Theorem. *See* Arrow's Theorem
Chicago School economics, 16, 22, 71
City of Richmond v. J.A. Croson Co., 122
Coherence. *See* Arrow's Theorem
Collective action, 23, 37, 72, 141–42, 146
Commerce clause, 73–75
Committees. *See* Legislative committees
Common law, updating of, 139–42
Congress. *See* Due process of lawmaking;
  Legislative power, delegation of;
  Legislators
Constitutional law, federal, 8–9, 55, 62–87,
  145–53; review of political process and,
  73, 116–43. *See also* Abortion;
  Affirmative action; Commerce clause;
  Contraception; Due process; Due process
  of lawmaking; Federalism; Gender
  discrimination; Homosexuality;
  Legislative power, delegation of;
  Legislative veto; Taking clause
Consumers, political organization of,
  24n.52, 37
Contraception, 145–49
Corruption. *See* Election financing; Interest
  groups
Cost-benefit analysis, 34–35
Council of Revision, 71
Cycles. *See* Arrow's Theorem
Cy pres. *See* Statutory interpretation

Dahl, Robert, 17
DeBow, Michael, 25–27
Delegation. *See* Legislative power,
  delegation of
Deliberation. *See* Legislative deliberation.
  See also Due process of lawmaking

Democracy: arbitrariness of, 3, 7–8, 38–42, 47–62; judicial review and, 63; nature of, 7–8, 37, 57, 61–62; pathologies of, 11; republicanism and, 44–47. *See also* Constitutional law; Due process of lawmaking; Legislator; Pluralism
Desuetude, 148
Dole, Robert, 96–97
Due process, 64, 138–39. *See also* Due process of lawmaking
Due process of lawmaking, 118–43, 148, 150–52; effectiveness of theory, 128–29; hierarchy of instituticnal legitimacy model, 122–24, 130–31, 136, 138–39; legal evolution and, 139–43; legislative deliberation model, 122–25, 129–30, 136, 137–38; procedural regularity model, 125–28, 130–31, 136, 138–39

Easterbrook, Frank, 2n.3, 4, 41, 41n.7, 47, 50, 54–55, 89–102, 111
Economic efficiency, and social justice, 34–35, 69, 76–77. *See also* Rent-seeking
Economic regulation, 4, 8–9, 63–87, 145. *See also* Rent-seeking
Election financing, 4, 14, 23, 133–35. *See also* Interest groups
Epstein, Richard, 67, 68, 76–77, 132
Equal protection, 119–222, 138–39. *See also* Affirmative action; Due process of lawmaking; Gender discrimination
Eskridge, William, 114

Federalism, 63, 73–78; public choice and, 75–78
Federalist Papers, 10–11
Federalists, 44
Fenno, Richard, 21
First amendment. *See* Election financing
Frankfurter, Felix, 147
"Free rider" problem. *See* Collective action
Friendly, Henry, 99–100
Fullilove v. Klutznick, 121–22, 124–25

Gender discrimination, 139–40
Grassley, Charles, 97
Griswold v. Connecticut, 146–49

Hampton v. Mow Sun Wong, 119–23, 139, 148
Harlan, John, 141, 147

Harrington, James, 43
Hart, Henry, 99
Hatch, Orrin, 100
Hayes, Michael, 18
Heart of Atlanta Motel v. United States, 74
Hefflin, Howell, 97
Hirschey v. FERC, 95–97
Holmes, Oliver Wendell, Jr., 65, 153
Homosexuality, 146, 150–52

Ideology: in politics, 7, 23–33; in popular voting, 24–27
Immigration & Naturalization Serv. v. Chadha, 84, 129–31, 136
Incoherence. *See* Arrow's Theorem
Interest groups: collective action problems of, 23, 37, 72, 141–42, 146; covert delegations of legislative power to, 136–39; economic theory of, 21–37; effects on politics, 7–11, 17–21, 21–37; legislative power, delegation of, and, 80–83; factors affecting political influence of, 18–20; interest group theory as part of public choice, 12–13; judicial perception of, as influencing public law, 13–14, 68; legal scholars' perception of, 12–17, 77, 83; narrow economic interests and, 18–20, 23, 37, 141–42; normative implications of group power, 33–37, 132; political science and, 17–21; public choice models of, 14–15; public perception of, 12; reducing power of, through public law, 132–39; religious, 146; risk aversion and, 82–83; Schlozman/Tierney study of, 18–20; sexual privacy and, 146; size and influence of, 19–20, 23–24, 70; support of legislators, 23. *See also* Economic theory of legislation; Election financing; Rent-seeking; Statutory interpretation; Taking clause
Interpretation. *See* Statutory interpretation
Interstate competition, 75–77

Johnson v. Transportation Agency, 112
Judicial activism, 8, 13–14, 63–87
Justice, and economic efficiency, 34–35, 69. *See also* Public interest

Kennedy, Anthony, 109
Keystone Bituminous Coal Assn. v. DeBenedictis, 72

K Mart Corp. v. Cartier, Inc., 108–10
Kozinski, Alex, 97–98

Landes, William, 15; interest group theory and, 15, 111n.67
Lee, Dwight, 25–27
Legal pragmatism, 6, 9, 106, 116–18, 142–43. *See also* Practical reason
Legislation, economic theory of, 21–33; deregulation and, 68; empirical studies and, 28–33; federal constitutional law and, 63–64, 67–73, 75–83; normative implications of, 33–37. *See also* Interest groups; Legislator
Legislative apportionment, 73
Legislative committees, 56–58, 100–101, 117. *See also* Legislative history
Legislative deliberation, 7, 8, 14, 16, 55–62, 100–101, 117–43. *See also* Due process of lawmaking
Legislative history, 88–102; defined, 89; interest groups as check on, 98; Scalia's critique of use in statutory interpretation, 95–102; legislative staff and, 95–99; public choice and, 100–102
Legislative intent. *See* Legislative history; Legislator, motivations of; Rent-seeking; Statutory interpretation
Legislative power: delegation of, 63, 78–87, 136–39; public choice and, 79–87
Legislative procedure, 4, 38–42, 49–50, 55, 57–60, 117–43. *See also* Agenda; Due process of lawmaking
Legislative veto, 84, 129–31, 136
Legislator: constituents and, 22–23, 27–33; interest groups and, 23, 27–33; median, 53–54, 101n.41; motivations of, 3, 20–33, 67–73, 76–78, 80–83. *See also* Legislative committees; Legislative history
Liberalism, defined, 43
Linde, Hans, 119
Lochner v. New York, 64, 67–68, 71
Loretto v. Teleprompter Manhattan CATV Corp., 65, 66, 72
Lowi, Theodore, 18

Macey, Jonathan, 79, 84
Madison, James, and Madisonian theory, 9–11, 13, 44, 143, 145–53
Marbury v. Madison, 123

Mashaw, Jerry, 42, 55, 61
Mayhew, David, 20–21
Mikva, Abner, 2–3, 4
Monitoring costs, of lawmaking activity, 81–82
Moragne v. States Marine Lines, Inc., 140–42
Mueller, Dennis, 7

National League of Cities v. Usery, 75
New Deal, 63, 64, 73–75, 86
Nollan v. California Coastal Commission, 65–66
Nondelegation doctrine. *See* Legislative power, delegation of

Occupational Safety and Health Act, 79, 85
Olson, Mancur, 23

PACs. *See* Election financing
Panama Refining Co. v. Ryan, 78
Pennsylvania Coal v. Mahon, 65, 66, 72
Personal preferences: Arrow's Theorem and, 38–42; pluralism and, 13–14, 44–47; republicanism and, 14, 44–47, 58. *See also* Pluralism; Public interest; Republicanism
Pluralism: as influencing public law, 13–14, 16; defined, 13; economic theory and, 22; public choice as undermining, 58, 61; public choice interest group model and, 15; political science and, 17–21. *See also* Interest groups; Rent-seeking
"Pogo effect", 36. *See also* Collective action
Political action committees. *See* Election financing
Political parties, 49, 54, 56–58, 135
Posner, Richard, 15, 41n.7, 92, 102–6, 113; interest group theory and, 15, 111n.67
Powell, Adam Clayton, 126–27
Powell, Lewis, 121
Powell v. McCormack, 125–27
Practical reason, 6, 60, 106, 116–18, 142–43. *See also* Legal pragmatism
Prisoners' dilemma game, 36
Private law. *See* Public law
Property rights, 8–9
Public choice: abstract nature of, 3; appropriate use in law, 9, 11, 63–64, 73, 77–78, 86–87, 116–18, 126–27, 131,

Public choice (*continued*)
132, 140–43, 145, 146, 148, 152–53;
cynicism about politics, 1–3, 37, 54–55,
57; defined, 1, 6–7, 63n.1, 86;
descriptions of legislative process, 2, 15,
38–42; federalism and, 75–78;
importance of, 3–5; interest group theory
of, 14–15; judicial selection and, 71;
normative implications of, 2; potentially
undermining respect for democracy, 2, 37;
republicanism and, 44–47, 57–62;
unrefined nature of, 6, 53. *See also*
Arrow's Theorem; Economic regulation;
Interest groups; Judicial activism;
Legislation, economic theory of;
Pluralism; Statutory interpretation;
Voting, popular
Public interest: Arrow's Theorem and, 38–
42, 58–62; legislature as representative
of, 1, 21–22, 38, 58–62; nature of, 9, 59–
60; republicanism and, 8, 14, 16
Public law: defined, 1, 6–7; relevance of public
choice to, 1, 3–5, 13–17, 116–18, 132,
140, 142–43, 145, 146, 148, 152–53
Public values. *See* Public interest;
Republicanism

Redistribution of social wealth, 34–35. *See
also* Taking clause
Reelection, as goal of legislator, 3, 20–33
*Regents of University of California v.
Bakke,* 121
Rehnquist, William, 79, 85, 112, 120–21
Rent-seeking: constitutional law and, 67–
73, 76–77, 83; cost-benefit analysis and,
34–35; defined, 15n.10, 34; interest
groups and, 23, 145; normative
implications of, 33–37. *See also* Judicial
activism; Legislation, economic theory
of
Republicanism, 8, 10, 14, 16, 42–47, 57–
62; defined, 8, 42–44; judicial review of
economic regulation and, 67, 69–71;
statutory interpretation and, 105n.49.
See also Pluralism
Riker, William, 3, 4, 7, 40–41, 47, 54–55
Roe v. Wade, 149–50
Roosevelt, Franklin, 64. *See also* New
Deal
Rose-Ackerman, Susan, 82

Scalia, Antonin, 4, 9, 65–66, 89–102,
109–10, 114
Schattschneider, E. E., 17
Schechter Poultry Corp. v. United States,
79
Schlozman, Kay Lehman, 18–20
Sexual privacy. *See* Abortion;
Contraception; Homosexuality
Simon, Paul, 97
Single-subject (germaneness) rule, 55, 57–
59, 127–28
Smoot-Hawley Tariff, 17, 18n.23, 86
Sodomy. *See* Homosexuality
Special interests. *See* Interest groups; Rent-
seeking
Stability. *See* Arrow's Theorem
Stare decisis, 110–15
Starr, Kenneth, 97
States' rights. *See* Federalism
Statutory interpretation, 4, 9, 40–42, 53–
54, 77–79, 82, 88–115, 121, 125;
changed circumstances and, 106–15,
139, 141–42; decision theory and, 102–
6; judge as legislature's faithful agent,
93–94, 102–8; legislative inaction and,
106–7, 109–10; public choice and, 88–
89, 92, 95, 100–102, 106–7, 114–15;
stare decisis and, 110–15; statutory
evolution and, 106–15, 139, 141–42.
See also Legislative history
Steelworkers v. Weber, 112–15
Stevens, John Paul, 120–21, 122
Stigler, George, 22
Structural due process. *See* Due process of
lawmaking
Structure-induced equilibrium, 50, 83–86,
101. *See also* Agenda
Sunstein, Cass, 10, 16
Supreme Court of the United States:
pluralism and, 14; presidential veto
power and, 71; public choice and, 63;
republicanism and, 14. *See also*
Constitutional law, federal; Judicial
activism; Statutory interpretation

Taking clause, 64–73; safe harbors for, 72.
See also Interest groups
Tariffs. *See* Interest groups; Rent-seeking;
Smoot-Hawley Tariff
Theory, role of in law, 5–6, 9, 13–14,
116–18, 132, 148, 152

Tierney, John T., 18–20
Tullock, Gordon, 33n.90
Twain, Mark, 1–2

Uncovered set. *See* Arrow's Theorem
*United States Railroad Retirement Board v.
   Fritz,* 136–39
United States v. E. C. Knight Co., 74

Virtue, civic. *See* Republicanism
Veto, presidential power of, 71. *See also*
   Structure-induced equilibrium

Voting. *See* Arrow's Theorem
Voting, popular: economic rationality of,
   24–27; participatory norms and, 24–27,
   37; reflecting voters' self-interest, 22–23

Weingast, Barry, 3, 4, 5, 7
Wickard v. Filburn, 74
Wilson, James Q., 18
Wrongful death actions, 140–42

Yolk. *See* Arrow's Theorem